SAVANNAH LIVES

# Savannah Lives

Animal life and human evolution in Africa

STAFFAN ULFSTRAND

TRANSLATED BY CHERYL JONES FUR

OXFORD

UNIVERSITY PRESS

# OXFORD
**UNIVERSITY PRESS**

Great Clarendon Street, Oxford OX2 6DP

Oxford University Press is a department of the University of Oxford.
It furthers the University's objective of excellence in research, scholarship,
and education by publishing worldwide in

Oxford  New York

Auckland  Bangkok  Buenos Aires  Cape Town  Chennai
Dar es Salaam  Delhi  Hong Kong  Istanbul  Karachi  Kolkata
Kuala Lumpur  Madrid  Melbourne  Mexico City  Mumbai  Nairobi
São Paulo  Singapore  Taipei  Tokyo  Toronto

with an associated company in  Berlin

Oxford is a registered trade mark of Oxford University Press
in the UK and in certain other countries

Published in the United States
by Oxford University Press Inc., New York

© Oxford University Press 2002

The moral rights of the author have been asserted

Database right Oxford University Press (maker)

First published 2002

British Library Cataloguing in Publication Data
Data available

Library of Congress Cataloging in Publication Data
Data available

ISBN 0-19-850925-1

10 9 8 7 6 5 4 3 2 1

Typeset in Scala and Meta
by George Hammond Design
Printed in Great Britain by T. J. International Limited, Padstow, Cornwall

3/05

# *Contents*

# *Preface*

ONE JULY DAY IN 1997 I decided to try to write a book about the African savannah. I wanted to share the fascination I have harboured for the region since I first set foot in Africa almost forty-five years ago.

Much has changed in Africa since that first trip. The changes in the large cities have been the most radical. In those days, Dar-es-Salaam and Nairobi were peaceful if not sleepy little cities where few buildings were more than two stories high. In October 1958, when I stayed several nights at the Norfolk Hotel in Nairobi, I noticed some sturdy iron rings set in the building's foundations. 'What are these for?' I asked my friendly host. 'So that the guests will have somewhere to tie up their horses.' Ah!

That particular July day in 1997 I thought about everything I had experienced and learnt about the biology of Africa and all that I wanted to share with other people. I crawled out of my tent, blew life into the fire, and looked out over the enormous Ngorongoro Crater in northern Tanzania watching the sunrise. The crater was partially hidden in a fog that was trying in vain to escape the early beams of sunlight. The night's raindrops glittered on the leaves of the bushes and in spider's webs, and bright yellow and black weaver birds in the tree over my tent huddled quietly, gathering energy to begin their day's work of continued construction of their half-finished nests. The sound of rustling wings announced the passage of twelve sacred ibis as they flew low over the tops of the

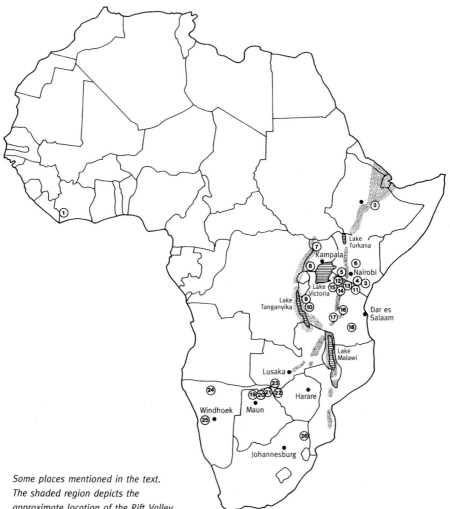

Some places mentioned in the text.
The shaded region depicts the
approximate location of the Rift Valley.

1. Tai Forest (Ivory Coast)
2. Lucy's home region
   (Ethiopia)
3. Tsavo (Kenya)
4. Amboseli (Kenya)
5. Masai Mara (Kenya)
6. Samburu (Kenya)
7. Murchison Falls (Uganda)
8. Queen Elizabeth (Uganda)

9. Gombe (Tanzania)
10. Mahale (Tanzania)
11. Kilimanjaro (Tanzania)
12. Serengeti (Tanzania)
13. Ngorongoro (Tanzania)
14. Laetoli (Tanzania)
15. Olduwai (Tanzania)
16. Mtera (Tanzania)
17. Ruaha (Tanzania)

18. Selous (Tanzania)
19. Okavango Delta (Botswana)
20. Moremi (Botswana)
21. Chobe (Botswana)
22. Hwange (Zimbabwe)
23. Victoria Falls (Zimbabwe)
24. Etosha (Namibia)
25. Namib (Namibia)
26. Kruger (South Africa)

lichen-covered trees and soared over the herds of wildebeest and zebras down towards the marshlands in the basin of the crater. They landed near a huge elephant lost in its own thoughts as it stood on the shores of a lake almost completely hidden by pink flamingos.

Everything I saw could have happened hundreds of thousands of years ago just as easily as it happened on 16 July 1997. These are the kinds of things I want to share – the African habitat that is our own species' original home. We are adapted to it and in it our roots are securely fastened.

I have several biologists among my circle of friends who share my interest for Africa and its biology, and many of them are much more knowledgeable than I am in many subject areas. They have generously provided their expert knowledge and their time in reading and commenting on one or more of the chapters in this book. In alphabetical order I would like to express my appreciation to Ingvar Backéus, Mats Björklund, Jan Ekman, Torbjörn Fagerström, Göran Spong, Bo G. Svensson, Bo Tallmark, and Nils Uddenberg.

As always however, my greatest appreciation goes to Astrid Ulfstrand. Without her generous support, there would not have been a book.

# 1

## *The curtain rises on the final act*

IN 1758, CARL VON LINNÉ gave our own species the scientific name of *Homo sapiens*—wise humans—and almost all evolutionary biologists agree that we have lived most of our history on the African savannah. Living in the shadow of acacia trees and congregating around receding water-holes underneath the African sun, those species that included the direct ancestors of modern humans also originated, evolved, and perished. First, *Homo erectus*—upright humans—and then later our own species, *Homo sapiens*, spread out of Africa in waves across the habitable reaches of the globe. Today's six thousand million people, a number that increases by almost 90 million each year, are the result of the last of these waves. There is scarcely a square metre of land or a cubic metre of water or air that is unaffected by the myriad individuals belonging to this one dominating, resource devouring, and uniquely successful species. Such global domination by a single species is unparalleled over the several-billion-year history of life on our planet. Directly or indirectly, we humans use over a third, possibly up to a half of all captured solar energy for our own purposes, leaving the other ten or twenty million species to compete for the remainder. Our species has power, which we exercise diligently, over the lives and deaths of our co-species on this isolated planet. In fact, this is not the first but the sixth time that life has approached a wave of mass extinction on earth. However, it is the first time that it will be caused by a single species.

Ecological dominance by humans is a fairly recent phenomenon—just the blink of an eye from the perspective of biological evolution. Did our position as a biological superpower originate during that time, tens of thousands of years ago, when humans began to cultivate certain useful plants and tame certain edible animals? When we literally began preparing the ground for the population growth that in more recent times has become a threat to our species' well-being and even our survival? Or did we establish our position of power much later? Perhaps it is only through the technological advances of the past hundred years that we have been able to overcome many of the factors that previously limited our population growth by restricting our exploitation of the world's resources?

Regardless of which of these alternatives we prefer, humans have begun to replace the living environment and lifestyle that has dominated 99 per cent of our species' history with a very different one; one where many tried and tested adaptations will fail, and will instead cause problems.

Maybe some information and eyewitness accounts from our original home will provide the key to a better understanding of human nature within modern evolutionary biology. The African savannah has permanently marked each and every one of us for life, and given us our species-specific nature. Our species, just like all other species, is shaped by the world around us. The world unremittingly picks and chooses among differently endowed individuals and, through natural selection, gives us our specific set of adaptations—adaptations that improve the chances for the survival and production of new generations in a highly dangerous world. By familiarizing ourselves with what our original home looks like and how it functions, where through millions of years our lineage collected most of the adaptations we carry with us, we should be able to obtain a better understanding of how today's humans function and behave towards each other. Our behaviour has been marked by hundreds of thousands, or even millions of years of hominid life on the savannah, and the new environment that modern science has created for us has existed only long enough to have influenced the pattern of adaptation of our species marginally. Newly awakened, we explore—hunter-gatherers who have landed in Manchester, Calcutta, Shanghai, or Chicago.

Our ancestors lived on the African savannah together with many other animal species that were important to them—as competitors, dangers, or food. Most significant were the big game species—the large herbivores and their predators (carnivores). Like us, they evolved their particular lifestyles in response to the savannah environment's trials and opportunities and therefore provide interesting comparisons. They have also been actors in the play in which our ancestors acted, and in that way have been significant in our own evolutionary history.

My aim with this book is to describe a series of interconnected evolutionary dramas that have been acted out and continue to be acted out on the ecological stage constituted by the African savannahs. Many characters have roles in this drama, and one of them is our own species. Will it stand alone on the stage when darkness falls and the show is over? Will the stage itself endure?

In order to accomplish my goal, I have set myself three tasks. The first of these is briefly to sketch the historical origins of the African savannahs and to explain those factors influencing the savannahs' present design and dynamics. The second is to describe several different animals that have been objects of qualified ecological research and whose ways of life illustrate different aspects of the problems and opportunities of life on the savannah. I willingly admit that my own impressions and experiences from numerous visits to the savannah regions of eastern and southern Africa have influenced my choice of species.

My third task is to provide a few glimpses into the biological research that aims to improve our understanding of our own species' behaviour and adaptations. In light of modern evolutionary biology, this research (often called biological anthropology) attempts to establish how our own species originated and evolved, and how our specific ways of life can be explained as a consequence of the process of natural selection in the African savannah environment with its particular opportunities and difficulties. Can our species-specific behavioural patterns, our response criteria, in short, our human nature best be understood as a complex of evolutionary adaptations that evolved during our long past on the savannah? Can the origins of our behaviour be traced even farther back into the depths of time before our species originated? Can we find counterparts to our behaviour among other animals, especially among the primates, the order of mammals to which we also belong? Until now the natural sciences have identified only a single biological mechanism with the ability to result in the remarkable and well-adapted wonders such as our brains and our minds—that is the natural selection of genetically variable individuals. Since this mechanism works in the same way for all living organisms, the comparison between us and other species is logical. Our species belongs within zoology. Twenty thousand generations ago most of the genes present in today's humans were not found in humans, but in another species.

Although we have every reason in the world to take care of our original home, a dark shadow lies over Africa's savannahs. They are quickly being transformed into more or less productive agricultural regions where, in an ever increasing degree, corn from America and lean livestock from Asia characterize the land-scape more than the naturally occurring plants and animals. Africa's population is growing at an alarming rate, more than in many other places around the world. In addition, most of Africa's inhabitants have perfectly valid reasons for striving for a higher standard of living for themselves and for their descendants, which automatically increases the strain on natural resources. Consequently, every indication points towards Africa's lions and elephants following the same fate as Europe's wolves and North America's bison. They may not die out, but they will only survive out of mercy—as tragic ancient relics from a time gone by.

Human teeth and hands are wearing down the original home of humankind. However, the show is not over yet. The curtain is rising on the final act...

# 2

# A significant digression

*'I am fully convinced that species are not
immutable; but that those belonging to what are
called the same genera are lineal descendants of
some other and generally extinct species, in the
same manner as the acknowledged varieties of
any one species are the descendants of that
species. Furthermore, I am convinced that
Natural Selection has been the most important,
but not the exclusive, means of modification.'*

CHARLES DARWIN (1809–1882) wrote these words in the introduction to his book
about the origin of species through natural selection, published in 1859. The
conclusions he drew were based primarily on impressions gathered during a
five-year voyage around the world on board HMS *Beagle*. What he saw during that
long voyage caused him to question the concept of the immutability of species.
He adopted the budding idea that, with certain modifications, species currently
living (very probably our own species as well) had evolved from other species
and—most importantly—he suggested a mechanism which could explain how
these modifications originated and why their designs were so well adapted to
their purposes. It is difficult to think of any other book that has had such a
comprehensive and lasting influence on human thought as Darwin's *On the
Origin of Species*.

Today's biologists do not need to suffer five years of seasickness on a poorly constructed ten cannon brig from the British navy in order to check Darwin's conclusions. Even if his theories have needed one or two corrections and additions, especially as a result of the dramatic advances in genetics during the last half century, it has stood up to numerous attempts to refute its main features and thus won credibility. Darwin's influence on evolutionary biology is so complete that this science is often called 'Darwinism' or 'neo-Darwinism'. His influence pervades all parts of current evolutionary biology: genetics (life's mechanisms of variation and change), ecology (factors governing these changes), systematics (the ensuing patterns of biodiversity) and phylogeny (life's history on earth).

*Figure 1. The experience and knowledge gained in the course of five years on board HMS* Beagle *inspired Charles Darwin to develop his revolutionary theory of the evolution of life and how living organisms have adapted to the world around them via natural selection.*

This book describes adaptations of animal species to life on the African savannah, including those of humans, from an evolutionary biology perspective. A summary of some of evolutionary biology's more important components is outlined for those readers who may not be familiar with these thoughts and ideas.

The most characteristic features of life are the special molecules that have the ability to build copies of themselves, to reproduce, as well as to vary, carry, and transfer information. These molecules are nucleic acids, and the most important one is deoxyribonucleic acid, DNA. Through generation after generation DNA transfers information about how one builds the most diverse creatures: aurelia jellyfish, blue whales, tortoise-shell butterflies, spruce trees, and humans. The outer shell, in the form of a body, which DNA builds up around itself and is primarily composed of proteins, delivers energy, makes a protective layer against the outside world, and provides transportation. Every cell in the body contains DNA molecules that are composed of a large number of distinct units or genes, which sit in long rows on several chromosomes. Humans have 46 chromosomes with a total of, at the most, 40 000 genes—a very normal number for a mammal.

To reproduce, DNA molecules in most organisms have an extremely ingenious way of organizing things. First, special sex cells (gametes) are produced with half the number of chromosomes (23 for humans). In some individuals, these bundles with half the amount of DNA are packaged in rather large, stationary gametes called eggs, and the individuals that produce eggs are called females. In other individuals (males), the sex cells (sperm) are small and mobile and will be sent on a long and laborious trip to find and unite with an egg. When this occurs, a cell with the full allocation of DNA is created, and the foundation is laid for a new individual—for example an aurelia jellyfish, a blue whale, a tortoise-shell butterfly, a spruce tree, or a human.

Occasionally small random changes (mutations) may occur within the DNA molecules. Although the frequency of such changes in each gene is quite low, there are so many genes that every individual contains a certain number of new manufacturing flaws. In addition, a rearrangement (recombination) of genes occurs in conjunction with those cell divisions leading to the creation of sperm and eggs. Since the number of genes is so large, this reshuffling causes every sex cell to be unique. Consequently, every individual is also unique as we are created through the combination of genetic information from two unique sex cells (one from the mother and one from the father). It is an extraordinary thought that every individual is a unique being. Neither good nor evil people, nor for that matter we who are quite average, can expect to be reproduced as replicas in the future. In principle however, genes are immortal and move from generation to generation, part of an eternal dance.

The above explanation applies to organisms with two sexes involved in sexual reproduction. In this summary, we have ignored all the interesting creatures that do not have two sexes and do not reproduce sexually, and those individuals that practice natural cloning, such as identical siblings who are genetic copies of one another.

Mutations and recombinations lead to a practically unending genetic variation. In addition, every unique collection of genes (genotype) will construct its own unique casing (phenotype) in a continual interplay with the existing conditions of the surrounding world. In turn, these phenotypes will vary in their ability to avoid or postpone death and, most importantly, to multiply. It is this variation between individuals in relation to relative reproductive success that is the mechanism Darwin suggested as the explanation for species' continual modification and obviously well-adapted design: natural selection. Under existing conditions, certain variations may be slightly better adapted than other variations, enabling them to produce a larger number of offspring. 'Unequal reproductive success' is natural selection's mechanism in three words. It leads to evolution, which is the gradual change of the average genetic information content of a group.

Sexual reproduction is a method that greatly increases genetic variation among offspring. The likelihood of individuals to have at least some offspring who are adapted to survive in new situations improves with this increased variation. Since the surrounding world is continually changing it is advantageous to produce offspring who are all just a tiny bit different from one another. One of them might survive. The more stable the world is, the less profit there is in changing the arsenal of adaptations (adaptive traits). Alternatively, the more quickly the surrounding world changes, the greater the pressure to modify adaptations. Necessity is the mother of adaptations.

Evolutionary processes lack any shred of design, purpose, or long-term planning; all creatures are last year's models. Among all the randomly generated variations that appear in every generation, the surrounding world discards the majority. Thus, adaptively designed creatures originate: whales acquire their fusiform shape, deer acquire their horns, and apes acquire their intelligence.

The evolutionary process began in the ancient sea with life's molecules, nucleic acids, and has produced the diversity of adjustments or adaptations that are the prerequisites for life in a dangerous world. Describe an organism's living conditions, and I can tell you what it looks like and how it behaves. Or, describe what it looks like and how it behaves, and I can figure out where it lives. Chance comes up with proposals. The surrounding world discards most of them but accepts a few. If it is cold, then become cold hardy. If it is dry, then become drought resistant. If you live in water, become fusiform shaped. If you live on the savannah—that is what this book is about.

But what about new species? How do they originate?

As concisely as possible, the answer is—through the dividing of populations and, following that, isolation. From continental displacement, climatic changes, or desertification, to flying in the wrong direction in bad weather, all kinds of events can cause a population to divide into two or more daughter populations. When contact between the two populations is broken, they will adapt and evolve in different directions based on the nature of the surrounding environment. After some time, they are so different that, even if they should come into contact again, they would not be able to hybridize. This is precisely the accepted definition of a biological species—a group of organisms that is genetically isolated from all other groups. Alternatively, one could say that a species includes all individuals that can potentially have genetic contact with one another. Humans and chimpanzees, for example, are two separate species since we are composed of groups of individuals lacking any genetic contact with one another. Within the entire group of organisms that we call humans, however, there are no genetic barriers, and thus—naturally—humans are *one* biological species.

This book does not offer the final truth. Its aim is much more modest: to present the results of some recent research to improve our understanding of this branch of biology. The underlying principle for this work is the theory of evolutionary biology for which Charles Darwin drew up the blueprint. Currently, it appears free from contradictions and is therefore credible. As a basic scientific explanation for the origins of life, diversity, and adaptive patterns, it currently lacks an alternative. However, as to the interpretation of several separate details, there is certainly no complete agreement. In addition, new data are continually collected, accepted interpretations are criticized, and new ones put forward, sometimes requiring the reappraisal of accepted ideas. Scientific research does not construct a well-stocked warehouse of concrete knowledge and eternal truths, but can be seen as a never-ending process of observing, speculating, testing, measuring, counting, modelling, experimenting...

Is there then any reason to take notice of the claims of researchers? Indeed, there is no other way to approach the truth about the origins of life and evolution on this earth. It is a long story that was primarily enacted before the human species had made its entry onto the stage. Reality is not a human invention, although it sometimes—amazingly enough—is argued as such. The laws of nature are realities even for buffaloes and baboons.

It is now time to travel to Africa. That is where the search must continue to discover our roots.

# 3

## Formation of the savannah

### THE BIRTH OF AFRICA

Africa has not always existed, at least not as a separate continent in the shape we recognize today. During the Mesozoic era the Earth's land masses were joined in two enormous blocks: a northern landmass called Laurasia, and a southern landmass called Gondwanaland which included Antarctica, Australia, Africa, the Indian subcontinent, and South America.

At the beginning of the last geological period in the Mesozoic era, the Cretaceous, Gondwanaland split into several separate landmasses that slowly drifted apart giving rise to separate continents and subcontinents. One of these fragments of Gondwanaland became Africa. Subsequently, contact between Africa, Australia, and Antarctica was broken. During the same period, Africa either retained or periodically established new land connections with Asia, including India, as well as connections with Europe, and North and South America. In addition to the continent's tectonic (structural) movements, contact between the different landmasses has been influenced by fluctuations in sea level. The African continent has had land connections with other continents lasting for long periods of time enabling plants and animals that originated elsewhere to immigrate into Africa as well as to emigrate to other parts of the world. During a large part of its 100–125 million-year history as a separate continent, Africa

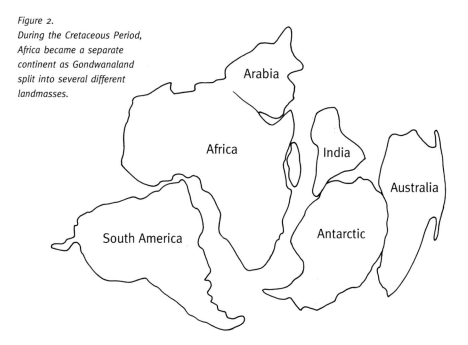

*Figure 2.*
*During the Cretaceous Period,*
*Africa became a separate*
*continent as Gondwanaland*
*split into several different*
*landmasses.*

has been less isolated from Asia than would be predicted from looking at an up-to-date world map.

The end of the Cretaceous period is characterized by the extinction of Africa's, and the rest of the world's, most conspicuous 'big game', namely, dinosaurs. However, there were a few important exceptions: birds and crocodiles are actually living descendants of dinosaurs.

Apart from this highly significant and interesting exception, the transition (65 million years ago) from the earth's Mesozoic era to the present Cenozoic era signified the end of the Age of Dinosaurs and the beginning of the Age of Mammals. Mammals actually evolved as early as 200–300 million years ago at the beginning of the Mesozoic era from animals that represented a kind of preliminary stage to the dinosaurs. Thus, 'The Age of Mammals', that is the last 65 million years, is only a quarter of the time during which mammals have existed. It was perhaps the geologically rapid disappearance of dinosaurs that gave the comparatively small and insignificant mammals their opportunity—an opportunity of which they took full advantage. If an asteroid had not fallen from the sky above Mexico about 65 million years ago, or some other catastrophe had not struck a deathblow to the last of the large dinosaurs, then biological evolution might have had a very different outcome. Who knows—perhaps humans would never have made their appearance here on earth.

## Savannah Origins

The newborn Africa was wet, warm, and covered by steaming marshes and immense rain forests. It remained like this during the entire Cretaceous period as well as during the first 10–15 million years of the earth's most recent geological period—the Tertiary period. After that, a dramatic climatic change began.

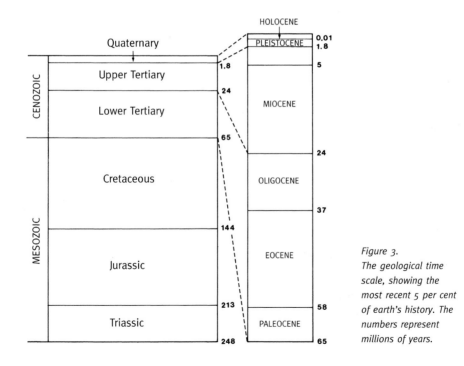

Figure 3.
The geological time scale, showing the most recent 5 per cent of earth's history. The numbers represent millions of years.

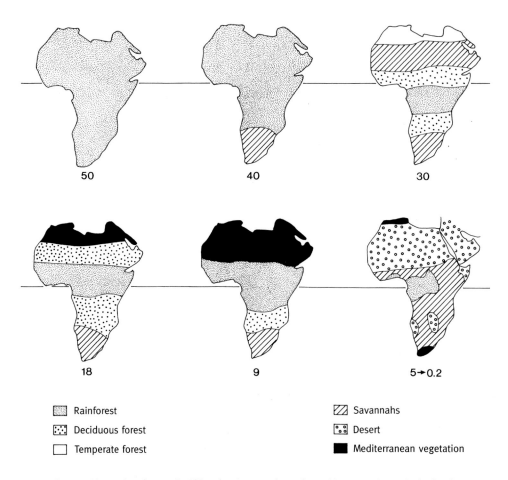

*Figure 4. Vegetation changes in Africa showing a prolonged transition to an increasingly dry climate. The numbers represent millions of years.*

These time spans, although short in comparison to the age of the earth (4–5 billion years) or the age of life (almost 4 billion years), are almost unimaginably long from a human perspective. The time that elapsed between the breaking up of Gondwanaland and the great climatic change in Africa—about 75 million years—reduces our human perception of time to a fraction of a second. Nevertheless, 98–99 per cent of the history of life occurred before the disintegration of Gondwanaland.

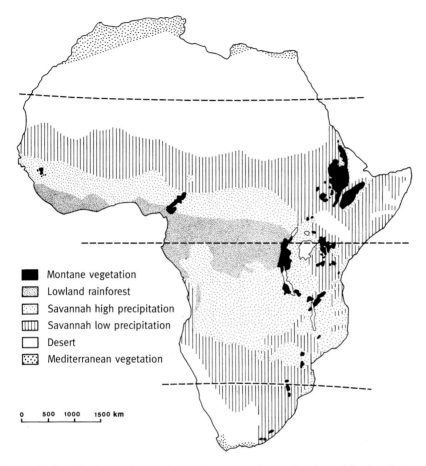

*Figure 5. Modern Africa's most important vegetation zones—disregarding the modifications that humans have made during the last few hundreds of years.*

Montane vegetation
Lowland rainforest
Savannah high precipitation
Savannah low precipitation
Desert
Mediterranean vegetation

0    500    1000    1500 km

About 50 million years ago the temperature of the earth began to decrease substantially and in many places rainfall decreased. Temperature extremes occurred and precipitation became more unevenly distributed. At certain times of the year in Africa and elsewhere, there were large areas where the climate was too dry and too cold to support rainforest. Instead, different kinds of savannah vegetation developed in these regions. The total area covered by savannahs gradually increased at the cost of rainforest, and sometime after the middle of the

Miocene (about 10 million years ago) savannahs had reached proportions equivalent to the current situation in Africa.

As a result of these changes in climate and vegetation, the African savannah became modernized at an accelerated rate; baboon-like apes, elephants, giraffes, and hippopotamuses evolved, and several different kinds of bovines (antelopes) wandered in from Asia and horses from North America (via Asia). The latter part of the Tertiary is also characterized by a modernization of the carnivorous mammal fauna through either evolutionary changes within Africa or immigration from other continents.

Last, but not least, a number of different early humans or hominids (*Australopithecus* and *Homo*) emerged during the last 5–7 million years of the Tertiary period. They carried within them the seeds of humankind and the story of these hominids is continued in Chapter 13.

The transition from the drier, cooler climate that characterized the Miocene (24–5 million years ago) and continued into the Pliocene (5–2 million years ago) had various direct and indirect effects on vegetation. Plant-eating mammals (herbivores) can be divided roughly into leaf-eaters (browsers) and grass-eaters (grazers). Browsers eat leaves, buds, and twigs from bushes and trees, whereas grazers forage on grass. There is an interesting difference between most grasses and sedges on the one hand, and trees, bushes, and herbaceous plants on the other which has to do with the mechanism used to capture the sun's energy and how they construct organic substances—carbohydrates—from carbon dioxide and water.

Many of the grasses that grow on tropical savannahs use a mechanism called C4-photosynthesis, whereas most other plants use C3-photosynthesis. Recently, researchers have found that during and after the radical changes in climate during the Miocene, a larger percentage of plant life was of the C4 type, which must have been a result of grass becoming an increasingly dominant component of the total vegetation. In turn, this meant that life became easier for grazers but more difficult for browsers. However, munching on grass also has its problems: grass contains copious amounts of small silicon granules which strongly abrade the teeth of grazing animals. Substantial changes in the design of the dentition of grazers accompanied the transition from browsing to grazing. Consequently, within the evolutionary line of horses (equids), all species existing prior to the beginning of the Miocene had low crowned teeth (brachydont), whereas after this period all equids had high crowned teeth (hypsodont), including the equids alive today. Similar changes also occurred among the elephants and their relatives. If you want to eat grass, then you must have high crowned teeth which will tolerate prolonged wear and tear.

This is a simple example of how natural selection works. First, a change in climate affects the vegetation, those changes then force modifications in the foraging tools of herbivorous animals. Gradually the plants evolve defences against becoming dinner for plant-eating animals.

You might wonder how we know that at a particular point in time millions of years ago, one specific mechanism for photosynthesis was more common when compared with other mechanisms, and that plant-eating animals underwent a change in food habits. The answer: by studying proportions of different carbon isotopes in plant fossils and in the microscopic plant fragments that can be picked from fossil teeth. This measure provides us with a hint as to how the grazed or browsed plants captured solar energy and built up their tissues.

And why were C4 plants suddenly favoured at the cost of C3 plants? Because there was less carbon dioxide in the atmosphere and because the somewhat more complicated C4-photosynthesis is more effective at lower levels of carbon dioxide. But why did the carbon dioxide levels in the atmosphere decrease? According to a recent hypothesis, it was because the central Asian mountain massif rose, altering the course of the atmosphere's jet streams. This caused more intensive monsoon systems and greater amounts of precipitation, which in turn caused the mountain rock to weather down more quickly. It was this latter chemical process that led to global cooling via its consumption of part of the atmospheric carbon dioxide. Today's greenhouse effect—except in reverse.

Since the Oligocene (24–38 million years ago), Africa has become increasingly diverse regarding its climate because its topography has become increasingly more 'violent'. Mountains rose and valleys sunk. From a geological point of view, the most dramatic event, which began 25–30 million years ago, was the birth of the Rift Valley with its surrounding volcanic mountains. From the Dead Sea to the Mozambique Canal (the strait between the African continent and Madagascar), is an enormous rift valley with tall mountains on either side. These mountains snare most of the rainfall that blows in over Africa on the west winds coming from the Atlantic Ocean. In the past, the rain-laden clouds crossed the entire African continent, but since the Rift Mountains arose, eastern Africa lies in their rain shadow. According to many researchers, this played an important role in reducing the forested areas east of the Rift Valley and replacing them with increasingly dry-tolerant vegetation types, while the rainforests in the Congo basin remained unchanged. In turn, this created one of the conditions for our own species' evolutionary origins. In due time we shall return to this scenario, which has been entitled 'East Side Story'.

Following a gradual decrease, a threshold value for atmospheric carbon dioxide was passed at about the time of the Miocene–Pliocene boundary. This triggered a comprehensive change of vegetation: from C3 to C4 plants. Forests diminished, grasslands (savannahs) expanded. This resulted in great upheavals for herbivorous animals, as well as for the interplay between vegetation and herbivores. Those herbivorous animals adapted for eating leaves, buds, and fruits from lush forest vegetation met with hard times and many species died out. Our own predecessors (the apes) generally belonged to the losers, as did swine, rhinoceroses, and elephants. However, the favoured groups included the monkeys (currently represented in Africa by the guenons and baboons), antelopes, and hippopotamuses.

Today, as a result of the enormous over-consumption of fossil fuels by modern humans, levels of carbon dioxide in the atmosphere are rising. This means that C4 plants are becoming less favoured by nature whereas C3 plants are gaining an advantage. Our own species has evolved in a C4 world, a world we are now in the process of phasing out. The increasing levels of carbon dioxide in the atmosphere are certainly not an environmental problem to be taken lightly. When C3 replaced

C4 it was the starting point for an evolutionary change that led to the origin of our own species. With C4 losing out to C3—what will the consequence be for us?

## THREE KINDS OF SAVANNAH

Definitions of savannah tend to vary depending upon the interest of the author. However, grass is always a characteristic and significant component of all vegetation types classified as savannahs. The word *savannah* simply means 'grassland', and comes (via Spanish) from a language that at the time of the conquistadors' arrival was spoken by the Taino people of Cuba. Soon, no one remained who spoke this language since the Spanish conquerors on Cuba, as colonizers in so many other places, promptly eradicated the native people.

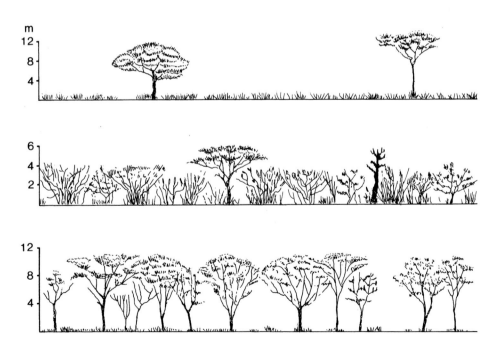

*Figure 6. Silhouettes of three kinds of savannah: grass savannah (with solitary acacias), bush savannah, and woodland (or forest) savannah.*

The GRASS SAVANNAH is composed primarily of vast grassy plains, with a few dispersed bushes, solitary trees, or small groves here and there. The Serengeti plains in northern Tanzania are one of the better-known examples of this kind of savannah. In fact, the word Serengeti means 'vast plains' in the language of the Masai.

Talk about open landscape! Nowhere, with the exception of a desert or at sea, is the horizon as distant as it is on the grass savannah. Empty and desolate? Not at all. An umbrella acacia on a distant ridge, a cluster of bushes in a shallow basin, a wind-cut cliff formation with tight brush in the crevices—all give depth and content to the unending expanse, whether it spreads out newly dampened after an afternoon shower or flickers in the grasp of drought and wind, revealing a palette containing all the different shades of gold. Gold, like on the skin of the lion suddenly discovered in the grass, or in the striped wing-covert feathers of the savannah larks which transform the sound of the howling wind into bird song.

The BUSH SAVANNAH is completely different. As the name implies, it is characterized by medium to tall thickets, sometimes so thick that they are completely impenetrable, sometimes so sparse that you can zigzag your way through them on foot or in an all-terrain vehicle. Here and there, expansive areas of grass lie interspersed in the bush savannah; particularly where the soil conditions retain water long after the rainy season has passed. Many of the dominant bushy species are extremely thorny. The only way to fight your way through really dense bush savannah is to follow the paths which elephants and other large mammals have worn down on their wanderings between water holes and grazing grounds. This activity can be exciting enough, as your field of vision is generally no more than a few dozen metres. Tsavo, halfway between Nairobi and Mombasa in Kenya, is a famous national park in which bush savannah is the predominant vegetation type.

'*Nyika*' is the East African word for bush savannah, 'thornbush', a region where even the most experienced pathfinders can lose their bearings only fifty metres from their tents. Luckily, over the sometimes verdant, sometimes parched and leafless brushy vegetation, the colossal baobab tree towers with its magnificently sculptured, many metres thick, ash grey trunk. Each has its own individual appearance and because of this, they are quite useful as landmarks. But watch out! If a herd of elephants has travelled through during the night and dug into the soft tissue of the trunk to reach the water hoarded inside, then yesterday's giant may have disappeared and been replaced by a pile of yellowish chips. It is black rhinoceros and slender gerenuk country, a place for the perfectly designed bateleur eagles that glide under clouds with rigid wings in constant readiness.

WOODLAND SAVANNAH, the third type of savannah, comprises connected, but never dense woodlands with trees that seasonally drop their leaves (deciduous trees). Because the trees are without leaves during part of the year, some sunlight reaches the ground; during the rest of the year the foliage gives shade and thus lessens the evaporation of water from the surface layer of the soil. Together these conditions make it possible for the ground in the woodland savannah to be covered by a more or less continuous grassy layer. The most expansive woodland savannahs are dominated by tree species that are collectively called *miombo*, a word that has also come to be used when describing the specific vegetation type. Enormous areas of miombo are found in Tanzania, Zambia, and Zimbabwe. In dryer regions and in relatively rich soils, miombo is replaced by another type of tree savannah dominated by mopane, *Colophospermum mopane*, a species of tree that, like the miombo species, belongs to the leguminous plant family.

Rain clouds may gather every afternoon, towering up in the north over Victoria Falls and the Zambezi river valley, whilst not a drop of rain falls in south-western Zimbabwe. Despite these dry conditions, the miombo forest cannot wait and instead seems to use the coming water in advance. What cascades of colour are thrown down the steep slope of the hills! The different tree species seem to compete with one another in presenting the greatest possible display of colour in their new foliage: burgundy, blood red, pale pink, orange, bright yellow, and in addition, every possible shade of green. A dozen or so sable antelope move about on the desiccated ground around a near-dry waterhole. A few of the males, dressed in a sober black, fence with one another using their impressive metre-long sables. It is to no avail however, as it seems that the dominant herd male has already achieved obvious success with one of the stylish light brown females. The rains come. Water gives life.

There is wide variation within each of these kinds of savannahs and there are great differences in the species composition of vegetation between the different geographic regions. However, at a more local level, savannah vegetation also varies as a result of differences in, for example, bedrock, soil, precipitation and drainage, frequency of fire, grazing pressures, and the actions of humans. Transitions from one type of vegetation to another may be abrupt or more gradual, with the dominant plant species seeming to decrease imperceptibly and being replaced by others. Savannah is not static or monotonous. Neither is it sharply delimited in relation to other vegetation types. For example, some plant ecologists do not accept woodland savannahs as a type of savannah. I prefer to use a very broad definition of the concept of a savannah.

In one direction the savannah changes into desert, in another into dense forest with the increasingly complete shading of ground vegetation. Between these two extremes lie the different kinds of savannahs, all more or less suggestive of parks with groves of trees, woodlands, and copses spread out over the grasslands that are the most important characteristic of all savannah types. When humans decide to transform some land for pleasure purposes, what is the result of our endeavour? Nothing other than a fragment of savannah that is called a city park. In Bangkok and Harare, Uppsala and Quito—everywhere, when our goal is to produce an environment in which we feel at home, we create a savannah.

## WATER

Botswana is an enormous country, much larger than France, for example. Dry grass and bush savannahs cover much of its expansive land area. The Kalahari Desert, not technically a desert although its climate is hot and dry, spreads out over a large part of the country. In Botswana, the Bush or San People knew that they should value water, which to them was a matter of life and death. In today's Botswana, one result of new economics and technology is that the fragile ecosystem is on its way to being trampled under the hooves of hundreds of thousands of cattle, demanding massive exploitation of the scarce water resources. The situation is serious, but one thing is certain—San People and beef producers, bureaucrats, and biologists all agree that Botswana's continued development depends above all on the availability of water. It is revealing that the country's currency is named 'pula', which means 'water'.

Some people maintain that there are no seasons in tropical regions. These people definitely have not been on the African savannah when the rainy season replaces the dry season. This event provides a much more dramatic impression of life's rebirth than the very gradual appearance of spring in the northern parts of the Northern Hemisphere. There is nothing quiet or gentle about the arrival of the rainy season. At 2 o'clock the ground is dry and dust flies up behind the jeep. At 3 o'clock you are stuck in the mud and have plenty of time to contemplate how fast the water is rising in the dry riverbeds and flowing over the road on which you had planned to drive. Termites begin swarming, impalas stand with outstretched tongues voluptuously drinking drops of water, and many species of small insect-eating birds immediately begin to sing and gather nesting material. Only the lions look sullen and displeased, resembling Scandinavian holidaymakers surprised by rain at the beach, feeling cheated because the travel brochure guaranteed sunshine.

The amount of precipitation and the length of the seasons are of crucial significance for life on the savannah. Across the entire African continent, it rains most when the sun is at its highest point in the sky or shortly thereafter. Thus, near the Tropic of Cancer, along the southern edge of the Sahara for example, the rainy season culminates some time during July to September, whereas closer to the Tropic of Capricorn, for example Botswana, rains culminate during February to April. At the equator, including much of Kenya, there are two rainy seasons, one after the vernal equinox and one after the autumnal equinox. Closer to the tropic circles, the dry season is longer and the rainy season shorter. Deserts spread out at both tropic circles, in Africa as well as on other continents, and weather stations exist in these regions that have never reported any precipitation at all, in spite of dozens of years of weather observations.

Latitude is not the only determinant of how much rainfall there will be in a certain area. Topography, or more specifically, elevation also plays an important role. There is a general rule wherever you are which says that the higher the region, the more rainfall there will be. Some of the more characteristic features of the African landscape are the mountains, often of volcanic origin, which sometimes rise thousands of metres above the savannahs. A succession of vegetation types line the slopes resulting from the increasing amount of rain and decreasing temperatures at higher elevations. The vegetation might change from woodland savannah at the foot of the mountains followed by other diverse forests, then a zone of bamboo stretching up to the timberline at about 3000–3500 m, above that mountain heaths, and finally, at the top, snow. In addition, precipitation is heaviest on the side of the mountain or plateau facing the prevailing winds, whereas a dry zone of rain shadow occurs in the lee of the mountains.

Another significant factor that influences the effect of precipitation on plant life is temperature. The warmer and windier it is, the quicker the small amounts of precipitation will evaporate. In the northern temperate zones levels of precipitation between 400 and 1400 millimetres would give rise to lush forests, expansive wetlands, and thousands of lakes and water systems. In Africa however, they result in dry bush savannah or an even poorer kind of vegetation, as the average yearly temperature may be 15 °C warmer than in northern Europe. African savannahs receive approximately the same levels of precipitation as northern Europe. If rainfall amounts drop below 300–400 millimetres, the savannah becomes steppe or desert; if rainfall exceeds 1500 millimetres and falls regularly throughout the year, the forest becomes too dense to be classified as woodland savannah.

In many parts of Africa's savannah regions, the fact that precipitation undergoes enormous yearly variations is of great ecological significance. More often than not, rain, either completely or almost completely, fails to fall during one or sometimes several rainy seasons in a row. There may be a long-term periodicity, with a 6 or 10–11-year cycle of wet or dry years respectively. The present climate trend is moving towards the warm and dry regions of the earth becoming warmer and drier. This is bad news for all people living on the African continent who support themselves through a pastoral way of life.

## FIRE

When I close my eyes and think of Africa, a variety of impressions from different places and different times come to mind. Visual impressions such as the procession of nine superb male elephants moving through the dry mopane forest in Moremi just east of the Okavango Delta. Another impression—later the same day—fifty thousand open-billed storks wheeling around in the thermals over the Chobe River. Then there are auditory impressions—why not the ground hornbill's serenade for bassoons performed at dawn one morning in Selous in southern Tanzania? As far as visual and auditory impressions are concerned, I have millions to choose from. When I think about African olfactory impressions however, the same one always comes to mind: the smell of fire.

Savannahs are often ablaze, like much of the cultivated land in the arid regions of Africa. In most cases today, it is humans who intentionally or unintentionally set fire to the dry vegetation. Fire has affected the savannah vegetation ever since the climate change during the Tertiary created conditions for the savannah's expansion over a large part of Africa. Lightning strikes must have been the most common cause of fire before the origin of the human species. When humans first learned to use fire—or Prometheus gave them the fire he had stolen from the gods—no one knows; perhaps it was no more than 60 000 years ago, perhaps twice as long ago as that. In any case, for a very long time the hunter-gatherer people have lit camp-fires and ignited dry vegetation to drive game, for example, in a desired direction.

Perhaps the most significant result of frequently occurring fires is that the grassy ground layer is favoured at the cost of bushes and trees. Fire kills a large number of the young bushes and tree shoots and thus counteracts rejuvenation, although adult trees and bushes are fairly resistant to the flames and the heat. However, the relationship between fire and vegetation is far from simple. For example, precipitation plays an important role in the balance between how much grass there is in relation to the number of bushes and trees. When precipitation is abundant, grasses become thick and high, and are therefore inflammable when drought comes and fires occur accidentally or are set. In drier regions however, grass grows too sparsely for fires to attain hot enough temperatures to affect the bush and tree vegetation. Quite a bit of research has been applied to these problems, especially in South Africa and Zimbabwe, where there is a strong interest from livestock producers to check the spreading of bushes unfavourable to their grass grazing herds. Fire seems to be an exceedingly important factor in the spread of different savannah and forest formations.

Because fire is a natural ecological factor in arid environments, many species of plants have evolved different adaptations in order to evade its effects. Examples of such adaptations are underground 'tubers' with a nutritional store and increased protection against overheating, as well as fruit-setting at the very end of the drought period, when fires have usually already occurred.

It is an error caused by our civilized environment that we regard fire only as threatening and damaging. Many plants and animals—on the African savannah as well as in the Nordic coniferous forests—do not have this negative outlook, but instead, possess adaptations which have evolved because they allow their owners to benefit from fires. Many of the savannah's tree species have a built-in draught that increases their flammability. They also retain abundant dead twigs and branches in a markedly dense tree crown, have high levels of volatile and inflammable oils in addition to flaky, inflammable bark. Why this built-in draught that would worry any competent fire inspector?

By bursting into flame so intensively and generating so much heat, neighbouring trees of the same or other species also burst into flame and die in the blaze. Perhaps the 'fire tree' meets its fate here, but during its lifetime it has sown countless seeds which are now able to germinate and grow without the competition of established trees nearby. And even if this murderous plan were not to work, perhaps the ageing tree increases the survival probability for one or more of its descendants by arranging its own cremation and fertilizing the ground with its ashes.

The effect of fire on the local savannah is diverse and involves almost everything: soil conditions, water evaporation, the composition of the plant community, and the living conditions for a number of animal species. How great an effect the fire has depends in turn on factors such as the amount of rainfall and its seasonal distribution. In particular, a complicated interplay between fire and grazing animals arises, most notably elephants, which if they are numerous have a profound influence on vegetation.

It is fascinating to watch what happens around a savannah fire. Many animals simply leave the area; others have to remain and try to survive, perhaps by seeking shelter in a deep hole in the earth. Sometimes there are signs of a tragedy of sorts—a turtle that did not escape and now lies in the ashes, cooked in its own shell only a dozen metres from the fire's edge, or a young raptor that has fallen out of its nest, burned alive in the still smoking crown of a fire-ravaged tree. These kinds of accidents in particular lure many animals to the site of the fire where they can find a crispy fried snake or chameleon for dinner. Marabou storks are opportunists who do not like to miss such free meals, and usually one or two tawny eagles or a black-shouldered kite also take the chance to peruse the menu. Yellowbilled or redbilled hornbills devour burned beetles and crickets as quickly as they can.

I remember one particularly wonderful spectacle that occurred in a place just outside Lusaka in Zambia. A large flock of carmine bee-eaters and European bee-eaters came to a smoking savannah fire and began feasting on the insects that were fleeing the flames. Suddenly, two or three hobbies turned up, migrant birds from Europe, who having devoured several dazed grasshoppers suddenly turned instead on the bee-eaters. They did not manage to catch any, however, and were forced to return to their insect-eating—but the bee-eaters decided that the area was unsafe for further hunting and chattering noisily departed for a more peaceful place to eat.

## THE SAVANNAH'S UNDERGROUND CULTURE

Big cities safeguard their inhabitants against most dangers and adversities. Inhabitants live in houses with carefully adjusted and healthy indoor climates, and food and water brought in from the surrounding countryside available either for immediate consumption or for storage. It is therefore unnecessary for the entire population to work incessantly for their own immediate provisions.

Specialists raise the new generation, and organizational effectiveness is their hallmark. There is extensive division of labour among the population. From the moment of every new citizen's birth, to that time when he or she finishes the course of his or her life and is laid to rest, life goes on as usual under the protection of a well-developed social network. Additionally, there is an effective defence organization ready to step in if external enemies should start pounding on the city gates.

Is this a 1960s dream of the perfect welfare-state society? Is this a well-meaning politician's description of the advantages of an inner-city housing project?

Not at all. It is a fragmentary description, just as biased as an election manifesto, of a termite community. In reality, termite colonies are characterized by everything except welfare, democracy, equality, individual integrity, and similar concepts meant to guide human relationships in western societies.

A short account of termite life and their manner of living must be included in any description of savannah ecology. These insects are vital to the functioning of the savannah ecosystem. Through their consumption of living and dead vegetation, they accelerate the circulation of many important nutritious substances. In addition, they turn over large quantities of soil and thus function as farmers ploughing the fields. Moreover, their lengthy underground systems of tunnels aid in the aeration of the soil and in allowing water to reach deeper levels than it would otherwise. In tropical and subtropical regions, termites fulfil a similar role of working the soil, as do earthworms in temperate regions.

Although important in the productivity of natural ecosystems, they commonly cause enormous problems in agricultural areas. Ripe grain and stored vegetables are food that termites do not turn down. Dead plant material is the primary food source for most termites, and in many parts of the world humans build their houses and other buildings with timber, which is a termite delicacy. Because of this, wooden houses in the tropics have very short life spans. The word 'termite' comes from a Latin verb meaning to abrade, thresh, and crush, as well as torment and wear out. It is a word with many facets and it fits these insects well.

On the other hand, farmers in some regions have learned to take advantage of the enriched soil around the large termitaria produced by the diligent little animals' transportation of soils rich in nutritive salts from deeper layers. The ring shaped areas of cultivation that farmers in some regions establish around the termite mounds can even be observed from aircraft flying at high altitudes.

Termites have two useful characteristics. They have evolved the ability to break down cellulose, although, just like the grazing mammals, they have to recruit microorganisms in order to manage this intractable chemical process. They either keep an abundant intestinal flora of bacteria and a menagerie of single-celled protozoa armed with the enzymes needed to break down cellulose, or they gnaw their way into decaying wood and return with it to their termitaria where it is deposited in the form of 'undigested' excrement. This in turn makes up the growth substrate for certain species of fungi that the termites grow in rigorously climate-controlled chambers and that have never been found elsewhere. It is these fungi which constitute the termites' diet.

The second characteristic of termite biology is that they are not at all related to ants, in spite of many similarities in their way of life and in spite of the fact that they are often referred to as 'white ants'. Within the insect family tree, the closest relatives of termites are cockroaches, although the original split between these two groups occurred more than 150 million years ago. Shortly after their origin, termites evolved a strict social way of life and are without a doubt the oldest group of animals with a eusocial system. This means that reproduction is turned over to a small minority of the society's members, while most spend their time doing everything else: finding food, growing fungi, defence, cleaning, repairing, building, caring for eggs and young, etc.

Although termites and ants come from opposite corners of the multiform insect class, the process of biological evolution has led to surprising similarities between them. The eusocial system, with a division into fertile and sterile castes, is present in both groups. In the termitarium, and usually in the anthill, only one queen reigns, and she is nothing more than a gigantic egg-laying 'machine'. Up to one decimetre long, she lies there, completely immobile and completely dependent on the care of others. An ant queen collects sperm during her short mating flight which she then uses to fertilize her eggs, whereas in the termite 'birthing hall', the termite queen has the company of a king—a small creature that continually delivers sperm but is otherwise just as care-dependent as the female. These two meet during a short mating flight that ends with the casting off of their long wings, after which they creep down into the soil and together establish a new termite society. It is said that they can live in their dark apartment for over a decade. If one of them should die, then another individual in the society, either a young individual or an adult, can be upgraded to a new sexual being—

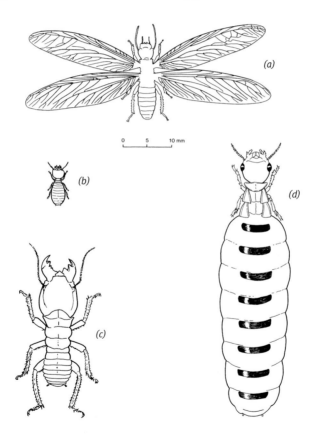

*Figure 7. Termites have different roles in their society: (a) a winged sexual termite, (b) a tiny fungus-farmer, (c) a heavily armed soldier, and (d) a female egg-laying 'machine'.*

a transformation that takes place by putting the individual on a special diet. Similar to ants, termites communicate with one another using chemical substances, and they engage in mating swarms on sporadically recurring occasions, which are synchronized across several communities. One big difference however, is that the sterile caste among termites is composed of both males and females, whereas among ants it consists only of females.

Where similar living conditions have led to a similar design in structure and behaviour in unrelated groups of animals, it is known as convergent evolution. Ants and termites are an excellent example of this; fish, penguins, seals, and whales (and submarines) are another example. From completely different starting materials, similar designs are constructed. Scientists often point towards such convergence as particularly striking evidence of the fantastic creative power of natural selection.

Although dead vegetation (sometimes via fungus farms) makes up the diet of most of the world's 2200 termite species, many of them also eat living, though often withered, plant material. Through devouring dried grass, they cause damage to agricultural crops and grazing land or compete with wild herbivorous mammals for food. Their enormous numbers, in spite of their small size, make them powerful ecological factors in the African savannah ecosystems. In South Africa, there may be up to 1.5 tons of termites per square kilometre that consume between 20 and 200 times their own weight in living and dead plant material per year. Other estimates indicate that up to half of all dead plant material in an ecosystem ends up in a termite's stomach. A study in the Tsavo region of Kenya showed that termites transported almost 9 tons of elephant droppings down into their nests, per square kilometre, per year. As is usually the case, the relationship is complicated. According to some studies, the influence termites have on the savannah ecosystem is insignificant or modest during abundant rain years, but quite radical during long periods of drought.

Termites are also important for life on the savannah in other ways and on other scales than as soil cultivators and ecosystem engineers. Their gigantic building constructions, up to 8 metres tall, make attractive nesting sites and dens for many other animals. In many places in Africa, monitor lizards can be seen sticking their heads out of termitaria ventilation shafts. Even more commonly, a large family of dwarf mongooses may play around a termite mound—energetic, playful, vigilant, and constantly interacting with one another. Hole-nesting birds are drawn to the concrete-hard termitaria where they use existing holes as nesting sites. Alternatively, they might peck out a new hole of their own, something they can do only during the intensive rainy periods when the stone-hard mud softens. Red-and-yellow barbets and woodland kingfishers are two of the species that can be seen suddenly peeking out from a hole in the red wall of a termitarium.

The food-filled termitaria with their stable climates are strong enticements for many different kinds of scavenger. Since insects are fairly skilled at chemical warfare, it is not surprising that at least one species of termite has evolved a special anti-pest preparation that can keep some of the thieves away from the pantry and nursery. The substance they have developed is simply naphthalene, which is what we use to protect our clothes from moths, dermistids, and other pests.

Termites are composed primarily of fats and proteins and are of course a very attractive food for many of the savannah's animals. Several animals have become exceptional specialists in breaking into termitaria and slurping up the small, but countless delicacies. The aardvark has gone the farthest in its specialist adaptations for termite eating, but pangolins, aardwolfs, and honey badgers also partake of termite titbits.

Termites are particularly vulnerable to predators during their short swarming period. When millions of fat insects stream out from the termitarium's special exit gates, a wave of a magician's wand produces multitudes of barn swallows, European swifts, two or three species of rollers, yellowbilled kites, marabou storks, tawny eagles, fiscal shrikes, and carmine bee-eaters. Different birds on each different occasion, but always with the same enthusiasm. Even various mammals enjoy the feast—spotted hyenas, black-backed jackals, savannah baboons, warthogs, and even duiker antelopes taste the goodies. And in some regions, humans also share the abundant delicacy. One simply does not refuse freshly toasted termites.

Moremi, just east of the Okavango Delta. A heavy rain had fallen all afternoon, but towards nightfall it stopped as expected and the sun shone in a narrow streak between the horizon and the slowly retreating rain clouds. Drops of water sparkled in tufts of grass and in spiders' webs as we left to try to locate a leopard that had been seen in the area. However, we were forced to stop only a few hundred metres from the campsite, enthralled by what we saw. In the evening light, an unending river of termites streamed up out of a hole near the base of a giant termitarium and fluttered with their long, glass-like wings slowly towards the heavens. Not one of them had more than a second of life remaining. A host of barn swallows had just arrived, thousands of migrants born perhaps only six months earlier in Sweden, Scotland, Ukraine, or Russia, and they darted about among the slowly rising swarm of termites. Apart from a faint snapping when a swallow beak closed around a termite body cutting off its four wings that floated down towards the ground, the swallows were absolutely quiet, emphasizing their professionalism. Against the light of the disappearing sun, we could easily see that not one termite escaped more than five to eight metres off the ground before it was devoured by a swallow.

There was a lengthy discussion around the camp-fire that night about how remarkable it is that life can go on against such odds. But, if termite queens down in their dark apartments, every day, year after year, can produce thousands of eggs, then mortality among their descendants can reach nearly 100 per cent without leading to a population decrease.


## HERBIVORES AND VEGETATION

Grass, bushes, and trees, all in various proportions and abundance, give the African savannah its characteristic appearance. Countless herbivores—primarily insects, birds, and mammals—eat this vegetation, regardless of the season and whether it is sprouting, budding, seeding, or withering. Complicated relationships therefore exist between the large herbivorous mammals and their food plants.

Although it is easy to imagine an arms race between carnivorous mammals and their prey—cheetahs and gazelles for example—it is not so easy to see that everywhere in nature there are just as intensive and endless games of life and death occurring between producing plants and consuming herbivores. The difference between these two kinds of relationships is in how the game is played. The gazelle must spot the approaching cheetah, read its intentions as quickly as possible, and if necessary flee from the area, whereas plants are sitting prey. They do not react until they have been subject to direct damage; and they cannot run away. Their chance is in building their own powerful strongholds so that potential consumers cannot, or do not find it profitable to eat them. They have a good ability to repair and replace bitten off twigs, buds, and leaves as a last line of defence. Unlike most animals, plants can be partly eaten while continuing to live and reproduce.

Herbivores can be classified as either grazers or browsers. (In addition to leaves, browsers also devour twigs, bark, flowers, seeds, and fruits—any part of a tree or bush.) Characteristic grazing species include hippopotamus, zebra, wildebeest, buffalo, and white rhinoceros; browsing species include the greater and lesser kudu, black rhinoceros, dik-dik, and giraffe. Some species such as impala, eland, and elephant, consume large amounts of both types of plant material, and when food is scarce, most species can shift between the two types of food sources. For example, during the period just before the rains come, grass has usually been grazed down to stubble, trampled down, or burned, but several bushes and trees have already begun to produce leaves. During this time, their delicate leaves are irresistible even to the more dedicated grass eaters.

In general, grasses are small plants, compared with bushes and trees, having shallow roots that are dependent on soil moisture relatively near the surface. Their small size allows grasses to take advantage of brief showers containing only small quantities of rain. To survive the dry season, grasses are either short-lived, often only for one-year, so that every new annual crop starts from last year's seed production, or lie dormant in the form of resistant buds under the surface. In relatively dry regions such as the African savannah, grasses comprise a nutritional resource whose abundance varies greatly according to the season from near zero to being practically unlimited.

Naturally, such a variation in the supply of resources creates considerable problems for grazers. One solution is migration—annual commuting between two different areas. The most famous of the big game migrations is the wildebeest migration across the Serengeti—Masai Mara region of north-western Tanzania and south-western Kenya (see Chapter 6). These game species, which have the ability to migrate between two ecosystems rich in resources during complementary time periods, often attain far greater numbers than stationary populations. One reason for their success seems to be that by commuting, they leave behind many of the carnivores that, because of their territories, are tied to a stationary way of life.

But, what kind of protective adaptations have grass species evolved? Grasses contain small silicon particles that wear down the teeth of grazers. Thus, those elephants whose diet is dominated by grass are in worse condition and die younger than those who eat greater proportions of twigs, leaves, and bark— simply because their teeth wear out sooner. Plants from areas with high grazing pressure accumulate more silicon in their leaves than those from areas lacking large numbers of grazers. They have been programmed to increase their defence budget and produce a greater number of silicon grains compared with plants from areas experiencing lower grazing pressure.

To reduce their attractiveness and tempt herbivores to switch to other plants some grasses have minimized their nutritional content. Typical grazers need to spend a large amount of time shovelling in food, and they must pick and choose not only among different grass species, but also between different areas covered by the same grass species. The nutritional content and energy components in grass may vary greatly from place to place. In particular, pregnant females and females with small, fast-growing young must ensure that they have access to the best quality grass possible. As a rule, grass seeds are loaded with nutritious elements. This is something that humans learned to take advantage of about 10 000 years ago with the development of agriculture; however, zebras and many other grazers had started taking advantage of this fact much earlier. Zebras and certain antelope search out those areas containing seed-bearing grasses when the time for foaling or calving is at hand. Thus, in addition to annual migrations, animals must also take advantage of nutritional resources that are only sporadically available, a situation calling for a more nomadic way of life. Rainfall, which is the most important factor for the productivity of savannah vegetation, varies unpredictably. However, antelopes, zebras, and elephants, as well as many other herbivores have the impressive ability to smell moisture on the wind and register where rain has fallen and where lush vegetation can soon be expected. Despite all their attempts at defence, many species of grass suffer great losses at the expense of herbivores.

Why do grasses react to grazing not only by repairing the loss but also by making an extra effort, an effort generally called compensatory growth? Can cropping actually have a net positive effect on grass? Is it possible that grasses have evolved special reactions whose functions are to tempt the grazing animals to remain longer in the same area? These are controversial questions. The answers to these last two questions are affirmative. When grass re-grows after being cropped, it has a higher nutritional content and a more 'bite-friendly' structure than un-cropped grass. Instead of a single blade of grass, the grazed plant sends up several, each with its own grain ear. Some of the savannah grasses are known to produce seeds with an extremely low germination frequency (down to 2 per cent), and the function of these seeds may be simply to attract grazing animals. Have these reactions evolved as adaptations because they promote the reproduction of the grass plant? Or, are they simply side-effects of the increased nutrient and water availability resulting from the reduction of a part of the grass in addition to the fertilization offered by the grazing beasts? Much of the savannah's soil is extremely poor in nutritive salts, and a shower of urine or a pile of droppings constitutes an important nutritional contribution.

How could grass profit from being grazed? If grazing in some way increases vegetative or reproductive growth then grasses will have a competitive advantage over other plants that have not had this 'idea' of increasing their production capabilities. Some plant ecologists emphasize that the worst enemies of a plant are not necessarily plant-eaters, but neighbouring plants. Competition between plants cannot be ignored when trying to understand why they behave in such a self-destructive manner as to entice herbivores to remain in the same grazing area. Because grass has several growth zones (meristems) at every 'knee' along the blade of grass, cropping part of the plant does not necessarily have such ill-fated consequences as it does with most other herbaceous plants. Other herbaceous plants have a single meristem placed at the top of the plant. Is this an additional grass adaptation, evolving in response to the grazing problem?

The small size of grasses allows them to take advantage of the irregular rainfall in savannah regions. The grass that dominates the Serengeti's drier regions, African oats (*Themeda triandra*), manages just as well irrespective of whether rain falls in several short showers or in a few heavy rains, and irrespective of the time interval between them. As soon as a little rain falls, African oats can quickly initiate growth, blooming, and seed production. When the ground dries out again, the grass returns to a deep torpor, giving it a chance to survive through even lengthy dry periods. This resistance to desiccation (drying out), in combination with the ability to react quickly to sudden rainfall, is a vital adaptation to the irregular rainfall characteristic of the savannah.

Compared with the grasses, bushes and trees have evolved a completely different lifestyle. As a result of living over several years as opposed to only one, trees and bushes have other kinds of problems with herbivores, but they also have other methods of defending themselves against them.

How a certain species of tree or bush best defends itself against browsers depends on many factors. That they do succeed may explain why grazers outnumber browsers in almost all savannah ecosystems. A basic difference between grasses on the one hand, and trees and bushes on the other, is that grasses are monocotyledons whereas trees and bushes are dicotyledons. Monocotyledonous plants have a much less well-developed biochemical mechanism for producing grazing-repellent substances than dicotyledonous plants. Many trees and even more bushes are masters at chemical warfare. As by-products of their normal metabolic processes, they manufacture many different substances, called secondary metabolites, which taste bad and are poisonous.

Through browsing injured plants send out chemical signals that lead to the up-grading of the entire population's chemical defences against plant-eating animals, thus minimizing their loses. Why don't all plants make themselves invulnerable to the insatiable gluttony of herbivores? It is costly to produce chemical defences. Substances produced for defence are not useful for other important functions, such as growth and reproduction. Defence costs must therefore be balanced against probable need. A common solution in plants exposed to herbivores is to reduce the nutritive value in the organs that are most easily within reach. As the risk for consumption then lessens, the plant can reduce its chemical defences. An alternative strategy is to grow fast to reach a 'browsing-proof' height as soon as possible. Those tree or bush parts that are more than about two metres tall are unreachable for all plant-eating mammals with the exception of giraffes and elephants. Plants that struggle with extremely dry conditions or poor nutrition unavoidably grow slowly and are therefore exposed to browsing pressures over a long period of time and, as a result, must sacrifice significant resources for defence. In these cases, lasting defensive weapons such as thorns and other physical defence structures tend to have developed in preference to short-lived chemical substances.

An additional strategy used by plants to reduce their defence costs is to load their most important 'body parts' with poisonous substances, while allowing the herbivores to devour the less important parts. Old leaves, which are about to fall off anyway, are not worth fighting for, whereas buds and fruits are. The plant has a dilemma with new leaves. These are undeniably important for the development of new tissues and eventually for growth, and should be defended. On the other hand, there is profit in getting foliage started quickly, by investing all resources in growth, and putting defence on hold. It is a complicated balance.

The attractiveness of a plant to a browsing animal doesn't just depend on how poisonous it is, but is decided by the balance between its nutritional value and the negative aspects of the plant. Certain plants or plant parts have such a high protein content or contain so many important minerals that the browsing animals, at least in certain situations, brave the plant defences and devour them anyway.

Mopane (*Colophospermum mopane*) alone covers enormous areas of woodland savannah in southern Africa. Since this single tree species is so dominant, leaf-eating animals are extremely dependent on it. The youngest leaves or leaf embryos are covered with a thick layer of sticky resin, making them practically inedible. All herbivores interpret the bright red leaf embryos and the strong-smelling resin as meaning: don't touch me! Once the leaves are fully developed, however, all the forest dwelling leaf-eaters tuck into the tender greenery with ravenous appetites—impala, sable antelope, kudu... By then, the tree doesn't need to defend its foliage. Instead, it reacts by successively sending out new shoots to replace those that have been eaten. Such an investment in growth after cropping (as described for grasses) has been observed for many different plants, with no clear understanding of why it occurs. Knob-thorn acacia (*Acacia nigrescens*) trees that have been severely cropped produce numerous new shoots, which are of extremely high nutritional quality. The more of the tree that is consumed, the more and better quality animal fodder it produces. However some species may die out due to intensive browsing and be replaced by trees of other species that are less palatable to herbivores.

As far as the African savannah's characteristic acacia species are concerned, defence against browsing animals is not primarily chemical, but physical. Thorns so long, hard, and sharp that they puncture even brand new off-road tyres, and spines and hooks that scratch your arms and legs—the typical experiences of travelling in many types of savannah vegetation. However, the creatures they are aimed at are certainly not wandering, meat-eating ecologists, but all kinds of herbivorous animals.

Thus, natural selection has designed a defence that optimizes effectiveness within a given budget. Just how dangerous is the enemy? 'Why prepare for 'star wars' when the adversaries can't even make a hairdryer that works?' (To cite a famed statement during a defence debate in the American congress.) On average, bushes are more thorny than trees, and tall trees, particularly their highest branches, are relatively poorly armed. Consequently, thorniness in the umbrella tree (*Acacia tortilis*) is variably distributed so that it protects the branches. However, it doesn't protect the leaves to the same extent as they are cheaper and easier to replace. Production of branches and twigs requires a great deal of material, they are quite costly, and are intended to serve for a long time. In a comparison between different trees of certain acacia species, the degree of thorniness influences the size of a mouthful and the number of mouthfuls per unit of time in browsing kudus. Barbed thorns, which are found in the well-named 'wait-a-bit' acacia, are particularly effective as protection against the browsing of these animals.

The giraffe is specialized for eating acacia leaves and flowers, and no plant parts below 5 metres above ground are safe from the giraffe's long, muscular tongue. However, few giraffes can reach above 5 metres, and it is therefore quite logical that thorniness in both the fever acacia (*Acacia xanthophloea*) and the white-bark acacia (*A. seyal*) decreases above that height. A more unexpected observation is that, on average, white-bark acacia has longer thorns if there are more giraffes in the area. In a situation where tame goats were the herbivores and whistling acacia (*A. drepanolobium*) the 'food', the low-growing acacias had shorter thorns on branches higher than 125 centimetres, which the goats could not reach, and in addition, the bushes generally reduced their armaments when they were protected from browsing goats through manipulations by the researcher. Time after time, new research results indicate that plants are capable of reacting quickly and expediently to different disturbances and attacks. They don't just stand there and wait to be assimilated into the giant food chain. Several species of acacia have the ability to sense the actual browsing pressure and adjust their defensive investments accordingly. The usual expression explaining this phenomenon is that an increase in browsing pressure 'induces' an increased defence investment in plants.

When it is not possible to fight off the enemy alone, some plants recruit an army of mercenaries. Ants make excellent soldiers. They are fiery and, thanks to their characteristic social habits, they live together in large populations. Thousands of plant species around the world have more or less permanent relations with ants, but on the African savannah there is one special case of plant–ant co-operation that is quite remarkable—the whistling acacia—which recruits mercenary ants belonging to the genus *Crematogaster*. In this acacia species, some thorns swell into an onion-shape inside which the ants make their homes. This doesn't usually occur until the plant is at least a metre high. The plant provides excellent housing for the ants and supplies them with small, protein-rich growths, which the ants gratefully collect and use to enrich their rations.

These ants provide the acacias with a standing professional army which, on the one hand, repels or kills most other insects that come to the bush in order to eat its leaves and seedpods, and on the other hand, makes life difficult for those giraffes that have similar intentions. Giraffes are exceptionally fond of whistling acacia; however, younger animals in particular are greatly bothered by the ants and feed on other acacias that have fewer or no ants. In addition to its army of ants, whistling acacias also have a large store of piercingly sharp thorns; they definitely belong to those plant species with a proportionally large defence budget.

*Figure 8.*
*A branch of a whistling acacia*
*provides accommodation for*
*its guards—fiery-tempered*
*ants in a swollen thorn—*
*a symbiotic relationship*
*where both parties benefit.*

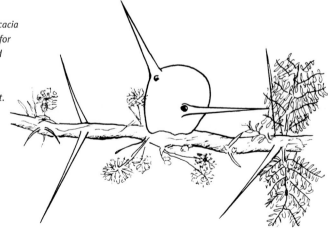

How does the whistling acacia whistle? Ants make small round holes in the swollen base of the acacia thorns to serve as entrances and exits to their homes. When the wind blows in regions with dense populations of whistling acacias, a faint whistling noise can often be heard.

Although there is often a continual battle between plants and animals, there are also more useful relationships between them. Many plants use different kinds of insects to transport pollen from flower to flower. In many cases, birds with a taste for nectar also act as polinators for the plants. In Africa, sunbirds and white-eyes are particularly good examples of this. Also, some mammals perform the function of pollen carrier: for example, bats and galagoes pollinate the large, white, fragrant flowers of the baobab tree (*Adansonia digitata*). (The genus *Galago* is a group of small prosimians often called bushbabies because of their whining calls.)

After the flowers are pollinated and the seeds have ripened, the seeds need to be dispersed throughout the region. Many plants allow their seeds to be transported by the wind, whereas others accept the help of larger animals, birds and mammals. Naturally plants must pay to get the animals to perform this service and they therefore pack the seeds in attractive and nutritionally rich wrappings of different kinds. When the acacia seeds are packed in their pods ready for distribution, a multitude of birds and mammals turn up and help themselves. Many seeds gallantly pass through the animal's digestive system; they then come out together with the droppings, fully or even super-fertile, and are sown in a well-fertilized germination bed. This is particularly true of seeds that end up in an ample elephant dropping: in one single such pile, an industrious researcher counted more than 2000 acacia seeds. However, the seed's travels need not end here. A great number of birds (hornbills, weavers, and starlings for example) and mammals (savannah baboons and various small rodents for example) habitually sift through elephant droppings and pick out seeds and those insects lured to the pile. In this way, the seeds may be carried an additional hundred metres away from the mother plant...

It can be very entertaining to sit down near a pile of fresh elephant droppings, enjoying the circus smell, and observe all the birds, butterflies, beetles, and other animals that have errands to this rich, but short-lived gold mine in the ecosystem.

## PARADISE IN PERIL

On a July day a few years ago, a couple of friends and I were sitting on top of a kopje, a castle-like rocky island, gazing out over the endless wide open expanse of the Serengeti. Far off to the north-east, towers the magnificent, but extinct volcano Ol Doinyo Langai. Towards the south-east, we could see the cloud-shrouded Ngorongoro Crater, and in the north and west, low ridges and shallow valleys reaching to the horizon, covered with grass, solitary trees, and walls of bushes. Looking like an ant, a Land Rover crawled along through the grass. We saw a herd of well over 400 eland antelope grazing on a slope—the largest herd of this heavy-weight antelope that any of us had ever seen. Although the dry grass and leafless trees indicated that a long time had passed since the last rain, a hundred metres from us was a small pool of water, and in and around it we saw a pack of 18 spotted hyenas—bathing, resting, slowly sauntering around with drooping stomachs. It had obviously been a real party night for this gang, who now lay resting beside the pool like tourists. Two shimmering points of silver, black, and white on a rocky precipice out in the water turned out to be a pair of blacksmith plovers, and silhouetted against a thunderhead building up in the west we saw a large spiral of circling white-backed vultures in addition to a pair of huge eared or lappet-faced vultures. Suddenly, a herd of Grant's and Thomson's gazelles grazing some distance from our look-out post suffered from an acute and collective nervous breakdown and they rushed off in all directions—all except two Grant's gazelles who remained in place, looked around, and then continued grazing. There is always one that doesn't lose its composure as easily as the rest.

Our peaceful conversation about all the interesting things we had seen drifted into a deeply philosophical topic: is paradise stable? That we were in the middle of paradise—of this we were all in agreement. However, was our impression of timelessness and balance a false impression, was it based on unscientific wishful thinking and on the sight (at that moment) of the peacefully grazing herds?

During the past hundred years the Serengeti region has been exposed to several influences that have brought about changes in the vegetation and animal life. There are no indications that this area is unique among Africa's savannahs. Disturbances of various kinds probably influenced the African ecosystems long before the short period about which we have direct knowledge.

The first Europeans who came to the Serengeti region over a hundred years ago were explorers, missionaries, and hunters. Their observations from the end of the nineteenth century describe a Serengeti that must have been very similar to the one we see today. They describe vast, open, grassy savannah alternating with sparse bush and woodland savannah, as well as dense gallery forests along the few permanent waterways that were lush even during the dry seasons.

A more lasting European presence in the Serengeti region arrived during the 1930s—some ten years after German East Africa became Tanganyika Territory. From those times, reports speak less of grassy expanses, and more of the unending 'bush'—which in this context means both bush and woodland savannah. Judging from these descriptions (in many cases made by knowledgeable and experienced biologists), quite dense forests covered large areas of the Serengeti.

Twenty years later however, the 'bush' had thinned out and even the disappearance of the woodlands was considered a serious problem. It was during this period, approximately fifty years ago, that the expansion of the present-day vast grassy savannah occurred. What factors brought about these powerful landscape dynamics? What is causing this peril in paradise?

During the last quarter of the nineteenth century—and a long while before that—a large population of Masai lived in north-western Tanzania. As today, the

Masai based their livelihoods on large herds of livestock. At the beginning of the 1890s however, a terrible catastrophe occurred for these people—a deadly virus, rinderpest, infected their livestock. The virus came to Africa via cattle imported from India and destined to supply Italian troops with meat during their campaigns in Somalia and Ethiopia. The Masai sank into extreme poverty as 95 per cent of their livestock died of rinderpest within a few years. Rinderpest also affects ruminants other than domesticated livestock. Consequently, populations of many herbivores such as wildebeest and buffalo also declined. Simultaneously, a smallpox epidemic raged among the already devastated Masai tribes.

The dramatic decrease in grazing pressure brought about by the unchecked rinderpest problem, encouraged an increasingly dense bush and tree vegetation to spread out over the open grassy savannah. There was also no elephant population to keep the invading vegetation in check. Re-colonization by the Masai became more difficult due to the occasional outbreak of rinderpest and as the vegetation in the area became more dense it became an ideal habitat for tsetse flies (*Glossina*). Tsetse flies can transmit the fatal disease called nagana to livestock and sleeping sickness (trypanosomiasis) to humans.

By this time an understanding had emerged of the importance of conserving nature and protecting it from the far too brutal effects of humans. Initially, the British colonial administration had worked energetically towards preserving the bush and woodland savannah in their 'original' condition; however, only half a century later they appeared completely different. (Enormous gratitude is owed the British colonizers for these early conservation efforts.)

In the 1950s the grass savannah again began to increase in area. Because grazing pressure was still quite weak, there was an abundance of dry grass at the beginning of the dry season. This often led to recurrent and extraordinarily intense savannah fires—sometimes spontaneous, sometimes intentional. Fire is a friend to grass and an enemy to bushes. Vaccination of the Masai livestock on a large scale resulted in a very quick increase in their herds, and also of their own numbers. Like fire, the herds of livestock are friends to grass and enemies to bushes. In addition, since the 1960s, the average rainfall has greatly increased in these parts of Africa; the amount has doubled outside the regular rainy season. Another important factor is that elephants—the foremost savannah architects— entered the scene (or made a comeback). As a consequence of heavy hunting pressures and an increase in agriculture, together with other disturbances in adjacent areas, in the 1950s, elephants wandered into the Serengeti, which was then relatively free from poaching. When I visited the Serengeti for the first time in 1958, my travelling companion—Hugh Lamprey, who was later to become legendary among wildlife researchers—and I saw two groups of over a dozen animals each and, in addition, two gigantic males with tusks so long that they reached the ground as the animals stood resting. The perpetual topic of discussion around campfires in the Serengeti at this time was 'the elephant problem'. In a research report based on fieldwork in the Serengeti during 1965–67, the authors wrote in summary that 'the speed with which the forests are being destroyed makes it clear that if the Serengeti's different habitats are to be preserved in approximately their current states and proportions, then time is short—perhaps only two or three years—to gather a scientific foundation for important decisions on the national park's future management'. In particular, the authors were worried that the magnificent and ecologically significant population of fever acacias would be ruined by the elephants, especially as elephants have the habit of pushing over or breaking off considerably more trees than they actually consume. In 1971, there were no fewer than 2500 elephants in the Serengeti, and these large consumers had an enormous effect on the vegetation. When possible, elephants eat bushes and trees rather than grass and thus contribute to 'deforestation', 'de-bushing', and the expansion of the grass savannah. In doing so they are literally sawing off the branch on which they sit, since they cannot survive as well in a pure grass savannah.

However, the Serengeti's elephant population crashed during the 1970s and early 1980s. Poachers killed about two-thirds of the elephants, and most of those who escaped the slaughter fled over the border to Kenya, to the Masai Mara region where tourist density was greater and protection better, preventing the criminals from acting as freely. Consequently, the Masai Mara region began to develop an 'elephant problem', as this quickly growing and confined elephant population began to 'deforest' their new homeland.

During the 1980s, in addition to the decline in elephant population, the other herbivore populations quickly increased in number and in several cases reached record highs. At the end of the 1980s, the Serengeti ecosystem (which is usually taken to include the Masai Mara region on the Kenyan side of the border) harboured approximately two million large herbivores, with wildebeest making up the greatest numbers. Despite the almost complete disappearance of elephants, the grass savannah remained open thanks to the tremendous population of grazers.

Owing to the terrible slaughter of elephants in East Africa during the 1980s, a number of large-scale experiments were unintentionally conducted on the effects of elephants on vegetation. During the 1970s, elephants in Tsavo, Kenya, caused a massive destruction of umbrella acacias and corkwood bushes (*Commiphora*) in particular. In both cases, an almost explosive 'resurrection' occurred during the 1980s when poaching and severe drought removed three-quarters of the elephant population, and in some places the numbers were even greater. Both acacias and corkwood produce seeds that are not wind dispersed, but are transported from their points of origin in the stomachs of, for example savannah baboons, impalas, and hornbills. Quite clearly, these seed-dispersers are extremely effective since the acacias and the corkwood reclaimed lost ground so quickly.

The perilous see-saw in paradise is a complicated phenomenon. The shape and extent of grazing pressures influence the vegetation, both directly and indirectly. In turn, changes in the vegetation provide new opportunities for different plant species. When elephants increase in an area of dense bush and woodland savannah, the nutritional basis for typical leaf-eaters such as black rhinos and both kudu species decreases, whereas it increases for grass-eaters such as wildebeest, zebra, and both gazelle species, all of which thrive in the open landscape.

Elephants are of great significance as architects of the savannah but even lightweight species can have a great influence, not necessarily in eliminating trees and bushes, but in preventing their re-establishment. Impalas for example have been found to eat so many seedlings that the establishment of new umbrella acacias can be hindered for decades. Rinderpest gave the vegetation a chance: when pressure from browsers was reduced, or in some places almost eliminated, bushes and trees shot up in great numbers. Even today, the traces of rinderpest can be seen in the age distributions of many tree populations.

As one gazes out over the Serengeti's wide-open spaces, it is easy to imagine that balance and stability characterize the savannah. This impression evaporates quickly in the light of the all too few published long-term ecological studies. These show how completely natural events, occasional or more frequent, give the ecosystem a push, allow various things to happen, and after a time a new pseudo-balance is reached that lasts until the next disturbance occurs. Extremes in amounts of rainfall are perhaps the best examples of natural events with a significant influence on plant and animal life. Even relatively small events expand and influence increasingly large sections of the ecosystem—sometimes a cascade effect is mentioned where a little 'nudge' reproduces itself throughout the system with increasingly greater effects.

Since humans have become the dictators of development in Africa's savannahs, the ecosystem has unavoidably become subject to disturbances that recur all too often and are all too profound and irrevocable. Humans, for example, can introduce diseases that affect both wild and domestic populations of animals—consider rinderpest, which devastated the ruminating herbivores. Our domestic animals such as dogs can spread infections like rabies and distemper to wild carnivores—with obvious consequences for the herbivores and, through them, the vegetation. Within a decade, humans have demonstrated their ability to exterminate elephants in a large area and thereby eliminate one of the most important players in the savannah's dynamics. Above all, we have reached a position as total dominators of the global ecosystem such that we, for our own consumption, have appropriated or taken charge of increasingly larger portions of the entire accessible capacity for production. Seen from a longer perspective, through a global restructuring of the ecosystem, we appear to be in the process of eliminating the living conditions for a great number of our fellow species.

Humans seem to have a catastrophic effect on the megafauna—the larger mammals—when they arrive on a new continent. Most of the larger mammals in Africa have been decimated or pushed aside into small pockets of their previous areas of distribution, although few species have been completely exterminated thus far. 'Out of the way, move aside—because here we come'.

It is quickly darkening over Africa's savannah. Those areas of relatively natural savannah still in existence today will probably decrease from the pressures of an overcrowded humanity. This is happening in much the same way as has already happened in Europe, where 'natural nature' is a rarity and most large mammals have been forced to retreat, are few in number, or are already exterminated. Perhaps Zimbabwe's, Namibia's, and Kenya's cheetah and lion populations will come to be as paltry as Sweden's wolf and wolverine populations. This is a depressing prospect.

# 4

## Pillars of the earth

*'There were two or three fine males, however, one of whom evidently acted... militarily speaking, as a General of Division. This particular elephant was standing in a position outskirting the rest, but his shoulder, unfortunately, was partially hidden by two large calves, which the jolly old patriarch was busily caressing. A very slight change of attitude was all I required to enable me to send him to the land of shades... To my intense disappointment, however, the huge brute all at once tossed his trunk on high, and, giving his sides two or three smart slaps with his monster ears, turned abruptly round and made off, instantly followed by the whole herd. But it would never do to allow them to escape thus. Springing, therefore, to my feet, and advancing a few steps, I levelled and fired at the second in size of the males... The bullet struck him, but very unsatisfactorily...'*

Thus writes the famous Swedish adventurer Charles John Andersson in 1861 in his book entitled '*The Okavango River*'. During the 1850s, this remarkable man travelled in the area now known as Namibia and Botswana, and his book is a virtual gold mine, especially for those who appreciate gruesome hunting tales of wounded animals.

Theodore Roosevelt was also a great hunter. The following is an a report of one of his elephant encounters: 'Then we saw that it was a big bull with good ivory. It turned its head in my direction and I saw its eye; and I fired a little to one side of the eye, at a spot that I thought would lead to the brain. I struck exactly where I aimed, but the head of an elephant is enormous and the brain small, and the bullet missed it. However, the shock momentarily stunned the beast. He stumbled forward, half falling, and as he recovered I fired with the second barrel, again aiming for the brain. This time the bullet sped true, and as I lowered the rifle from my shoulder, I saw the great lord of the forest come crashing to the ground.'

Like Andersson's book, Roosevelt's 'African Game Trails' (1910) is the perfect book for one who is looking for horrible and grisly hunting stories, and—as the author so rightly points out—'the death of an elephant is always a great event'.

Throughout time, many have preferred to see elephants just so: through a gunsight with the bead aimed at the spot just beside the eye which marks the doorway to the brain, or aimed at another significantly larger target, the heart and lungs, which my sources recommend for 'amateurs and tourist hunters'. Today, an increasing number of people find such pleasure-shooting ethically offensive. However, it is not individuals like Charles John Andersson or Theodore Roosevelt or their successors who are behind the declining numbers (about 80 per cent) of African elephants during the past century.

No, the reason for this radical decline is not depredation by early explorers, regardless of how unbelievably brutal many of them were. Neither is it the fault of more recent 'amateur and tourist hunters', who in most African countries hunt under at least somewhat controlled forms. Instead, there are two reasons why the African elephant has become one of the world's greatest conservation problems. First, the decline in elephant populations can be blamed primarily on the organized and mechanized mass slaughter aimed at obtaining their valuable ivory. Second, additional problems are currently developing because a rapidly increasing number of poor farmers find themselves forced to co-exist with elephant herds.

For thousands of years, humans have coveted the elephant's two upper incisors. Those constantly growing, wonderfully formed, brilliantly white (especially by the light of the full moon) ivory tusks. The elephant's all-purpose tool that acts as a pickaxe, a pitchfork, a lever, a weapon, and an ornament.

The light creamy whiteness of the ivory and its exceptional hardness provides inspiration to artists to carve all kinds of objects—jewellery, dagger handles, chess pieces, statues. Both Asians and Europeans have been enthralled with this raw material, which for a long period comprised Africa's most important export commodity, along with the slave trade. Thousands of slaves were driven from their home districts to shipping ports in West and East Africa, weighed down under ivory tusks with the same destination. Approximately 50 000 elephants per year were killed for the sake of their ivory at the beginning of the twentieth century. In easily accessible areas, such as the open savannah of East Africa, elephants had already been decimated or exterminated during the first third of the twentieth century. In those days however, there was a reserve which could be plundered. In large parts of Africa, transportation and communication were non-existent, or at least not suitable for large-scale exploitation of natural resources until after the Second World War, and there was plenty of land available that was not coveted by land-hungry farmers.

That situation changed drastically during the last quarter of the twentieth century. It is estimated that a total of about 700 000 elephants were killed (80 per cent illegally) on the African continent during the 1980s. This represents a removal of about 8 000 000 kilogrammes of ivory, most of which was destined for Hong Kong and Japan. Across vast areas, in entire countries, the elephant populations have been decimated in this incomprehensible massacre. Increasing prosperity chiefly in Eastern and Southern Asia increased the clientele and raised the prices, which led to an increase in profitability for the illegal ivory trade and made it comparable to the ruthless international narcotics trade. An additional similarity between these two operations is that in many countries their organizers manage to corrupt politicians and public authorities and thus make themselves untouchable by society's policing authorities.

One effect of the ivory passion has been that elephants with small or almost no tusks have had significantly better chances of surviving and reproducing than those with large tusks. In East Africa, it is now extremely unusual to see one of those mighty 'tuskers', with tusks almost scraping the ground in front of the elephant. Such individuals were far from rare until the 1960s and early 1970s. Since the growth of tusks is a highly heritable trait, today elephant young are born with small tusks or no tusks at all. A characteristic that was previously advantageous—large tusks—has suddenly become a disadvantage, and consequently, the elephant population has undergone a modification (not a deterioration, which is sometimes suggested) in genetic make-up. In other words, the elephant population has undergone rapid evolutionary change.

The ruthless exploitation of Africa's elephant herds has certainly not ended. However, there is some hope. Resolutely and successfully, politicians and public authorities in several countries have combated the illegal hunting of elephants, especially since they have understood the economic potential elephants hold. Many African countries earn—or could possibly earn—considerably more money from tourism than from any other industry. This insight, urged on by international pressures and economic subsidies, is why elephant populations have begun to make comebacks in Kenya, Tanzania, and Uganda, three countries where poaching had been particularly widespread and disastrous in the past. Many rulers in these, and in other African countries, view the increase in elephant populations with satisfaction since tourism is an important factor for their countries as well as (sometimes) for their own entirely private economies.

Unfortunately, a positive result in the minister of finance's budget in Nairobi, Harare, or Lusaka is poor consolation for the impoverished farmer who sees his corn crop completely destroyed by a nocturnal visit from an elephant herd in the Kenyan, Zimbabwean, or Zambian countryside. If the meagre harvest fails, starvation and misery threaten him and his family. It is no wonder he is tempted to take up his weapon to try to rid himself of the colossal food bandits. How can the interest for keeping vigorous elephant populations be combined with the legitimate needs of humans for food for their daily survival?

One of the more successful attempts at solving this dilemma is a project called

*Campfire*, which hopes to enable the co-existence of small-scale farming and robust big game populations, especially elephants, in different parts of Zimbabwe. The theory is simple. If a village agrees not to shoot at marauding (or any other) elephants, then they receive a sum of money or some wished-for installation (for example, a better road, a clinic, or a school). The government rakes in the money for this 'encroachment compensation' through hunting fees from those who, like Charles John Andersson and Theodore Roosevelt, get a thrill from shooting elephants or other big game—and are willing to pay generously for the thrill.

Naturally the farmers are unwilling to trade away their traditional way of life. In addition, the money that should be sent to the village from some public authority in Harare commonly fails to arrive. The money is probably pocketed by officials along the way.

One thing is certain: in order for elephants to roam freely over Africa's savannah in fifty years time, tourism must continue to grow. Each year, new throngs of poor people want to claim a piece of the African soil. Their most pressing concern is not conserving large wild animals, but instead, scraping out a harvest from the meagre soil, thus supplying food that will keep starvation away from them and their families.

From our origins in Africa, the radiating waves of modern humans across the world led to the decimation or extinction of large mammals (the megafauna) on one continent after another. There were no sanctuaries for the large scrumptious mammals when the new primates turned up with their craving for meat, their effective teamwork, and their long-distance weapons.

Our species originated in Africa, the same African continent where our predecessors also had their headquarters. The reason why Africa's megafauna has managed to survive this human craving for meat more successfully than the fauna in any other part of the world is perhaps because we evolved together on the African continent. Because of this co-evolution, we have ended up in a kind of balance of terror, which has not threatened most prey species until the present century. With the exception of Africa, humans, *Homo sapiens*, are intruders every-where, newcomers with exotic habits and deleterious effects—akin to how we look upon starlings, minks, or fire ants in the countries that they have invaded.

Among large mammals in Africa, elephants have been given the most attention and their numbers have undergone a catastrophic decrease during recent decades. Their survival in a natural state is in danger. There are many reasons for this. Elephants are big, and a full-grown elephant bull is enormously so. When you meet one on foot instead of from the relative security of a car, it is inconceivably huge.

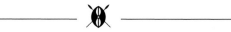

I was once driving in Ruaha National Park in the heart of Tanzania with my Tanzanian assistant, Boniface, at my side. The elephants had pulled up and overturned lots of thorny bushes and small trees, scattering them across the road. Since it would not have been very amusing to have a flat tyre in the middle of that sparsely inhabited region, Boniface jumped out and pulled the bushes and trees aside. After the umpteenth time this happened, I decided that it was my turn to lend a hand, so I climbed out of the car and approached the bush that was blocking our way. It was hard work; I pulled with all my strength. Suddenly, I heard Boniface rapping on the window from inside the car, pointing excitedly towards my left. There stood two enormous bull elephants—I thought that they were as big as two-storey houses and I remember their light, ash-grey colour—and from a distance of 50 metres, they observed my struggle with the thorny bushes. They stood stock still, they had stopped chewing even though they each had a twig protruding from their mouths, and they scrutinized me with what looked like amused expressions. As quickly as I could, I retreated to the car where I could watch them more closely. After a while, they shook their heads so that their trunks swung back and forth and little clouds of dust rose from their necks. Then their jaws began grinding and they slowly walked across the road in front of us and disappeared among the bushes and trees. I wondered what they were thinking—though perhaps it is best that I do not know what their comments about my pathetic struggle would have been.

Everything on an elephant is enormous. In the old days, the biggest males could attain a shoulder height of at least 4 metres and weigh 6 tons. However, since both legal and illegal hunters prefer to shoot the biggest animals, such giants hardly exist anymore. Elephants are one of the terrestrial mammals that exhibit the greatest size difference between the sexes (sexual dimorphism). The largest females are only, at most, half as heavy as the largest males. The largest tusk ever weighed was 106 kilogrammes, and the longest was 3.55 metres long. Sexual dimorphism of tusks is even greater than for body weight, as the heaviest tusk recorded from a female only weighed 25 kilogrammes. An erect penis on a full-grown elephant is S-shaped, about 1.20 metres long, and weighs 25 kilo-grammes. His heart weighs 30 kilogrammes. Is any more evidence required to show that everything about an elephant is colossal?

It is no easy job constructing legs that can support and move an elephant body that weighs as much as three or four medium-sized cars. Natural selection has solved this problem by shaping their legs like columns, replacing their bone marrow with a porous, but effective shock absorbing 'filling', and making their feet big and circular. The fact is that these huge animals walk on their toes and only the front part of their feet. The fibula and tibia are twisted around each other as our radius and ulna are when we place our hand on a table in front of us with the palm facing up. This configuration stabilizes the extremities. The cost of being able to maintain necessary stability is that elephants cannot move their legs laterally and they can neither gallop (with apologies to Andersson the big game hunter) or jump. The elephant's gait is hard to describe—even when it is in a hurry, it glides or drifts over the terrain, shuffling or lumbering, although seem-ingly light on its feet and dignified. It is effective: elephants move 40 times more economically than mice do, relative to their weight. An elephant is also fast: no human has been able to run away from an elephant that really wanted to catch them. It moves quietly: these three to four ton giants can move soundlessly across the savannah. Many times I have had several elephants only a few metres from my tent and not had any idea they were there until the moon was suddenly hidden behind one of their bodies. There is an almost spooky atmosphere about a night with elephants around the campsite. In some places, the darkness was darker than black: it was probably an elephant. Tusks glimmer as streams of moonlight reflect off their ivory surfaces. Suddenly a palm tree falls to the ground. Who did that? With its tiny grating call, a Scops owl makes more noise than three elephants.

Their appetites are huge. An elephant eats food equivalent to about 5 per cent of its own body weight, which means between 150 to 200 kilogrammes per day for an 'average' elephant. Elephants eat all kinds of plant material, but prefer mostly bush and tree greenery to grass. Different kinds of succulent fruits and seeds can also be very desirable. The hard, apple-sized fruits of the doum palm are apparently irresistible. It is quite a sight to see an elephant butting the tree trunk trying to make them fall to the ground. What a satisfied expression when a bunch of

*Figure 9.*
*A local specialization: in some places in Zimbabwe older male elephants in particular have learned to stand on their hind legs to reach high branches. Quite a feat for a five-ton giant!*

those delicacies come thudding down on and around the elephant! Sometimes the entire palm is knocked over with one big shove. It doesn't seem to be intentional, at least judging from the expression of 'uh oh' that one imagines on the elephant's face.

This enormous consumption means that a large elephant population will change the vegetation, decimating the trees and bushes and encouraging the open grassy areas to expand. Since vast, open grass savannah provides poor nourishment and no shade the elephants move on to 'greener pastures'.

That was how it was before. Nowadays however, most elephants are enclosed in some kind of wildlife preserve and they are met with gunfire at every attempt to migrate. Consequently, they return to the national park or wildlife preserve, which results in further damage to the trees and bushes as well as, sooner or later, their own deaths. If not sooner, their deaths come when the area is hit by a series of several dry years in a row.

Everything is on a large scale when dealing with elephants: including the problems they cause in a changing environment increasingly dominated by man. Should we or should we not eradicate elephant populations to prevent them from causing drastic environmental alterations and crop damage outside reserves as well as in national parks? This question has no easy answer. It is here that ecology, economy, ethics, and politics become part of the decision-making process.

The elephant population has already been decimated through culling and is still declining in many African countries. By the winter of 1997–98, one of the last big undisturbed elephant populations in Africa started being culled, namely the elephants living in north-eastern Botswana, Namibia's Caprivi corridor, and the western most regions of Zimbabwe.

Elephants are extremely gregarious and communicative. All attempts at reducing elephant numbers must take this into consideration. If you shoot one or more individuals from a herd, the survivors will flee the area in a state of shock and spread their experiences of humans, vehicles, and aeroplanes to all the other herds that have yet to be targeted. The region will soon be filled with nervous, socially rootless and aggressive elephants—not a good situation for those who have the job of culling or for tourists whose credit cards are necessary for the fragile economies.

For these reasons, culling generally occurs in the following manner. A herd is chosen that seems convenient to 'take out' (kill) via aerial reconnaissance. The aircrew provides directions to the ground-based culling crew so that they can approach the herd. For the last kilometre, the shooters and their assistants proceed on foot, carefully observing the wind direction since elephants have a keen sense of smell. The aeroplane continues to roar above the elephant herd, which allows the advancing shooters to approach stealthily as close as possible.

Three or more experienced marksmen, each with a 'gun-loader', try to get as close as 20 metres. When the herd's matriarch discovers one of the men, she trumpets her warning call, folds out her huge ears, and goes to attack to protect her family. Ideally, it is best to shoot her first because then complete confusion spreads through the herd. Elephants rush this way and that in panic, screaming in terror, often running into each other, one after another toppling or sinking to the ground, dead or dying, paralysed by a bullet in the spine. The mothers do everything they can to defend their young from the gunshots and they place themselves between their young and the marksmen. Dead and dying elephants prevent those still alive from being able to flee and many of them do not even try to leave: elephants do not leave their loved ones willingly. The last rifle shots extinguish the lives of those not yet dead and of the very young elephants that paralysed from terror, lean against their dead and dying mothers. On successful hunts, twenty, thirty, or perhaps forty elephants can be cut down in less than ten minutes. Would you like to join an elephant hunt? Unlikely.

When the echo of the last rifle shot has died away, the bearers come forward and begin taking care of the cadavers. The ivory, meat, and skins will all be used for some purpose or another. One can take the penis of a young male and make a nice lamp-stand from it, and from the penis sheath, one can make a durable and functional golf bag. Eventually, only a pile of termite-eaten and hyena-gnawed bones bear witness to the massacre that has taken place. The mowing-down of an entire elephant family seems to have made no impression at all. Or, has it?

The various elephant herds in any specific area have closely knit social ties and frequent infrasound communication across long distances. They live in clans or tribes, with hundreds of members divided up into small nuclear groups that for the most part move about on their own. In these smaller herds, the oldest female takes on the responsibility of leadership. A common age for such a matriarch is between 40 and 60 years old. Most likely, it was just such an old, experienced, elephant grandmother that Charles John Andersson described as 'Division General' and 'patriarch' and tried to send to the 'land of shades'. The other adult females in the herd are her daughters, granddaughters, sisters, and perhaps a cousin or two—as well as their offspring of both sexes. The females live their entire lives within the herd into which they were born, and maintain special lifelong relationships with their mothers. The males however, leave the herd and their mothers permanently when they become teenagers. This pattern is repeated in many other species as well: the young of one sex emigrate, the young of the opposite sex stays at home. There is no risk of inbreeding.

It is a difficult decision for a young male elephant. On the one hand: leave mother and all the other nice aunts and friends who have been so good to play with. On the other hand: what is there over that hill, and wouldn't it be nice to be just one of the guys...?

One afternoon, near the Chobe River in northern Botswana, we saw a young male elephant wrestling with exactly this dilemma. Down along the banks of the river, absorbed in resting after a thoroughly enjoyable bath in a delightfully muddy pool, was an elephant herd of about twenty individuals—adult females of different sizes and their offspring. A young male elephant moved uneasily back and forth just on the edge of the herd. Every now and then he tried to nudge his way into the herd, but was met in an unfriendly fashion. Then, with his trunk waving and his ears flapping, he ran a couple of hundred metres up the sandy bank of the river towards the forest. He stopped, turned around, and looked at the herd. 'A prisoner of his emotions...' After a minute, he lumbered down to the herd again and tried to force his way in among them. Again, he was rebuffed—not brusquely, but rather 'reprovingly'. They continued in this manner until the sun began to go down and we were forced to leave.

It is captivating to witness the reunion of elephant females and their young when they have not had contact with each other for a while. A wild greeting ceremony and a storm of emotions break out. Old and young run towards each other under loud trumpeting and rumbling, they smell and touch one another with their trunks, and two by two, they twine their trunks around each other. The youngsters bugle and jostle against one another. How could you describe happiness without including the greeting ceremony of elephants?

Most elephant herds, at least if they contain more than half a dozen individuals, are like ladies clubs. Every club is part of an extended regional network. If one of the nuclear herds should suddenly fail to appear at one of the more or less regular gatherings that elephants in a particular region have, they would without a doubt be 'missed'. The matriarchs, who have good memories, would notice that one group in the network had stopped coming to the conferences. Thus the complete annihilation of an entire nuclear herd might spread anxiety in an area and influence the elephants' behaviour.

Some professional biologists have observed that elephants have a mysterious concept of death. Elephants react very strangely when, during their wanderings, they discover dead elephants or parts of elephant skeletons. Elephant researcher Cynthia Moss wrote: 'Elephants may not have a graveyard but they seem to have some concept of death. It is probably the single strangest thing about them. Unlike other animals, elephants recognize one of their own carcasses or skeletons... When they come upon an elephant carcass they stop and become quiet and yet tense in a different way from anything I have seen in other situations... They seem particularly interested in the head and tusks... I would guess they are trying to recognize the individual.' They do not behave at all in this manner when they encounter other dead animals.

Cynthia Moss, as well as other elephant researchers, has described how passing elephants have strayed from their course and come into a research camp when part of a dead elephant has been brought in to determine its cause of death. She writes: 'Recently one of the big adult females in the population died of natural causes and we collected her jaw after a few weeks and brought it to the camp. Three days later her family happened to be passing through the camp and when they smelt the jaw they detoured from their path to inspect it. One individual stayed for a long time after the others had gone, repeatedly feeling and stroking the jaw and turning it with his foot and trunk. He was the dead elephant's seven-year-old son, her youngest calf. I felt sure that he recognized it as his mother's.'

'Death by natural causes', for that matter. What do elephants die of when they are not executed by a firing squad? Definitely not because of predation, other than on the rare occasion when a young elephant becomes separated from its family. On the contrary, it is a great pleasure to observe the combination of nonchalance and superiority that elephants demonstrate towards even large predators such as lions. Neither a herd of elephants nor a solitary male elephant shies away from such a triviality as a pride of lions. Every now and then a lion might growl and show its teeth at an approaching elephant. The elephant's reaction, at the most, is a lazy swing of its trunk and an irritated glance. Predators are certainly not a common cause of death for an adult elephant.

A study from Hwange National Park in western Zimbabwe provides a partial answer to the natural causes that can result in the death of an elephant. Accidents seem to be the most common reason: getting stuck in the mud, drowning, falling down a precipice, and breaking a leg, all are incidents that lead to a more or less immediate death. During fights between males, the elephants sometimes receive unpleasant wounds that can become infected, and in the worst cases, life threatening. The role that disease and parasites play is difficult to determine. Unlike most wild animals, it seems as though an appreciable number of elephants die from different kinds of age-related changes, especially those affecting their teeth. Although elephants have a unique secondary dentition mechanism, where one after another of the teeth is pushed forwards in the jaw so that they can successively act as millstones, their teeth wear down. The cause of death for these elephants could be that they are no longer able to chew their food well enough to supply them with the nourishment they need. However, since most elephant populations are now subject to hunting pressures, it is rare that elephants reach the age when the last of their teeth fails them.

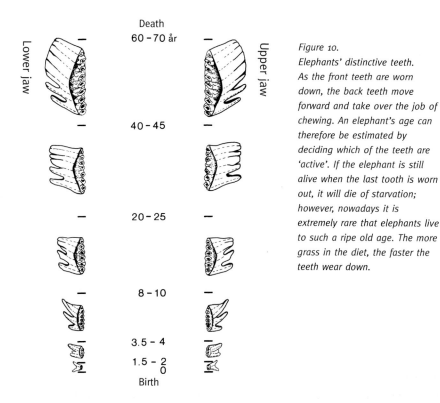

Death
60 – 70 år

Lower jaw

40 – 45

20 – 25

8 – 10

3.5 – 4

1.5 – 2
0

Birth

Upper jaw

*Figure 10.*
*Elephants' distinctive teeth. As the front teeth are worn down, the back teeth move forward and take over the job of chewing. An elephant's age can therefore be estimated by deciding which of the teeth are 'active'. If the elephant is still alive when the last tooth is worn out, it will die of starvation; however, nowadays it is extremely rare that elephants live to such a ripe old age. The more grass in the diet, the faster the teeth wear down.*

Female elephants normally live within the circle of their families until their last days. Some of them might have passed menopause and act as full-time grandmothers. Several times, researchers have seen how their relatives try different measures to keep them alive after they have sunk to the ground, unable to rise again. Elephant herds never abandon an individual—young or old—who for one reason or another moves at a slower speed. Instead, the pace is adjusted to allow for the slowest member of the family.

On rare occasions, elephants may kill carnivores that have not reacted appropriately to the elephants' threats. My good friend Hugh Lamprey (at that time a game researcher and gamekeeper in Tanzania) once told me about the following episode that he had witnessed during his fieldwork in Tarangire, south-east of Ngorongoro in northern Tanzania. Nowadays, the Tarangire National Park is popular with tourists, but then it was only a sparsely inhabited reserve, similar to the surrounding savannah. The region provides an important haven for many of the big game species that are dispersed across the southern part of Masai land during the rainy season, but are dependent on the Tarangire River during the dry period.

Hugh was standing at the edge of a grass-covered glade that was as big as two football fields and surrounded by dense brush. Across the glade he saw two elephant mothers, each with an offspring of about 3–4 years of age. The young elephants played and romped about moving farther and farther out towards the middle of the glade and away from their mothers, who continued feeding on the acacias along the edge. Suddenly, Hugh heard a bushbuck bark from somewhere close by and as he looked towards it he saw, a bit further off, a crouched lioness with her gaze fixed on the cavorting juvenile elephants who were slowly moving closer to both Hugh and the lioness. When they were about fifty metres from the lioness, she rushed towards them with amazing acceleration. With a violent body-tackle, she brought the smaller of the two young elephants to the ground and in the same split-second the other juvenile gave out a terrific scream and ran back towards the two mothers. They had already noticed what was happening and one of them, most likely the downed elephant's mother, came racing like a Fury towards the spot—trunk raised and ears spread wide. The lioness must have suffered a momentary mental block because instead of fleeing, she crouched, growled, and prepared to defend her prey. The next minute, the elephant grabbed the lioness around her middle with her trunk, lifted her so violently that all four feet were pointing straight up, and then threw her crashing to the ground. Then she lowered herself onto her knees, thrust her tusks through the body of the already dead lioness, stood up and then repeatedly trampled the body of her enemy. She screamed incessantly throughout the whole episode while the other female—perhaps her sister—with her panic-struck offspring pushed closely against her, stood quietly and unmoving beside her. Darkness fell and the scene faded away.

While female elephants spend their time in ladies clubs, the males wander between different feeding grounds and watering holes, alone or in small groups. The young elephant that I described earlier having difficulty leaving his mother, if he is still alive, is probably part of a small male herd somewhere on the savannah south of the Chobe River. Right now, perhaps, he might be bathing in the fresh, clear water of the Okavango Delta. I hope he is all right.

These herds of male elephants usually comprise unrelated individuals, they wander about more than female herds, and their groups are more loosely cohesive. Unlike the female herds which are led and ruled by a matriarch, in the male herds there is no leader and each elephant does as he wants. If a male does not enjoy the company, then he leaves and lives alone or finds another group to join. Of course, there is a social hierarchy within the male herds with the biggest male occupying the dominant position. However, there is rarely trouble between the males in these herds. They eat, rest, sleep, and wander slowly between different locations; if they encounter a herd of females, they smell the females to check if any of them are in heat. If not, they move on. Normally, the males are the most peaceful of all elephants. They fear nothing.

A herd of females with their young provides much more lively entertainment for observers (social interactions between males are less obvious). Except during the hottest part of the day when mothers stand and fan themselves with their ears in the shade of a tree and the young ones lie down and rest there is almost continuous social interaction. Apart from baboons, chimpanzees, humans, and other primates, elephants are unparalleled in their individuality.

For the benefit of wildlife and tourists, Hwange National Park in Zimbabwe has constructed a number of artificial waterholes. During the dry season these attract many thirsty animals of various species. Feeding and trampling the surrounding vegetation gradually creates a clearing. At one particular waterhole, water ran from a pipe protruding from a wall—clear, fresh water forming a muddy pool, five metres across. In the heat of the midday sun, a magnificent bull elephant stood in the middle of the pool. He was 40 or 50 years old and had long, heavy tusks. He had his backside up against the water inlet and his feet in the mud, and he looked very comfortable. His eyes blinked sleepily, his ears flapped in slow motion, his trunk slowly descended so that the two prehensile fingers at its tip were moistened, and then lifted again.

A little adolescent elephant moved around nearby—well, small only in comparison with the huge male, as he was at least as tall as a horse. He walked back and forth—he badly wanted to get into that little pool, but there sat the big guy, parked for a long stay. After several minutes of fussing, the little one stopped in front of the big elephant and tentatively stretched his trunk towards him. The big elephant stretched out his trunk in reply and they gently touched trunks with one another. After that, the little elephant walked around the big fellow to the place where the clear water was flowing from the pipe—and he drank and drank and drank.

'Grandfather, can I have a drink?'

'Sure my boy, of course you can.'

Sometimes, however, the pulse of life changes for male elephants, for example when they enter 'musth', which happens about once a year (at different times for different males) and may last from several weeks to a couple of months.

*Musth* is an Urdu word (a language spoken in India) meaning drunkenness or intoxication. Indian elephants have been working for humankind for thousands of years and consequently much more was known about Indian elephants than African elephants. It was well known that Indian elephants went through musth every now and then, becoming intractable and unruly and, if possible, escaping from captivity to search far and wide for a willing female.

However, it was less than twenty years ago that musth was noticed among African elephants as well. It was a young researcher, Joyce Poole, who with Cynthia Moss as her advisor, began a research project in the Amboseli National Park in Kenya. This park looks out towards the Tanzanian border and the astoundingly beautiful snow-covered peak of Kilimanjaro—the unmistakable backdrop of countless nature films. Moss was conducting research into the social system of female elephants and advised her younger colleague to 'take care of the males'.

Individual elephants are identified through characteristic marks such as scars or notched ears. One of the first things Poole discovered was that certain males behaved differently to others. They did not display any of the majestic movements, philosophical vegetativeness, or the academically striding processions for which male elephants were generally known. Instead, these males tended towards unprovoked violence (for example charging Poole's Land Rover). They rushed back and forth attacking other males who, terrified, yielded to them in spite of the fact that they might be bigger, older, and generally more dominant than their attacker. The troublemakers continually leaked urine and had greenish foam at the end of their penis sheaths. A thick secretion dripped from their temple glands. Their testosterone levels indicated an amount five times higher than normal.

It did not take long to discover the connection: African elephants also enter musth during certain specific rutting periods. During this time, they leave their groups and race around in solitude, testing the winds and listening. Females in heat signal their condition via scents and special infrasounds, which can be heard over long distances, and all males in the area respond to the enticing signals. Even older males who are not in musth and adolescents who are not yet old enough to experience musth, flock around a signalling female, chase her, and try to gain access to her. Sometimes one of them might manage to mount her. However, he does not usually succeed in his copulation attempt because the vagina of a female elephant is located in such a position that a successful copulation requires her full and active co-operation. And as is so often the case, it is also a question of experience: older females cannot be forced into unwanted copulation, whereas younger females seem less capable of refusal or perhaps less discriminating.

This circus of activity, which occurs around a female in heat and in which her female club associates are also active, comes to an abrupt end when a bull 'in musth' turns up. He might not be the biggest male in the area. Normally, he would never dream of behaving as he does now: he rushes into the crowd like an angry and randy tank (if that is imaginable), butting, bellowing, shoving, and belligerent... I feel sorry for anyone who gets in his way. Even males twice his size move out of the way with terrified expressions on their faces. When he has established respect, he tries to drive the female in heat away from the crowd and she willingly complies, relieved that she finally has a bodyguard to protect her from all the other pushy suitors. During one or two days, the male in musth and the female in heat remain together, mating once or twice, often under the curious, but respectful gaze of the crowd. Soon, however, he tires of the company and storms away across the savannah, searching for new females. The object of his passion returns to her ladies club with an abated sexual appetite and lengthy and lively greeting ceremonies erupt. ('Now you just have to tell us everything...')

That is how a female elephant is fertilized, and 22 months later a baby elephant is born, weighing around 100 kilogrammes (certainly heavy, but proportionally smaller than our own species). Twins are exceptionally rare.

Researchers have only very rarely had the privilege of witnessing the birth of a baby elephant. When the time approaches, the expectant mother withdraws to an isolated place, but when the young one enters the world, it becomes the centre of the herd's attention. The matriarch or some other older female sometimes helps to remove the fetal membranes from the young. Within an hour, it is on its feet and looking for mother's nipples: there are two, located just behind the front legs. The mother guides the baby in the right direction with her trunk. Although a baby elephant is born into a closely-knit group of females, it is completely dependent on its mother during the first two years of its life. If its mother should die before that, the herd's care is not enough to keep the young one alive.

Elephant young are dependent on their mothers and other experienced herd members in many different ways. Like any other mammal offspring, they need to suckle. In addition, they must be schooled in the conditions of their surrounding environment. Old elephants know where the paths to the waterholes are, how to dig a water hole in a dried-out riverbed, where to find food even during extremely dry periods, where the poachers usually are, and with which neighbouring groups they have a shared history. Elephants carry with them many memories and form many traditions. Elephants have a culture.

It is sometimes possible to re-introduce different kinds of big game, including elephants, into areas from which they were previously driven or eradicated. The situation is such that livestock-farming is becoming less profitable in many areas, whereas tourist numbers are increasing and they are willing to pay to watch, photograph, or shoot animals in their natural habitats. Thus, for some economically disposed land-owners, the re-introduction of different species of antelope, giraffes, black or white rhinoceroses, and elephants seems a satisfactory solution to their financial problems.

The special mental abilities of elephants have both advantages and disadvantages for such a comeback. On the one hand, elephants pass on to each other more or less hard-earned experiences, so that if a young elephant has received a shock from an electric fence, not only that elephant, but all his or her 'acquaintances' will avoid the fence in the future. On the other hand, young elephants might have problems adjusting their behaviour to life in a new, unknown area. They do not know where to find water or where different dangers lurk. Even their sexual behaviour may go haywire without positive examples. Once, when a group of young elephants of both sexes were introduced into a reserve in South Africa where there was an abundance of white rhinoceroses, the young male elephants started courting the female rhinos instead of the female elephants. I wonder which group of ladies were most surprised: the flirted-with rhinos or the neglected elephants?

Pachyderms in general have interesting inter-species relationships. One night, in the light of a full moon, I saw three black rhinos come to drink at a waterhole in Etosha: a female with her almost full-grown offspring and a male, who was obviously more interested in her than in her offspring. The interest, however, was not mutual, and his attempts at establishing contact were refused with affronted snorts and threatening swings of her horned head. The situation became more dramatic when a number of elephants also appeared on the scene. From the right, a splendid male followed by two younger adjutants—from the left, a small herd of five females and three or four young elephants of various sizes. It was easy to see that the male rhinoceros was in a bad mood as he turned and took a few steps towards the three male elephants, which stopped abruptly and parked themselves under a tree. They certainly looked dignified and collected in comparison with the ill-humoured rhino walking back and forth letting off steam with resounding snorts. The female elephants, however, walked in single-file down towards the waterhole, which caused the three rhinos to protest (although the young one's protests seemed only symbolic). Needless to say, the situation was tense… For a short moment, the elephant herd paused, lifted their trunks, and folded out their ears. Then the largest female broke out of line, took several quick steps towards the rhinos, trumpeted an exceptionally fierce roar, and rolled her trunk up between her tusks, ready for battle. Rhinoceroses, however, aren't so dumb that they don't know when they've met a stronger opponent, so they snorted, turned with amazing speed, and trotted off into the African night. The elephant herd then spread out and walked down to the water where splashing, cavorting, and contented gurgling indicated great satisfaction. On the opposite side of the waterhole, the three males also strode down to the water slowly and deliberately and began drinking.

I recently read an article that explained that this occurrence at the Namibian waterhole was quite typical. Despite their enormous size, elephant males are not generally willing or capable of putting a determined male rhino in his place, whereas female elephants with thirsty children and grandchildren don't allow themselves to be impeded in their important activities by any brazen old rhino.

Naturally, it is questionable as to what extent one should use words such as 'tenderness', 'shame', and 'disobedience' when one talks about species other than our own. However, it seems a bit forced to try to come up with (with the help of one's old Latin or Greek dictionary) more neutral terms, especially for those animal behaviours that have exactly the same background and motives as human behaviour. Two jealous rivals over the same partner—human or leopard, what is the difference? A mother, who without a thought for herself defends her offspring from danger—human or elephant: what is the difference? In the case of elephants, with their long lives, individuality, enormous memory capacity, and complicated social network, it is impossible not to see and accept the similarities with our own species.

The same day that we saw the young male elephant at the Chobe River preparing to leave his mother, a solitary young elephant, perhaps six or seven years old, plunged out of the bushes near our observation area and ran across the open, sandy ground towards the riverbank. It stood there and drank. We began discussing why it was there on its own, a dangerous situation for such a small elephant in an area full of lions. Last night, only a few kilometres up river, we had seen six lions surrounding the unfortunate remains of a young elephant that they had obviously managed to overpower. Our little elephant looked quite nervous as it gazed and sniffed towards the forest every now and then, and we started to realize that it had a terribly bad conscience. Thirst had become too much for it, it had left the herd, and now regretted its haste and was full of anxiety over how things would turn out. We were worried too.

We heard a crash in the bushes, a low rumble, and an elephant herd composed of nine individuals broke through the wall of bushes led by an ageing matriarch with no tusks. She and her herd stopped just at the edge of the bushes, all sniffing, listening, looking—the matriarch then growled her 'OK, let's go', and the herd continued slowly towards the river. At the river, the little elephant had heard the 'OK' and, recognizing his herd, gave out a small shrill cry. Behind the matriarch, one of the females who was not quite so large, paused and raised her trunk like a periscope. And then she broke away from the group and ran as fast as possible down to the little fellow who received a careful bout of 'smelling' and hopefully, in addition, several clearly formed opinions about how an obedient elephant child should behave. This storm of emotions became too much for the matriarch, who let out a mighty trumpeting signal and a growl so deep in tone that we felt rather than heard it. Then, followed by her small group, she rushed full speed down to the two elephants at the edge of the water, the mother and her young one. Immediately, they all began drinking, spraying water on each other's backs, and pushing and shoving in a friendly manner. The younger ones and eventually the older ones as well all lay down on their sides in the mud and shallow water. Finally, the matriarch joined them. The little escapee and his mother stayed close together the entire time, touching and caressing each other with their trunks.

We sat very still. Our guide, a man from Maun who has lived his entire life in the African bush, said very quietly: 'That, I will never forget.'

# 5

## *The long reach of a giraffe's neck*

THE WAR BETWEEN GERMAN SETTLERS and the Herero people in former German South-west Africa was one of the most terrible of all colonial wars. A visit to the little cemetery at Waterberg—halfway between Windhoek, the capital city of Namibia, and the well-known Etosha National Park—is a reminder of bygone evil days. Here, there are many gravestones with the names of young German men who died during those battles, while in another part of the cemetery a copper plate erected in the 1980s by a German war veterans association commemorates the memory of their fallen—but nameless—adversaries. There is a steep slope beyond the cemetery, and high up on the slope perches a large and impressive house, built long ago as a holiday home for the governor-general of German South-west Africa. The house is now a restaurant and centre for Waterberg's small, but species-rich, nature reserve.

An even more striking memorial from the time before the war—a war which was resolved through a bloody battle at Waterberg in 1904—is an old fort called Namutoni, in the eastern most region of Etosha National Park. At the end of the 1800s, the Germans built an easily defendable border patrol station in an attempt to control the restless, rebellious local population. The resulting fort, complete with towers and pinnacles, looks like a medieval castle—but in miniature. Eventually, during World War I, it was transformed into a military camp and was used as a camp for British prisoners of war. After a period of decay, Namutoni was restored at the end of the 1950s and became a field hotel for tourists—one of the most unusual hotels in the world. As a reminder of its military history, a trumpeter still blows reveille at dawn and taps at dusk from the highest tower of the little white castle.

Etosha National Park is one of Africa's largest parks with an area of over 22 000 square kilometres. Much of the park is covered by a gigantic salt basin, Etosha Pan, which looks like a snow-white desert. During the unreliable rainy season this basin fills to form a shallow lake. It stretches 130 kilometres from east to west, 75 kilometres from north to south, and has an area of almost 6500 square kilometres. This enormous basin sparkles with dried salt that is periodically caught up into spinning whirlwinds and spread out over the surrounding open country. Naturally, salt-loving and salt-tolerant plants thrive here—short, thick-leafed, and tough. West of Etosha Pan lies an area of open forest, which in Afrikaans is called Sprokieswoud—Ghost Forest. It is a sparse forest comprising primarily moringa trees (*Moringa ovalifolia*), which, because of their grotesquely swollen and crooked trunks have probably led the imaginations of many wanderers to thoughts of supernatural and frightening creatures. It is a peculiar place. East of the salt basin a completely different type of forest spreads out, dominated by honey acacia (*Acacia mellifera*) and large expanses with tight thickets of the three metre tall whistling acacia (*A. drepanolobium*). A third and very conspicuous vegetation type in Etosha is the woodland savannah, with mopane as the dominant tree type. It covers the entire southern region of the park.

———————————— ⚔ ————————————

One January day we were driving east along a dusty gravel road following the southern shore of the salt lake. Our destination was Namutoni, which eventually appeared on the horizon in all its splendour. This particular afternoon in Etosha was memorable for another reason: neither before nor since have I seen so many giraffes at one time. As we reached one of the low ridges we had a perfect view out across the plain. We got out and counted no less than 108 individuals. They were alone or in small groups of females with young, standing, or casually strolling about on the expansive plains. Several of the gigantic animals seemed to drift slowly towards the east and we knew that they were on their way to one of the permanent waterholes north of Namutoni. As usual however, they gave the impression that they were out for a stroll rather than on their way towards a definite goal. Giraffes always seem to have plenty of time.

It was certainly a strange sight—all those construction-cranes striding slowly. Although giraffes do live in herds, such large groups are rare. In fact, three, five, or eight animals in a herd are much more common. However, it is often difficult to define a giraffe herd clearly—more difficult than with the savannah's other large herbivores. Individual giraffes usually keep a good distance between themselves and other individuals and do not seem to react as a coherent herd when they are disturbed. If you happen to approach a herd of zebra or springbok or oryx too closely (just to name three other common species in Etosha), the whole company flees at the same time and in the same direction. Additionally, in an undisturbed herd of those same animals, individuals have regular interactions with other members of the herd—they seem to notice each other's existence.

Not so for giraffes. Whether a group of giraffes is close together or spread out over a square kilometre they do not appear to have any obvious interactions. If you happen to come too close to one giraffe, it will stop eating and may take a couple of frightened jumps or steps to the side while the other giraffes look as if they are thinking: 'That has nothing to do with us!'

'Giraffes live in groups—but do not seem to enjoy a social life', wrote one wildlife biologist. It is easy to agree. On the other hand, animals with eyes so high above the ground can undeniably see one another and keep a discrete eye on one another at considerable distances.

The giraffe is one of the most strangely built animals, chiefly because of its enormously long neck. Despite the long neck length however, the number of cervical vertebrae is the same in a giraffe as in, for example, a shrew or a Russian colonel—that is, seven. Up to 5.5 metres above ground for males, and 4.5 metres for females, the neck ends in an elongated head with beautiful dark eyes and remarkable horns that slant backwards, three for males and two for females. The horns originate during the embryo stage as cartilage-like loose 'buttons' under the skin. They fuse with the skull at about 4 years old for males and 7 years for females. Unlike both deer and hollow-horned animals (antelopes and bovines), the giraffe's horn is not attached to the frontal bone, but to the temporal bone. Another unique feature of the giraffe is that the outer layer of bone in the skull continues to grow and therefore increases in thickness throughout its life. In both cases, horns and heads, growth is much greater in males than it is in females. Old male giraffes therefore carry around a disproportionately large and heavy head on top of their long necks, and it becomes thicker with age. Giraffes in the wild have been reported to reach ages of up to 25 years old, and if they are in the best of condition, males can weigh 1200–1900 kg, whereas the corresponding figures for females are 800–1200 kg. Thus, as with many other large ruminants, sexual differences (sexual dimorphism) in weight and size are quite significant for giraffes.

It is sometimes difficult to find time to eat enough food, especially for the huge males. Giraffes are built for eating leaves and twigs from bushes and trees rather than grass from the ground. They enjoy different species of acacia tree and also eat eagerly from bushes and trees belonging to the *Combretum* group. Leaves and twigs provide a high quality diet and are much easier to digest than grass. However, the acacias try to reduce their losses to herbivores, including giraffes, by arming themselves with a most formidable thorny defence. When a giraffe eats from an acacia tree, it is difficult not to be amazed that its lips, tongue, and mouth are not completely perforated, or that its eyes do not get punctured by vicious thorns up to 5 centimetres in length. Giraffes have perfect table manners and eat neatly and calmly of this apparently dangerous food. Thorniness does act as a slight deterrent however. In an experiment, scientists have shown that giraffes browse more heavily on trees that have had their thorns removed than they do on trees that have not been de-thorned.

The large size difference between male and female giraffes has consequences for their dietary habits. Adult male giraffes prefer an environment with dense and tall acacia trees, whereas females, particularly those with young calves, prefer open terrain. Females probably prefer places where they have a good view in all directions in order to be able to detect any predators that might threaten their calves. If giraffes discover approaching predators in time, they have no problem escaping as they can reach speeds that leave predators lagging far behind. It may look slow when a galloping giraffe 'sails' away over the savannah, but the length of its gait is enormous (up to five metres for an adult individual) and compensates for its relatively slow rhythmic pace.

In many regions, the giraffe's diet is composed primarily of leaves, flowers, and twigs from the whistling acacia, a species that seldom exceeds two metres in height. It looks truly uncomfortable when an adult giraffe stands bent over, with its long neck stretched out horizontally, to eat from the low bushes in a posture similar to a waiter who is serving guests at a table—a particularly uncomfortable posture for the back and shoulders. The male giraffes, that prefer the taller forest vegetation with fever acacias and white-bark acacias, seem to eat more comfortably. But even these giraffes will browse at awkward lower levels, particularly when they wish to be near the females who are in heat; at these times the males choose to frequent the vegetation areas consisting of shorter bushes instead of the preferred taller acacias.

One characteristic of savannah vegetation is that many of the trees and bushes start coming into leaf or flowering (or both) before the rainy season begins. Consequently, these new leaves and flowers appear when it is most difficult for many savannah mammals and birds to find food. Magnificent throngs of sunbirds (of several species) can be seen in flame trees (*Erythrina abyssinica*) when bright red flowers bloom on their bare branches, changing the entire tree into a giant red sign in the middle of the scorched, brown savannah! Without a doubt, the red colour has evolved because it provides a dramatic signal to the sunbirds. They are not only consumers of the flower's sweet-smelling nectar, they also pay for the food by carrying the pollen from flower to flower. Plants with large

*Figure 11. A long neck can be rather uncomfortable. The posture of this foraging giraffe certainly looks strained. Might the giraffe's long neck be more of a weapon than an adaptation to reach high-up food?*

red or orange flowers or inflorescences are often fertilized by birds and they use different kinds of birds as flying inseminators.

Acacias, on the other hand, have small, yellow, wonderful-smelling flowers that occur in spike-shaped groups. The buzz of hymenopterans (bees and wasps) around a blooming acacia tree reveals the animals the acacias hire to spread their pollen. Many acacias produce an abundance of sterile flowers, probably to increase their power of attraction and entice pollinators. At certain times, when all the forest's trees are in need of their services, pollinators can be in short supply.

Unknowingly, even giraffes may act as pollen carriers for acacias, particularly for the knob-thorn acacia (*Acacia nigrescens*). Towards the end of the dry season, this tree produces an enormous number of flowers in bottleneck-shaped tubes. Knob-thorn acacias expose their flowers to the appetite of herbivores without restricting access with thorns or other obstacles. The flowers that are unusually pale-coloured, almost creamy-white, have presumably adapted to pollination by more or less colour-blind mammals rather than birds or insects, which have an exceptional sense of colour vision. Thus, there is a possibility that the giraffe, by coincidence, acts as a pollinator for one of the most important plants on its menu.

What can giraffes reach with their very long necks? The answer may be obvious: more food. The giraffe's long neck is usually seen as a textbook example of an adaptation with an easily understood function: to reach up into the tree crowns and allow its bearer to reach resources at which other herbivores can only gaze enviously. (Except for the elephant who can manage anything: if it cannot reach, it simply knocks the tree down.) During the dry season when resources start running low for savannah herbivores, the giraffe's long neck enables it to reach flowers, leaves, and twigs in a three metre wide zone stretching above the upper limit for species such as greater kudu and eland.

Recently however, some ecologists have begun to doubt that this 'dietary hypothesis' is the sole explanation for the fantastically extended neck of giraffes. The long neck would seem to be an inconvenience for eating from low trees and bushes. There are plenty of studies showing that they consume a considerable amount of food from lower levels where their long necks are of no particular help, whether or not there are competing leaf-eating species. In the Serengeti, for example, researchers have found that giraffes eat only from tall trees such as umbrella thorn acacias during the rainy season—when food is plentiful at all levels and competition with the more 'normal-necked' leaf-eaters is of little significance. During the dry season, the giraffe's main food source is, instead, the leaves and fruits of the short *Grewia* bushes, which are also a favourite with humans. (In Botswana, the dried fruits are ground into flour and made into a porridge, which when eaten together with dried grasshoppers is considered a delicacy. The fruits are also popularly used for producing beer and other alcoholic drinks.)

If the driving force behind the evolution of an extremely long neck had simply been to be able to reach food high in the treetops, one would have expected a more proportional extension of all the body parts. However, if you compare present-day giraffes with their predecessors, who looked a little like the giraffe's only close living relative, the okapi, one finds that the length of the neck has proportionally increased more than, for example, the legs. Interestingly, this does not apply to the giraffe calf's first year when it is relatively short-necked and okapi-like. The neck doesn't start growing until after their first year, leading to the bizarre body proportions that we see in adult giraffes. Surely a competent designer would have built giraffes with longer legs and shorter necks? If, however, neck length has a purpose other than reaching high into the trees, then the remarkable body construction becomes more understandable.

So, what is it that giraffes can reach with their long necks if access to the treetop's greenery is not sufficient as an adaptive explanation? Does the design of the long neck make it suitable primarily as a weapon? This is an idea suggested by behavioural ecologist Robert Simmons, working in Namibia and South Africa. He reasoned that giraffes fight by standing side by side and tackling or battering one another with their long necks. Normally giraffe aggression is dignified and absent-minded: suddenly the jostling stops and both males stare into the distance. Then, one of them remembers what he was doing and tries to twine his neck around his opponent's or pummels him with his head. Sometimes it gets very heated and the animals swing their powerful necks at one another like clubs. The heavy, horned head of the adult bull comes in handy, and such fights can lead to serious injury or death. One gruesome account describes how a male giraffe knocked out his opponent with a tremendous swipe and then kicked him to death. Like most species, male giraffes fight—either to attain dominance or to drive away a rival for access to a female in heat. As would be expected from this 'weapon theory', bull giraffes are armed with longer and thicker necks, bigger and heavier heads, and more and sharper horns.

Animals fight only when they must. If a conflict can be solved by signalling, using for example various types of threatening actions or calls, then so much the better for both individuals, including the likely winner. After all, each match can result in an injury and cause an unavoidable loss of energy and loss of time better spent. We humans demonstrate our willingness to fight—depending on our resources—by threatening someone with our fist, for example, or ordering the navy to make an appearance just outside the enemy's territorial waters. According to this idea, the giraffe's neck and head simultaneously act as weapons and signals of power. As a rule, males determine dominance relationships without fighting and base their decisions on the theory that 'the biggest weapon wins'. Consequently, it is advantageous for adolescent male giraffes to invest in the fastest neck development possible and thus lay the foundation for high status in the giraffe gang. Still, he has little chance in achieving a heterosexual mating until he is about eight years old. The largest and heftiest of the bulls have a monopoly on that entertainment. Homosexual mountings, however, occur between both younger and older males, and seem to be a behaviour that helps in establishing rank. Dominant animals mount, subdominant ones are mounted. For many species, sexual behaviour can sometimes have a function completely separate from reproduction.

If the giraffe's long neck is primarily a weapon only used by males in their battles, then why have peaceful females also developed an absurdly long neck? In all animal species, there is a high level of genetic correlation between the two sexes. Males and females have an almost identical set of genes. Assuredly, certain sexual genetic differences exist, but they comprise only a very small portion of the total genetic make-up. If natural selection favours evolution of a specific characteristic in one sex, a long neck for example, then due to genetic similarities, the same characteristic will also develop in the other sex. Although striking sexual differences can arise in superficial details, such as the extremely long tail feathers in some species of birds, this kind of structural difference would involve such a complete reconstruction of the entire animal that a genetic separation of the sexes would be impossible.

The enormous neck and head of the giraffe (bull giraffes in particular) has developed at a cost. In order to pump blood up to a brain that is three metres or more above ground, the giraffe requires a proportionally large heart; and in order to manage the record high blood pressure, the arteries must be specially reinforced. There is a system of valves in the neck blood vessels that prevent an acute drop in blood pressure in the brain when the animal quickly and precipitately rises after having taken a drink. Think of the dizzy spell it would otherwise experience!

The extra large necks of giraffe bulls make them more vulnerable to predators, primarily lions. According to a study from South Africa, lions kill twice as many adult male giraffes as they do females, leading to a surplus of females in some giraffe populations. It is unclear why lions are able to kill proportionately more males than females. Possibly the long neck functions best when browsing on tall trees, and male giraffes are known to spend more time in forests than females. It is easier for lions to stalk giraffes in a more dense, rather than open, terrain. Another possibility is that the enormous front-heavy giraffe bulls are late out of the starting blocks and therefore slower than their attackers. Or it may be that the strong sexual scent of adult males can reveal their whereabouts to the sensitive noses of hungry lions, even at long distances. Whatever the reason, the giraffe's neck illustrates the recurrent theme that an advantage always carries a price. Whether the giraffe has evolved its long neck because of an expansion of its diet or because it uses it to fight, problems occur. It is very common that a structure or behaviour which functions as an announcement of an actor's splendid qualities and desirability as a partner must be paid for through greater risk of a nasty and sudden death. Live fast, die young, and end up a handsome corpse.

For a giraffe bull to remain in one piece in spite of carrying around an extremely long neck and heavy head, he must be an individual of high quality. The individual who reaches a mature age in spite of the handicap of his tall front half is a living example of his own excellence. Wise is the female (well adapted that is) that obtains for her offspring genes from such a prime beast. According to this model, competition in attracting females has led to sexual selection of the male giraffe's surrealistically built body, despite the fact that natural selection acts in opposition. In order for the signal 'I have good genes, choose me as your mate' to be true, it must be of such a nature that not just any male can send it. That is, it must be costly or act as a 'handicap'. Death in the jaws of a pride of lions is thus the price that a giraffe bull must pay in order to have luck with the ladies during his life.

Such evolutionary biological reasoning did not occupy our thoughts when we emerged suddenly from a dense bushy savannah thicket and looked out across the Linyanti River at the surrounding open, lush territory. We were in Botswana, looking into Namibia's northernmost corner. A spiral of twenty or so wheeling vultures had drawn us to this location. On closer examination, we saw that there were twenty white-backed vultures and two white-headed vultures: the latter, smaller in size and decidedly more elegant with their elegant black and white attire. We soon found the object of the vultures' interest—the dead body of a huge bull giraffe, distinguished even in death, and guarded by a magnificent male lion with a yellowish-gold and black mane and a snow-white bearded chin. A few spotted hyenas sauntered nearby, but if they came too close, they were shooed away with a lazy swipe by the lion. The white-backed vultures parked themselves in a dead tree some distance from the kill. Not the two white-headed vultures. They dropped down right beside the giraffe's head, an event that caused a stubborn and piercing protest from the gorged lion. A flock of Egyptian geese grazing on the coastal meadows in the distance thought that they were the cause of the angry protest, so just to be safe they flew over the river and into Namibia.

When we let our binoculars scan the edge of the thicket from which we had just emerged, we saw the rest of the lion pride lying in the shade: one male, just as magnificent as the other male who had tried to chase away the vultures from the cadaver and who was probably his brother, as well as five females. He gazed, squinting, out over the vast expanse where small groups of puku antelope and lechwe were grazing peacefully. The antelope were safe in the knowledge that the lions were fully satiated and, in addition, had a pantry full of several hundred kilos of giraffe meat yet to be consumed. Suddenly, a couple of hundred metres beyond the dead giraffe, there was a movement at the edge of the thicket and a herd of 15 roan antelope—hinds and calves with one guarding buck—quickly trotted out onto the grassy flood plain. When they caught scent of the lions, they came to a dead halt and looked around, but like the other antelope, they soon saw that the lions were thinking of anything but hunting. The roan antelope calmed down and started slowly and cautiously approaching both the lions and ourselves. It was difficult to avoid the thought that the antelope wanted to take the opportunity to watch, and let their calves see, those demons of the night as they rested lazily in the bright sunlight, looking as terrifying as kittens on a couch. When they had approached to within 100 metres, however, courage left them and they turned suddenly and disappeared at full gallop in among the brush. The male lion nearest the giraffe lay his head on his front paws, closed his eyes, and began devoting his time to digestion, rest, and repose.

# 6

## Savannah ruminants: five different lifestyles

### Pathway through the Stomach

About 80 million years ago a group of archaic mammals roamed the earth, mammals that would in turn give rise to many of today's large savannah herbivores. As early as the beginning of the Tertiary (65 million years ago), one species within this enigmatic group divided and produced two evolutionary lines. Of these, one evolved into two of the orders of mammals alive today, namely, the artiodactyls (aardvark, swine, giraffes, camels, and the hollow-horned bovines) and whales, while the other lineage is represented today by perissodactyls (horses, rhinoceroses, and tapirs), sea cows, hyraxes, and elephants. Thus, a cow is actually more closely related to a whale than to a horse.

Today, there are about 200 different species of hoofed mammals. Of these, about 185 are artiodactyls, and of those, about 170 are ruminants. The fifteen species of artiodactyls that do not ruminate include the aardvark and the swine species. Perissodactyls never ruminate.

Being a herbivore has its problems. In general, meat is substantially more energy-rich and easier to digest than grass, leaves, bark, and twigs. Herbivores however, have solved this digestive problem in several different ways; ways that are so effective that the savannah is inhabited by a great variety of species that have entirely vegetarian diets. With their four stomachs (each with its own function and its own set of microorganisms), ruminants are highly efficient at assimilating the nutrient content of their food. Their one disadvantage is that re-chewing food takes time and thus limits their total dietary intake. Non-ruminants have solved the same problem either by assuming a diet that is relatively poor in fibre and easily digested (for example swine prefer roots and fruits), or by developing a very large caecum where an ample set of different kinds of industrious microorganisms spend their time breaking down large quantities of cellulose (as occurs within the horse family).

Consequently, a zebra's stomach makes the zebra a gourmand: a zebra devours an enormous quantity of food to compensate for the diet's poor protein and vitamin content. Zebras must spend two-thirds or more of their time grazing. Impalas however, like other ruminants, are pure and simple gourmets: they are finicky about the quality of their food and are satisfied with a significantly lower rate of food intake per day. During much of each day, impalas and other savannah ruminants stand or lie in the shade and ruminate. Four stomachs and a multitude of bacteria permit a typical ruminant to pursue a slower pace of life than the one-stomached non-ruminant, who must stand out in the burning sun and graze. Horse and cow manure are quite different in both odour and consistency— because they are waste products from two processing industries with fundamentally different chemical technology.

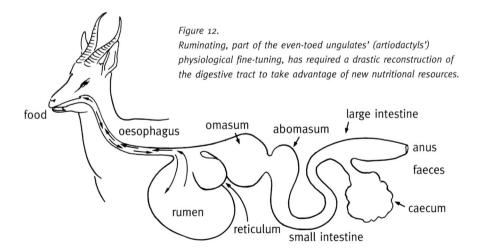

Figure 12.
Ruminating, part of the even-toed ungulates' (artiodactyls') physiological fine-tuning, has required a drastic reconstruction of the digestive tract to take advantage of new nutritional resources.

Chapters 4 and 5 looked at some of the African savannah's more specialized herbivores, the elephant and the giraffe. The following five species all belong to the family of hollow-horned animals (Bovidae) within the order Artiodactyla. The Bovidae family contains most of Africa's big game species. The five selected species—buffalo, impala, dik-dik, wildebeest, and springbok—have very different lifestyles. They are all fairly common, at least in some regions, and I have enjoyed numerous observations and encounters with them. Summaries of other species are included at the end of the book.

## BUFFALO: LIFE IN A HERD

Suddenly finding yourself very close to an African buffalo is an extraordinarily powerful experience. For me, it was an experience I remember exceptionally well— perhaps because it occurred during my very first trip to Africa over forty years ago. I had the opportunity to join a wildlife research project in Tarangire for a few days. Tarangire was a sparsely inhabited region at that time (it is now a national park visited by many ecotourists) not far from the famous Manyara Lake in northern Tanzania. My colleague (who was collecting data for his doctoral thesis on the ecological differences between different big game species), his two field assistants, and I walked as quietly as we could across the dry and thorny bush savannah, following a marked path and recording all observations and tracks of the various wild animals. Here, a herd of ten zebras; there, the footprint of a leopard. A warthog family raced away with their tails sticking up in the air like radio antennas and suddenly, behind a dense thicket, two enormous buffalo bulls appeared, with—at first glance—gigantic horns. They stared at us long and hard as only bovines can. We stood frozen in place for what seemed like ages until both buffaloes suddenly snorted, turned abruptly and began walking away; then they stopped and looked back, making sure we were not doing anything threatening before finally disappearing from sight down a dry river bed.

I let out my breath and felt the tension leave me. When we first caught sight of the buffalo, my three companions—more well-versed in buffalo encounters than I was—had quickly found climber-friendly trees to stand beside. I remembered that for next time.

The previous day we had seen buffalo under more relaxed circumstances in the lush countryside near Manyara Lake. Large herds grazed and rested, peacefully ruminating on the green fields between the lakeshore and the huge cliff which constitutes the western limits of the Rift Valley. The buffalo watched us with expressions that successfully concealed the considerable mass of knowledge and craftiness that are the most helpful qualities to them in their danger-filled world. If we came too close, they turned and jogged away. Their lives appeared worry-free: plenty of grass to graze upon, shade trees to protect them from the midday heat, and a number of springs, which ran from the base of the huge cliff and provided them, as well as many other animals, with fresh water. We had seen several of Manyara Park's famous tree-climbing lions, but in the midday heat they were not interested in hunting buffalo.

Buffalo are extremely social animals. While resting, they often lie quite close together. Sometimes you can see herds of several hundred or sometimes more than a thousand animals that, especially if they have been frightened, run so close together that the whole herd can look like a river of lava pouring over the ground. A cloud of dust rises above them when they are on the move, revealing their existence from a great distance. Oxpeckers—peculiar starlings that specialize in picking parasites from large herbivores—cling to the buffaloes' backs, but are forced to take wing when the ride becomes too rough.

For buffalo as well as many other animals one of the important advantages of herd life is, without a doubt, that the large number of individuals decreases the risk for any one individual to fall victim to a predator. Lions pose the most serious threat to buffalo. All the other buffaloes in a herd create a living shield for any one individual. Consequently, individuals try to stay in the middle of the herd as much as possible so that other individuals take the first blow, regardless from which

direction the predators attack. However, buffaloes are enormous animals—
a large bull can weigh up to 900 kilogrammes, a large cow up to 600 kilogrammes. Herds are quite capable of actively defending themselves against
attacks from predators by creating a front, and they can fend off attacks from lions
as well as hyenas with their horns. Buffaloes are known to have attacked solitary
adult lions or temporarily abandoned lion cubs without provocation. Buffaloes
have a lot to gain from killing or driving lions away from their home ranges.

Living in herds also has its disadvantages. For buffalo, the cost of living in a
herd is, first, competition for status and second, competition for food. Aerial
photographs show that every large buffalo herd is made up of a number of distinct
subgroups. Each of these units comprises several cows and their calves. As is so
often the case with mammals, females constitute the framework of the social
structure. The bulls—full grown, jet black, huge dominant fellows—move
around within these groups of females, testing the air to see if any cows are in
heat, and if they find a receptive female, they fight with each other for her attentions. In addition, younger males and bachelors in poorer condition who have no
chance of competing with the bigger fellows roam around within the herd. Under
certain conditions, especially when the food supply begins to dwindle, the herd
splits up into subgroups that live separately, as it is worth having a less effective
predator defence to reduce the competition for food. When food again becomes
more abundant, the subgroups rejoin into a unified herd. Human persecution
also leads larger herds to break up; against humans, it doesn't pay to live in large
herds. Buffalo, similar to many other species, are good at adjusting their social
behaviour depending on the type of threat.

Bulls that can't compete in the larger herd—due to youth, age, or poor condition—leave and form 'bachelor groups' where they are free from harassment by
superior competitors. These groups may comprise only two or three individuals
but may be up to several dozen. After regaining their strength during a peaceful
respite among like-minded individuals, these bulls may return to the main herd.
It is this herd that represents stability as the animals move within a limited area.
Bachelor herds tend to wander more than female herds. On the whole, the buffalo

is a very conservative animal, remaining in its traditional home range as much as possible, even when it is subjected to disturbances.

Despite its enormous size and the social cohesion of the herd, buffalo are far from being invulnerable to large predators. Lions prey particularly on calves that have for some reason or another become separated from their mothers, as well as on adolescents. The oldest males are another risk group, as they often spend their last days alone or in very small groups. Many buffalo end their days as lion food in Manyara National Park. Successful lion hunts mainly take place at night by the light of the moon or at dawn when it is still too dark for co-operation within the buffalo herd to be very effective, but light enough so that the lions can co-ordinate their hunting teams.

A strict hierarchy exists among buffalo cows and bulls. Consequently, buffalo herds are characterized by marked social inequality, something that might not be apparent at first glance. It is generally impossible to identify any one individual as the herd's 'leader'. The bulls spend only a part of their time with the female groups and, in addition, often commute between several such groups; thus, we can probably disqualify them as leaders. Neither are there any individual cows that seem to have the ability to dominate such large herds. Thus, it is not comparable with the system found amongst elephants, in which matriarchs act as enlightened despots. According to some researchers the daily movements of buffalo herds between various grazing grounds is in some strange manner controlled by 'the collective experience' of the herd. Different parts of a herd's home range have different productivity at different times depending on, for example, how long it has been since the herd grazed there. Returning to an area too soon is not a good decision. Regardless of the reasons for the variable food availability in the various parts of their traditional home ranges, buffaloes must not make a wrong decision and march from their midday rest location to an unproductive grazing pasture. They can't correct such a mistake as they are very unwilling to wander around in the dark. Wherever they find themselves of an evening is where they will stay until morning light.

Departure of the buffaloes from their daytime headquarters—preferably located in a windy area with few insects, a good view, and access to water—is preceded by behaviour that buffalo researchers have described as a 'voting proce-dure'. In a resting herd, cow after cow will stand up, assume a characteristic hunchback pose, and stare off in a particular direction for a minute or two, before again lying down. The cows engage in this behaviour during the hours just before sunset. The animals become very active just as the sun dips towards the mountain ridges far off to the west. Young bulls butt heads with each other while the really big bulls stand up, sniff in all directions, and check the odour of nearby cows. Calves nudge their mothers, trying to get them to stand so that they can nurse a while, and soon, the entire herd is up stretching their legs, scratching, urinating, and defecating—until suddenly, solitary animals or small groups wander off one after the other, seemingly towards a goal, all in the same direction. Soon they are gathered into one large herd with the bulls in front and on each side and, after a longer or shorter walk, they reach their goal—a glade with lush grass where they then spend the night alternately grazing and resting until they return to their daytime quarters at dawn.

It is at dawn, on their return, that buffalo run the greatest risk of lion attack. They must be very careful, particularly when they pass through the dense bushes, because amber-eyed lionesses may be waiting there in ambush.

Buffaloes are pronounced grazers and are very dependent on water and shade. Dry regions are not good buffalo habitat, but if there is water, then almost any kind of vegetation will do. Buffalo depend more on hearing and smell than on sight as other bovines do. Perhaps this reveals the savannah buffalo's recent evolution from life in dense rainforests, where sight is the least useful of the senses. After their establishment on the savannah, natural selection clearly favoured an increase in body size and disproportionately larger horns, which are used both as status symbols and as weapons against predators. Rainforest buffalo live in much smaller herds than savannah buffalo, and their colour has changed from reddish-brown to the slate-grey or black of buffalo on the savannah. Rain-forest buffalo and savannah buffalo are different in so many respects that they stand on the edge of becoming genetically isolated from each other, that is, of becoming two separate species. However, since there are certain areas where they can be found together, where they mate with each other and produce fertile hybrids, they are still considered to be races of the same species. A parallel situation occurs in elephants, where rainforest populations are characterized by smaller size, relatively smaller tusks, differently shaped ears, smaller herd size, and smaller sexual size dimorphism.

There are few savannah animals that look as threatening and dangerous as an old bull buffalo. When they leave the main herd and wander alone or in small groups, which occurs more often as they reach old age, they are vulnerable to lion predation, despite their enormous size and terrifying horns. Because of their weight, they can fend off most attacks by lightweight lionesses, but if the pride includes one or two muscle-bound males, then death is likely to catch up with them.

I lay awake half a night once, listening to such a final battle. It was in Tarangire, and it was the night after the buffalo encounter described at the beginning of this chapter. In the afternoon we had observed a very large old bull buffalo lying in the shade of a venerable baobab tree, and not far from it we had also noticed a pride of lions composed of two magnificent males, four rather lean lionesses, and two six-month old lion cubs. The buffalo was a couple of hundred metres from our campsite and the lions were a couple of hundred metres farther away. We had the feeling that the night was going to be eventful.

When we finally doused our fire and crawled into our sleeping bags, we first heard nothing more than the usual African night sounds: a stone curlew whistling lonely and forsaken, a Mozambique nightjar hacking and coughing, and a giant eagle owl that concentrated and amplified the atmosphere through its muffled hooting. Far in the distance a leopard coughed repeatedly—that was his way of advertising for a female companion. Zebras bawled nervously. A Cape turtledove had evidently dreamed a pleasant dream, and as it woke it began to coo. Probably because we knew that only a short distance from us there lay an old buffalo bull that had perhaps now caught wind of the approaching lions, it seemed as though the African night was holding its breath…

… when suddenly violent lion roaring, snarling and bawling shattered the night air so that our mosquito nets seemed to flutter on their poles. This continued, on and off, for two or three hours: first, a long period of silence (the shrill baying of the zebras was entirely out of place in the muffled, magical atmosphere), then another outburst, bawling and thuds from heavy bodies, again, quiet…

When morning arrived with its light and we had eaten breakfast (with leftovers from last night's ostrich egg omelette as the main ingredient), we drove over to see what had happened. The buffalo bull had been killed and was half-devoured; the tracks in the sand showed us that his last fight had been great, but there was no sight of the lions. They were probably lying a short distance away, digesting their food and planning on returning for another feast the next night. Perhaps they were keeping an eye on us to ensure that we didn't take any food from their pantry—something that we might have done if we weren't leaving that same day. According to my old edition of Brehm's classical animal encyclopedia 'buffalo meat competes in taste with fattened beef calf. It is coarser, but very juicy and tasty despite its lack of fat'. It would have been interesting to test the truth of that statement.

## Impala: The Perfect Antelope

Were someone to have the bizarre idea of arranging a beauty contest for African antelopes, deciding the winner would be difficult. Would it be the kudu, with its enormous spiral-shaped horns and subdued colouring? Would the oryx, with its javelin-like horns, its boldly contrasting and tastefully harmonic colour pattern gain the highest marks? Or perhaps the impala, with its velvety chestnut brown coat, graceful movements, and sensual gazelle-like eyes?

Field guides rarely contain emotional or aesthetic digressions; however, Richard Estes' expresses his enthusiasm in one section of his detailed and excellent '*Behaviour guide*' for African game species. He begins his description of the impala with the words: 'the perfect antelope'. In addition to its incontestable beauty, the impala also has many interesting biological qualities.

Many years ago one of my friends was involved in a study of the reproductive biology of a small African bird belonging to the same genus (*Cisticola*) as the European fan-tailed warbler. This African bird was unusually interesting in its behaviour although its plumage was dull. The study area was near the famous Naivasha Lake, west of Nairobi, Kenya. When I visited for a few days, I was recruited as a field assistant and sat in the shade of a leafy green fever acacia to observe and record the activities taking place in two nearby warbler territories. The birds had different coloured plastic rings around their legs making it easy to identify individuals. It was immediately enthralling to follow the continuous role-playing that occurred within and between the two territories.

The hours under the acacia passed quickly, especially since many other animals were also active around my observation post. One of the animals with which I became particularly familiar was a magnificent male impala with elegantly curved horns, easily identifiable due to a scar on his right shoulder. Had he had a near-death experience with a leopard in his younger days? For long periods of time he stood on a bare hilltop, which was really an abandoned termite hill, only fifty metres away in a clearing surrounded by bushes, constantly testing the wind. Every now and then he strolled over to some bushes and nibbled on some leaves. I considered asking him to leave those particular bushes alone since they contained the objects of my ornithological observations, but I kept the request to myself.

The second day began just as peacefully as the previous day had ended, but after a while, uneasiness invaded the camp. My scarred friend snorted and coughed (I gave a start the first time I heard this sound as the impala has a coarse, almost roaring bark that can sound very much like a leopard) and pawed irritably on the ground until he suddenly lowered his head and ran off, disappearing behind a thicket. With the risk of deserting my duty (watching the greyish brown warblers), I stood up and sneaked after him. It was easy to see what had disturbed him: an entire company of male impalas of various sizes had entered what he clearly thought of as his territory. With a curiously jerky gait, he walked towards them and made a sudden lunge at the closest impala—a half-grown adolescent—who, terrified, turned and disappeared in among the others. The entire herd of intruders slowly retreated, sullen and glaring, while 'Scar-shoulder' hopped back and forth, lunging with his horns at each of them in turn. One of the males evidently felt ready to test the seriousness of the territory owner's bold actions because he did not back down, but instead, lowered his horns and, casting his head back and forth, approached. 'Scar-shoulder' didn't hesitate, but immediately accepted the challenge. I heard a loud 'clang' when the horns clashed together—once was clearly enough, however, as the challenger quickly retreated back to the bachelor herd. Neither did 'Scar-shoulder' follow up on his success, but remained standing, seemingly quite startled over his simple victory. The intruders—29 in all—disappeared from sight after several minutes and 'Scar-shoulder' remembered his territorial defence and I my warblers and we returned to our respective positions.

Thus, a regular day proceeds for most impala males. A small minority manage to establish and defend a territory, the larger majority remain 'bachelors' and wander in herds, eating, growing, gaining weight, continually engaging in small disputes and sparring with each other—a bit like body builders.

Together with last year's calves, the females also wander about in herds, feeding as much as they can. For them, the rule is to spend time where food is most abundant. When they enter a male's territory, they are immediately 'captured' by him. He tries to force them to stay as long as he can. He circles them anxiously, smelling for signs of a female in heat, which then triggers his foreplay behaviour and mating attempts. However, he is also testing the wind for any sign of envious intruders. He has little time left for eating.

After a while he becomes so exhausted and emaciated that he doesn't have the energy to stand guard over his females any longer and they leave his territory. He then also leaves his territory and joins up with one of the bachelor herds in the neighbourhood. One of the costs he has been forced to pay during his period of territorial defence, besides a severe diet, is a significant increase in the number of irritating ticks on his body. Being on guard incessantly as a territorial male has resulted in the neglect of his personal hygiene. Considering all the diseases ticks and other ectoparasites can transmit, it is not only a source of irritation, but also most certainly a health hazard and thus, a serious cost.

In East Africa territory-holding impala males can be identified at almost any time of year, even if activity declines during the worst of the dry period. Every adult male alternates between active duty on a territory and recovery in a bachelor herd. The female herds decide their movements based on food abundance, whereas the males compete intensively over territories containing profuse and lush impala food. Consequently, the male having the most and best food resources available in his territory has the greatest chance of attracting females and will most likely mate with one or more of them.

Female impalas probably gather in herds to minimize the risk of any one individual falling prey to a predator. For similar reasons, the males also live much of their lives in herds. Only periodically does a male leave the relative security of the herd to become a risk-taking territorial male. During short periods, his territory may be visited by a group of females that eventually moves on, either when the food resources are exhausted, or when the territorial male can no longer prevent them from leaving. Previously, the impala's mating system was described as harem defence, where one male dominated a number of females. The truth is that the female herds roam freely about searching for food and males are nothing more than a pleasant distraction in their lives.

As with many other animals, impalas live in clans, that is groups based on kinship relationships. Results from one investigation conducted in Zimbabwe showed that clans of female impalas and their young were made up of 30–120 individuals and each clan moved within an area of 80–180 hectares. Occasionally, females dispersed from their birth clan to a neighbouring clan. The males are generally much more mobile and, on average, move over a kilometre away from the clan territory where they were born. Different dispersal distances for males and females are common for almost all kinds of animals and are usually interpreted as an adaptation originating because it reduces the risk of inbred offspring.

Researchers have been able to demonstrate that the social systems of many mammalian species vary both between different places and different times. This is certainly true for the impala. Most of the information above came from studies in an area in central Zimbabwe, where access to food resources was good and the population density of impala was high and even increasing. In regions where the nutritional resources are poorer and the population densities lower, the clan and territorial structure of the impala is significantly less stable and the exchange of individuals between different groups is greater.

The impala's diet is composed of a mixture of grasses and leaves, the former primarily during the rainy seasons and the latter during the dry seasons when the only food available may be the dry leaves of corkwood bushes (*Combretum*). This periodic shifting between dependence on grass and on bushes and trees constrains impalas to live in regions with a mosaic pattern of vegetation.

Like so many of the savannah's herbivores, impalas love to eat acacia shoots, leaves and twigs. On the whole, the impala is a very particular and cost conscious consumer, a fact that was demonstrated through another study from Mashonaland in northernmost Zimbabwe. The impala's favourite food in that region is the shoots and leaves of the blackthorn acacia (*Acacia nilotica*), which are present in abundance, interspersed in woodland savannah dominated by miombo or mopane. Researchers built observation towers from where they could follow the activities of the impala herds without disturbing them. As expected, impalas were careful in their choice of which acacia bush to visit, and they avoided to a greater extent than was expected those bushes that the researchers had labelled in advance as being of low value. The higher the quality a bush had (according to the researcher's pre-determined classification), then the longer time the impalas spent eating from that bush, as well as taking a greater number of bites. Perhaps the most interesting finding was that the size of the herd influenced the eating habits of individual impalas. The more individuals there were in a group, the fewer bites each individual took from every bush visited. A similar correlation has also been found in species other than impala. Researchers speculate that this behaviour might be due to competition between browsing individuals for the best bites, causing each of them to 'hurry up' and spend less time at each bush than they would if they had been alone. With the exception of the one or two dominant individuals in a herd, an impala that has found a particularly rich and productive bush must count on being shoved aside quickly by a superior. So instead, they choose to move quickly and orderly between bushes minimizing the risk of being abruptly 'rebuked' and forced to make a more awkward retreat.

In addition, each individual can't stay as long as it really 'wants to' at each bush, as those herd companions that don't find a good food source don't remain in the area, but instead choose to move on. Being left alone is not something that a herd-living herbivore accepts easily; it is better to be satisfied with fewer tempting morsels. Not being able to arrange one's own eating pattern as one would like is one of the costs of enjoying the other benefits of group living. As long as those benefits outweigh the unavoidable costs, an individual animal remains in its herd—but not a minute longer. Being together is the means, not the goal.

## DIK-DIK: TWO BY TWO

The road east through Etosha National Park towards the pleasant little town of Tsumeb in northern Namibia passes through an endless expanse of dense bush savannah. Because many of the bushes are covered with thorns, it is difficult to find one's way through the impenetrable thickets. The best strategy is to follow the winding elephant trails that connect feeding grounds with waterholes. As the hike becomes less difficult there is time to concentrate on the interesting species living on the bush savannah. Here, a termite mound with a clan of dwarf mongoose as lodgers; there, a pair of nest-building sunbirds; a bit further on, a pair of drongos furiously attacking a yellow-billed hornbill that approached their nest with dubious intentions. From the top of a hill the view opens up and far in the distance the thatched roofs of some huts in a little village are visible. But people don't live here, do they? No, I was mistaken. What I had seen were the giant nests built by the sociable weaver bird (*Philetairus socius*)—an extremely social species of weaver. The flock's hundreds or thousands of birds, each smaller than a house sparrow, build such an enormous collective nest in the treetops that from a distance it looks like the thatched roofs of a group of huts.

One of the animals that may be seen on the bush savannah is the dik-dik. It is one of the smallest antelopes, with adults weighing only about 5 kilogrammes. The males have a pair of small (7–8 centimetres), pointed, backwards-sloping horns; the females lack horns entirely. With its large eyes and ears, its long and moveable nose and its delicate build, the dik-dik is a beauty to behold in its dainty format.

For animals the size of dik-diks, life is full of predators—clothed in either fur or feathers. In many regions the mighty martial eagle is something of a dik-dik specialist. To hide from the keen-sighted and hungry predators, dik-diks rely on the grizzled colouring of their coat, which provides a perfect camouflage among the dry leaves, twigs, and grass. If you catch sight of a dik-dik, it usually 'freezes': it comes to an abrupt halt and stands motionless, often with one of its front legs poised in mid-air like an old equestrian statue. If you remain completely still, the dik-dik slowly 'thaws out' and begins walking around searching for food, continually listening, smelling, and keeping a lookout in all directions.

It is rare to see a solitary dik-dik. Unlike most other antelope species, dik-diks live in monogamous pairs—that is, one male and one female, who are occasionally accompanied by their most recent offspring. The pair stick close together, but the slightly larger female is the one who decides where and how fast they move. If she lies down in the shade of a particular bush, he lies down a short distance away. When she flees from a real or imagined danger, he rushes after. They never journey long distances; there is no need since dik-diks live in limited territories that are strictly private, where intruders are not welcome. Their boundaries are announced with scent marks made partly of a secretion from the pair of large scent glands near the eyes, and partly of faeces and urine. During a normal day, a dik-dik pair never stray from their territory, which can range in size from 5 to 35 hectares—depending on the food supply in the area.

Why do dik-diks live in territorial pairs, a way of life that is so different from most other hoofed mammals on the savannah? Food and water shortages often characterize the dik-diks' environment. Additionally, darkness at night and heat during the day prevent them from foraging during all except a couple of hours in the mornings and evenings. They are inactive both at night (probably due to the great risk of becoming a predator's meal) and during the midday heat. The smaller the animal, the larger its area relative to its volume; consequently, a small animal is more susceptible to overheating and dehydration than a larger one. Thus, dik-diks, to a much greater extent than the larger savannah animals, are forced to make sure they take a proper siesta in the shade during the hottest midday hours.

The change of seasons from the rainy to the dry season poses another problem for dik-diks. During the rainy season, dik-diks can fill their water and dietary demands fairly easily. They can even be fussy about their food and only eat certain special plants. Generally, dik-diks never eat grass but instead dine only on fruits, leaves, and shoots from woody plants.

It is difficult for a human observer to understand how plant-eating animals can survive on the withered vegetation and the lack of water that exists during the dry season. However, dik-diks manage. They browse energetically first thing in the morning when dew coats the plants, thus taking in quite a bit of moisture. In addition, they eat primarily from those plants they ignored during the rainy season, particularly fruits and other plant parts that are relatively high in nutrition and water content. Sodom apples (*Solanum incanum*) and wild figs are among their favourites, both of which have a water content of 80–90 per cent.

In general, the physiology of this little animal teems with interesting adaptations to harsh ecological conditions. A dik-dik produces three times as much heat per kilo as does a cow weighing 500 kg. In order to prevent overheating, dik-diks rely on the evaporation of water through their skin. Since water is a scarce commodity for much of the year, dik-diks are forced to be economical with the water they absorb via their diet. The dik-dik's extremely effective kidneys accomplish this task. With a minimal expenditure of water, their kidneys can cleanse their bodies of unwanted waste products. In addition, they have a water absorption mechanism in their large intestine that is so effective that their piles of excrement are drier than a desert camel's.

Plants don't grow during the dry season and the dik-dik must live on the vegetation present at the end of the rainy season until the start of the next. This can be a period of eight or nine months in those areas with the least precipitation in eastern and south-western Africa where the dik-dik lives. When resources are limited and non-renewable, territorial behaviour becomes advantageous. Every male dik-dik claims and defends to the utmost an area that contains enough resources to keep it alive through the merciless dry period. He tolerates no other male within his territory.

The territory's resources must feed not only the male, but also his female: the dik-dik pair bond is a permanent life-long relationship. Thus, territories provide both guaranteed access to resources as well as allowing the male to monopolize a mating partner. He follows her like a shadow as she wanders through their territory to guard her from other males, and energetically tries to prevent her from straying beyond the territorial boundaries. There are rivals out there—a threat to his own reproductive success. Therefore, the territory must be large enough to provide both dik-diks with sufficient food, but small enough so that it is possible to defend.

Dik-diks demonstrate that a monogamous lifestyle doesn't need to be associated with, or dependant on, both parents caring for offspring for reproduction to be successful. The dik-dik male doesn't share these responsibilities. He may provide some kind of assistance as a lookout for predators, but that is all. During the rainy season, their offspring accompanies the female who nurses it, and as a result, the female is less likely to leave the territory and is therefore easier to guard. This, in combination with the abundance of food, grants the males an almost vacation-like existence during the rainy season. Considering his exemption from helping with the care of the young, it is surprising that he doesn't try to acquire a more expansive territory so that he could have room for two or more females. This would seem to increase his reproductive opportunities at a relatively low cost.

The most likely reason why he establishes a 'one female territory' is that he would probably experience insurmountable problems in simultaneously guarding two or more females. If he were to fail in his guard duty, neighbouring males might sneak into his territory and steal matings with his females; consequently, all his efforts would benefit his rivals instead.

One of the mechanisms that upholds monogamy among dik-diks is that females are quite aggressive towards one another. A wandering female searching for a partner is anything but welcome when she encroaches on a territory that already accommodates a female. Sometimes the newcomer drives the established female away—something that doesn't seem to bother the territorial male in the least. He is more interested in his territory, because as long as he holds the territory, he needn't wait long for a partner.

Social monogamy is combined with sexual polygamy in many animal species, with females mating with one or more males nearby. However, the dik-dik is also sexually monogamous. With the aid of techniques from molecular biology, researchers have shown that the territorial male is always the father of the offspring found within his territory.

All in all, the dik-dik's fairly unusual mating system of monogamous pairs within a defended territory can be seen as a result of a series of concurrent adaptations to a periodically severe and harsh environment where dietary resources are non-renewable during most of the year and are thus worth defending. Females search out territories with the richest resources and males cannot guard more than one female at a time. Guarding is made difficult because the dense vegetation limits visibility forcing the male to stay very close to the female in order to ensure that she has no opportunities to mate with other males.

I once had the luck to watch the dik-dik's peculiar method of territorial marking—
the placement of faeces and urine at certain fixed localities along the territorial
borders. As I sat on the trunk of a fallen tree, I saw a dik-dik pair walking stealthily
through the bushes—the female first, as always, and the male following a metre
behind her. When she arrived at a place where there was already a flat pile of
thousands of faecal pellets, she squatted, urinated, and made her small contribution
to the pile. Then she got up and took a few steps forwards whereupon the male
approached the pile, smelled her contribution, kicked the pile, and then added his
own urine and faecal pellets. Then both animals proceeded to rub their scent glands
against a pair of dry branches, licked one another in the face, and then strolled off in
the same direction from which they had come.

Dik-dik dung piles can cover an area of up to two square metres and can
measure up to a decimetre thick in the centre. They are built by successive
territory owners over the years and provide a certain level of stability for the local
territorial pattern. One of the most important things for a young dik-dik male that
wants to establish himself as a territorial male, attract a female, and reproduce, is
to start a new dung pile or take over an existing one. A young dik-dik leaves its
mother and its home territory when it is six months old, at about the same time as
its mother gives birth to a new little dik-dik.

The natural explanation for these impressive dung piles is that they are signals
to other neighbouring dik-diks and thus have a similar function to, for example,
the song of a blackcap singing at the edge of a European wood. The strange dung
piles of the dik-dik can lead to completely different interpretations. I heard one
such explanation in Tanzania. Once upon a time a dik-dik came strolling through
the bush savannah. Suddenly he tripped and fell on his nose and crushed it, and
since then all dik-diks have had noses that are slightly down-turned like a little
trunk. Of course the dik-dik was so indignant when he discovered that his

accident had been caused by tripping over a pile of elephant dung that he immediately decided to take revenge—if he had tripped over elephant droppings, then he would make sure that they tripped over his. Ever since that day, all dik-diks have built their dung piles up high enough so that big elephants will trip over them...

## Wildebeest and Grass

What does paradise look like? It looks like Ngorongoro, Serengeti, Masai Mara, and Ol Doinyo Orok—evocative names from the grandiose system of national parks and reserves that together cover an area of almost 40 000 square kilometres in north-western Tanzania and southern Kenya between Lake Victoria in the west and the Rift Valley in the east. That is what an earthly paradise looks like.

Every year, directed by the climate, a splendid, incomparable, zoological drama is acted out in these wide expanses—the migration of the common wildebeest between their various grazing grounds.

Throughout the year, the tropic zone (that is the wide belt along the equator extending 23° north to the Tropic of Cancer and 23° south to the Tropic of Capricorn) is characterized by an abundance of light and heat. Precipitation, however, varies considerably between the different seasons. In general, precipitation is most plentiful at, or soon after, the time of year when the sun is at zenith. In the northern part of the tropic zone, for example in the Sudan, precipitation is most abundant during July and August, whereas in Zimbabwe and Botswana the rain period culminates in January and February. At the equator, there are two rainy periods annually—one after the vernal equinox and the other after the autumnal equinox. The Serengeti is located immediately south of the equator and therefore receives the largest amounts of rainfall during October (the short rain) and April (the long rain).

In addition to the seasonal variations, local differences in precipitation conditions may occur. Large lakes can affect the amount of precipitation in the

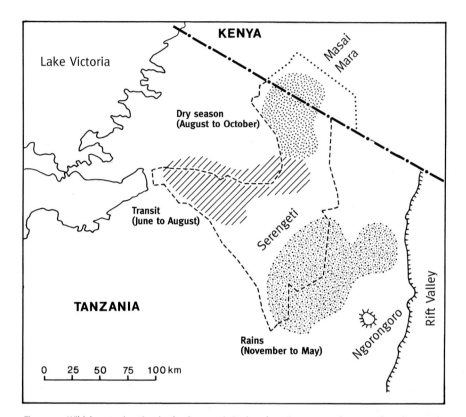

*Figure 13. Wildebeest migration in the Serengeti. During the rainy season these antelope live on the short-grass savannah of the south east while they spend the dry season in the more luxuriant mosaic savannah of the north. The west is an important transit area but the migrating herds are subjected to intensive poaching just outside the borders of the national park where there are heavily populated agricultural regions filled with meat-hungry humans.*

surrounding area. Due to the proximity of Lake Victoria, the Serengeti ecosystem in East Africa receives considerably more annual precipitation in the north west (1200 millimetres) than it does in the south east (500 millimetres). However, topographical conditions also contribute to this pattern. This gradient of decreasing precipitation eastwards plays a significnt role in the migration pattern of wildebeest.

The most abundant large herbivore in East Africa is the common wildebeest (wildebeest). During the 1990s, their population in the Serengeti ecosystem numbered somewhere between 1 and 2 million animals. The wildebeest is easy to recognize with its dark grey coat and black stripes (which are clearest on the front regions), short, thick neck, and crooked horns (in both sexes). Like the buffalo, the wildebeest is equipped with a broad muzzle, designed in the shape of a lawn-mower, for the effective clipping of short grass. As grass is a poor provider of both energy and important minerals, the wildebeest, more than any other large game species in Africa, has become a migrant who commutes between different regions depending on seasonal changes in climate and vegetation to fulfil its nutritional requirements and its demands for water. The wildebeest migration characterizes the Serengeti ecosystem and has laid the foundation for the world-wide fame of this region. '*Serengeti shall not die*' was the title of an epoch-making book by Bernhard and Michael Grzimek. When it was published at the end of the 1950s, it drew the world's attention to all the dangers threatening Africa's savannah and big game species.

I will never forget that special day in March when I, together with a group of like-minded Swedes arrived in the Serengeti. We had spent two exciting days in the Ngorongoro Crater and were now travelling across the short grassy plains of the Serengeti, hoping that before nightfall we would reach Ndutu, a camp near tiny Ndutu Lake where we were to spend the night. The wind-carved cliff formations or '*kopjes*' (a South African word) are typical features of many African savannahs, rising like castles over the plains and creating important signposts and splendid lookout points. To our right was Simba Kopjes and to our left, Moru Kopjes. We climbed one of the latter kopjes and the view from the top of the bare hillock was unforgettable. Without really noticing it, we had driven down into a gentle valley and could not see as far as we thought we should be able. From the top of the cliff, however, we could see out over the expansive savannah. Everywhere we looked we saw herds of thousands of wildebeest, all with their noses pointing towards the north-west, in unending columns reminiscent of an army on the march, all moving slowly in the same direction… There was something almost unreal about that remarkable mass movement.

The sun dropped quickly and we hurriedly returned to our vehicles in order to continue on towards the camp-site. Sitting outside our tents that evening and sipping tea, we witnessed another sight that is etched in my memory: as far as our eyes could see, wildebeest silhouettes lined the horizon. Most of the wildebeest stood still and awaited the night, when some of them would be set free from the hardships of migration by becoming a meal for hyenas, wild dogs, or a pride of lions. Several thousand went down to drink from the pitiful muddy pool of water, which was all that the drought had left of Ndutu Lake, but they were obviously nervous and were continuously looking around wearily. And not without good reason: the bushes were dense along the shores of the lake and danger lurked among the thickets. Crowding made flight difficult. Throughout the night, we heard the characteristic squealing or grunting calls of the wildebeest (which gives the species its alternative name "gnu" via the San language in the Kalahari).

Shortly after dawn the next morning, we couldn't see a living wildebeest from our camp-site. However, there were three or four half-eaten carcasses down by the lakeshore and a gang of marabou storks perched in some umbrella acacias looking out over their waiting breakfast. Three black-backed jackals were already feeding on one of the wildebeest before more powerful competitors could drive them away. The savannah larks were singing, the glossy starlings were chattering, and the clear tune of the chin-spot batis flycatcher resounded from the acacias. It was hard to imagine how eventful the past night had been.

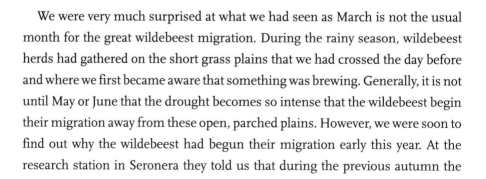

We were very much surprised at what we had seen as March is not the usual month for the great wildebeest migration. During the rainy season, wildebeest herds had gathered on the short grass plains that we had crossed the day before and where we first became aware that something was brewing. Generally, it is not until May or June that the drought becomes so intense that the wildebeest begin their migration away from these open, parched plains. However, we were soon to find out why the wildebeest had begun their migration early this year. At the research station in Seronera they told us that during the previous autumn the short rains had almost completely failed to arrive. Because of this, the drought had caused the vegetation to wither unusually early and the wildebeest herds had responded by departing on their annual north-westerly migration earlier than usual.

Where were they going? They were on their way to an area of abundant rainfall near the western regions of Serengeti National Park, an area that is actually outside the park's boundaries. The region is densely populated and many of the wildebeest will be killed, legally or illegally, and used as food, particularly biltong (dried game meat), which is an important food commodity in many regions of Africa (and an exquisite delicacy). Based on the rainfall's timetable and abundance, the herds depart from this area and move on towards the north and north-east and, during some years at least, arrive in great numbers at Masai Mara, a Kenyan National Park that borders the Tanzanian national park system. It is during this stage that the wildebeest herds must pass the Grumeti and Mara Rivers, home to a dense population of magnificent crocodiles. It is an unforget-table sight when the wildebeest hurl themselves into the water to cross the river, simultaneously offering the crocodiles their richest feast of the year.

On a visit during another year, I encountered the giant wildebeest herds when they were in the Masai Mara. It was August and according to the rulebook they shouldn't have been that far north yet. However, in Africa every year is 'abnormal' when it comes to precipitation. On the previous occasion, a rainy period fails to arrive in the plains area, causing the wildebeest to begin their travels unusually early. In the Masai Mara, however, the wildebeest were in a migratory kind of mood because the rains on the short grass plains nearby had begun to fall unusu-ally early in the season. Even though we don't know how they do it, it seems that many savannah animals can detect rainfall across great distances. Is it the smell of moist earth on the wind, or the rumbling of a distant thunderstorm, or simply the behaviour of other animals signalling that grass is sprouting and herbs and leaves are waiting just beyond those hills?

Undoubtedly, those wildebeest herds in the Masai Mara knew. From the top of every hillock they could be seen grazing in the valleys, all slowly moving towards the south, small herds, large herds, hardly in marching formation, but with an urge to migrate that could literally be felt on the wind. With the silhouette of the Ngorongoro Crater in the background, they seemed to long for open expanses, away from the dense thickets, the high grass, and the crowded valleys in the Masai Mara. Kongoni and topi antelope seemed to stare at them in perplexity— these species actually enjoy the high grass that waves in the lush Masai Mara throughout the year.

The migratory habits of wildebeest means that they can't possibly engage in permanent pair bonds or constant territory defence. Instead, adult males establish short-term territories to which they attempt to attract females or groups of females. Their breeding period occurs at the end of the rainy season when the animals are in the best condition. For those wildebeest that migrate between the Serengeti and Masai Mara, this means that practically all of them enter rut at the same time, during the initial stages of the migration in May. Thus, almost all the calves are born at the same time (90 per cent within a three week period) and in this way they unintentionally provide one another with a kind of protection against predators. Even if there is a feast among all the savannah's carnivores, from the jackals to the lions, from the baboons to the marabou storks, when 10 000 or 100 000 wildebeest simultaneously give birth to their calves, their numbers are so overwhelming that each one's chance for survival is better than if it was born outside the main calving period. Another defence against predation is that calving occurs in the most open terrain possible where the density of larger predators is lower. A third advantage is that the calves are able follow their mothers almost immediately after birth. However, mortality among wildebeest calves is still enormous: only those few who have received the best genetic specifications, who have the most experienced mothers and, in addition, have a lot of luck manage to survive the first months of life.

Is it food, water, predators, or perhaps something else entirely that is the ultimate reason for the evolution of the wildebeest's migratory behaviour? Perhaps all these factors play a part, but researchers have identified one very special factor: phosphorus. Phosphorus is a chemical element necessary for life processes in all living organisms. Researchers have found that the dry grass that remains on the plains during the dry season has an extremely low phosphorus content. If the wildebeest were to remain on the plains, they would not be able to fulfil their requirement of this essential element by eating the grass that they are adapted to graze upon. Thus, they benefit from migrating to other grazing grounds where the grass is richer in phosphorus. In other words, it may not be the quantity that is the key factor, but its quality.

In this region of East Africa with the Serengeti and Masai Mara at its heart, the wildebeest is unconditionally the most abundant of the big game species, whether one counts individuals or total biomass. Elsewhere in Africa, herbivores that migrate have been found to reach large population densities and appear to be quite successful in many other respects, for example the topi in southern Sudan, the kob, also in the Sudan, the springbok in southern Africa, and the common wildebeest in the Kalahari. (This was before humans intentionally or unintentionally encroached on the living conditions of these animals.) Why are species that migrate so exceptionally successful?

Ecologists have concluded that minimizing losses to predators is a significant contributing factor. Since the migrating herbivores are absent for part of the year in a given area, the predators in that region suffer a period of reduced prey supply. This keeps the carnivore population at such a low level that they have a relatively insignificant effect on the prey population. In many circumstances, carnivores can reduce prey species populations, but this is hardly possible with one that undertakes annual migrations. However, the primary reason that wildebeest migrate is not to ease predation pressure, but to ensure that they have access to large enough quantities of high quality food throughout the year. That their losses to predators are minimized is probably only a fortunate consequence.

Completely unintentionally, humans are in the process of conducting a grim experiment that will shed light on the consequences of preventing wildebeest populations from migrating. In the Kalahari (Botswana), the most important source of livelihood for the human population is raising livestock. However, since wild herbivores carry disease and can thus infect the domestic livestock with serious illnesses the Botswanan authorities have erected thousands of kilometres of fencing across the Kalahari's wide-open expanses. One of these fences blocks the migratory route of the wildebeest between the rainy season's vast grazing grounds and the dry season's limited water supply. Many tens of thousands of wildebeest died of thirst en route to their traditional waterholes during the first year after the fence was erected. Because of the lack of sufficient water, today's wildebeest population has dropped to less than ten per cent of its previous size and has refrained from its seasonal migrations. Will the carnivores succeed in regulating the Kalahari wildebeest population now that they have become stationary?

Recently, wildebeest populations have indeed declined in Africa due to the expansion of humans into new areas. In some places, however, wildebeest populations have actually increased, proving that a species can sometimes succeed despite dramatic changes in ecological conditions. The wildebeest's migratory behaviour constitutes one of the most important components of their lives: they exploit vegetation during the period when it is most nutritious, and their migrations prevent predator populations from reaching such high densities as would exert a threat to their prey. However, there are wildebeest populations that do not undertake seasonal migrations. Down in the Ngorongoro Crater, wildebeest live stationary lives, largely isolated from the migrating populations on the plains of the Serengeti. Similarly, there are stationary wildebeest populations in Selous, Hwange, and Etosha, just to mention a few of Africa's most well-known national parks.

To conclude this dramatization of wildebeest life is an interesting statistic. During the mating season (rut), male wildebeest establish tiny territories which they defend energetically from other males at the same time as trying to lure receptive females into their territory with metallic grunts and peculiar antics. There can be up to 300 of these territories per square kilometre within particularly attractive areas, each with its somewhat crazy owner; in other words, each territory is only about 3000 square metres. There is definitely a lot of quarrelling and squabbling on the plains during this time of year!

## Springboks in the Land of Thirst

In north-eastern and eastern Africa there are a number of closely related antelope species called gazelles. The word gazelle has become symbolic of delicate limbs, graceful manners, and sensual elegance. As they move across the open landscape with their lithe movements and velvety colours in the heat-induced mirages and quivering air that hovers over the dry white earth, they can almost be mistaken for illusions rather than animals made of flesh and blood. Thomson's gazelle and Grant's gazelle are probably the best known of the true gazelles, but there are several other gazelle species found in Africa, Arabia, the Middle East, and India.

In southern Africa, there is only one antelope species that fills the role of gazelle—the springbok—but opinion is divided as to whether springboks are, or are not related to gazelles. Springboks probably evolved in Europe 14 million years ago, their predecessors having already found a design that was very much like that seen in modern springboks. The springbok was clearly quite common in East Africa a couple of million years ago and is the most abundant species found in the fossil record.

The springbok has several characteristics that distinguish it from the true gazelles and may argue against it being a form of gazelle that became isolated in southern Africa. For example, the springbok's horn is hollow whereas the gazelles have solid horns, and they have different dentition. One of the springbok's unique physical characteristics is a fold of skin on its back that contains tufts of long white hair and a number of scent producing glands. (They produce a smell like burnt sugar.) Usually the skin fold is not visible, but in certain situations it opens up and the long tufts of white hair protrude. On such occasions the springbok is communicating chemically with its neighbours.

The Dutch immigrants who began colonizing South Africa during the seventeenth century gave the springbok its name. In both Dutch and German, 'springen' means jump, and this Boer designation refers to a very special springbok behaviour. Every now and then, in the middle of a good gallop, one or more individuals start jumping high, high into the air with feet together, necks curving downwards, and backs arched. The scented skin-fold on their backs turns inside out and the white tuft stands up and is visible from a great distance. After a while, the animals stop jumping and return to more sensible behaviour. In the jargon of behavioural scientists this is called stotting, and quite a bit of printer's ink has been squandered on trying to explain why springboks (and certain other gazelle-like antelopes) engage in this bizarre leaping behaviour.

One suggestion is that stotting is a way for the animal to get a good overview of its surroundings. Jonathan Kingdon, a South African zoologist and artist, maintains that it is chiefly animals that are new to a region and therefore unfamiliar with the terrain that engage in this high-jumping behaviour, and that they do this in order to collect information about their surroundings. He also thinks that springboks facilitate the spreading of their chemical signals by jumping up into the wind currents at the same time as they release scent from the glands in their skin folds.

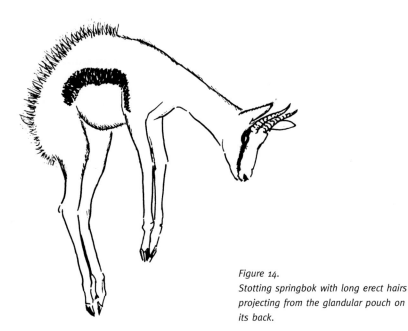

*Figure 14.*
*Stotting springbok with long erect hairs*
*projecting from the glandular pouch on*
*its back.*

The Israeli evolutionary biologist Amotz Zahavi suggests a completely different explanation, which he bases on his experience with the Arabian gazelle in the Negev Desert. Zahavi thinks that stotting acts as a signal to approaching predators: 'Look how alert and fit I am—go away and try to catch someone who doesn't jump as high as I do since you will never catch me anyway.' However, the signal could just as easily be aimed at other individuals of the same species: 'Look how superbly I am managing this situation, I definitely have some get up and go.' The honesty of the signal is guaranteed because an individual who sends the signal without actually being in superb condition would easily become a meal for a predator. According to Zahavi, the signal is thus associated with a functional handicap. The message that the stotting behaviour communicates is: 'I can survive despite performing this handicap behaviour.' In this way, individuals demonstrate that they are superior to those who may have escaped danger without tempting fate. The ultimate reward for this energetic stotting in the face of danger could also be that it bestows increased status within the herd, and thus, increased sexual attractiveness, which in time results in a greater number of offspring.

This handicap hypothesis has been put forward as an explanation for why so many animals engage in various strenuous or daring behaviours, or wear different cumbersome or costly ornaments that seem to do everything but increase the individual's chances for survival. You can imagine a gang of young boys competing over who will be the first to poke at the rattlesnake they find by the side of the road. If Johnny finally dares to lift the perhaps frozen stiff but still terrifying snake by the tail, isn't there just a sigh of admiration that goes through the little group, and doesn't Johnny become the hero of the day?

There is no definitive conclusion about stotting springboks. In fact the handicap hypothesis has become the subject matter for more widespread research as it may explain many puzzling behavioural patterns in our own species as well as in others.

The springbok's tremendous migrating behaviour is even more fascinating than stotting, although migration is unfortunately almost an obsolete springbok behaviour nowadays. As with the wildebeest in the Serengeti, migrating herbivore populations can be very successful and occur in great numbers. This used to be the case for springboks in the Kalahari. However, the wildebeest's regular annual migrations bear no resemblance to the springbok's more chaotic emigration from which very few individuals ever return to their area of birth. It is only during some years, with long unpredictable intervals in-between, that the springbok suddenly appear in great crowds far to the east and south of their usual home ranges in the heart of southern Africa. This occurs when the drought in their home range has become extreme at the same time as their numbers have increased due to a series of exceptional reproductive periods. This springbok migration behaviour can be compared to 'invasion' birds in Scandinavia. When spruce trees in Scandinavia fail to produce seeds, the crossbills and coal-tits emigrate to other parts of Europe in search of more food. Only a small minority of birds ever return from such journeys. (However, one could imagine that even fewer would have survived had they remained in their Scandinavian home regions.) Another parallel between the Scandinavian invasion birds and the South African springbok is that not all individuals embark on the journey. The ecological explanation is probably similar in both cases: those who remain at home have access to a resource that would be too costly to abandon, such as a nest hole for a male Tengmalm's owl or a popular territory for a male springbok.

Before European invaders started their exploitation, decimation, and in some cases extermination of South Africa's big game, springbok were so abundant that they completely overshadowed the Serengeti wildebeest. In 1947, Colonel J. Stevenson-Hamilton, then director for Kruger National Park in eastern South Africa and an expert on South Africa's wildlife, wrote of the springbok: 'In former days these treks were of almost inconceivable magnitude, consisting of hundreds of thousands of individuals, and naturally the country over which they passed was denuded of every blade of grass and for the time rendered useless for stock. Such an immense concourse of antelopes was followed by every description of carnivorous animal, which, together with wild creatures of other species, and

*Plate 1. Some African tribes used to have the pleasing belief that mankind was first created in the crown of a baobab. These savannah zebras are standing alert in front of an elephant-damaged baobab. Tsavo, Kenya.*

PHOTO ALLAN CARLSON.

Plate 2. (above) The elephant – Africa's primal landscape architect. Dense elephant populations can quickly reduce rich woodlands to tinder and eliminate their own food supply. Ruaha, Tanzania. PHOTO ALLAN CARLSON.

Plate 3. (left) This old gentleman elephant has seen everything and probably done most of it. Masai Mara, Kenya. PHOTO BO G. SVENSSON.

Plate 4. (top opposite) A whiff of danger? Worried elephant females form a defensive ring around their young. Amboseli, Kenya. PHOTO BO TALLMARK

Plate 5. (bottom opposite) When in transit between foraging areas and water-holes, older, experienced mother elephants bracket their young within the column of walkers. Other elephants cover the flanks of the column. Ruaha, Tanzania. PHOTO ALLAN CARLSON.

Plate 6. Contortions for a few buds of whistling acacia! Long necks do not necessarily make feeding any easier. Amboseli, Kenya. PHOTO BO TALLMARK.

Plate 7. The highly sociable savannah buffalo thrives in most habitats but requires daily access to water. Lake Manyara, Tanzania. PHOTO BO TALLMARK.

*Plate 8. Impala – the perfect antelope. This buck is guarding his territory and keeping a sharp lookout for potential rivals. Nairobi, Kenya.* PHOTO BO TALLMARK.

*Plate 9. (left) The dik-dik´s large eyes and ears and constantly sniffing nostrils indicate that it can never relax its vigilance – just too many predators. Samburu-Isiolo, Kenya.* PHOTO BO TALLMARK.

*Plate 10. (below) Napoleon´s Army marching across the Russian steppe? No, wildebeest migrating from the dry short-grass savannahs of south-eastern Serengeti to the greener pastures of Masai Mara across the border in Kenya.* PHOTO BO TALLMARK.

*Plate 11. (top left opposite) Less than ten minutes after its birth this wildebeest calf was able to run alongside its mother at an impressive speed. Serengeti, Tanzania.* PHOTO BO TALLMARK.

*Plate 12. (top right opposite) Wildebeest bulls fight intensely for possession of territory that is likely to attract plenty of females. Certain territories seem to be preferred by females because, among other things, they are relatively predator-safe. Amboseli, Kenya.* PHOTO BO TALLMARK.

*Plate 13. (bottom opposite) Waterbuck – a perfect specimen of one of the most beautiful African antelopes. Tsavo, Kenya.* PHOTO BO G. SVENSSON.

*Plate 14. This topi bull is making itself as conspicuous as possible by standing on top of an old termite mound. Masai Mara, Kenya.* PHOTO BO TALLMARK.

even domestic beasts, were often seen being borne irresistibly forward in the midst of the congested throng. When an inhabited district was passed, white men and natives turned out to the last man, and killed, until they had to stop from sheer exhaustion. These migrations, though less in magnitude than of yore, still occur in the north-western ranges of the species.' One account describes a single South African trader who exported nearly 2 million antelope hides, mostly springbok, during the three-year period of 1878–80. In addition to hunting, however, another factor contributed to the decimation of the springbok population—the rinderpest epidemic—which arrived in South Africa in 1896. It caused the deaths of at least 90 per cent of the hoofed animals both in South and East Africa, and in many areas the springbok never recovered from this catastrophe.

Since then, conditions in most parts of Africa have not been favourable for springboks or for other wildlife; not even in South Africa, which has pursued a comparatively far-sighted and effective conservation programme during the entire post-war period. For the springbok, however, the future looks brighter than for many other species. This is chiefly because springbok are used as semi-domesticated producers of meat and hides in the drier inner regions of South Africa. There, as in many places in Africa, ranches are enormous, and gradually an insight has developed that 'game ranching', the use of wild native species, can produce both ecological and economic benefits in these vast but fragile expanses. In addition, wild game meat has become not only a delicacy that is easily sold to gourmet consumers throughout the world, but is also thought of as a particularly nutritional food source in many of the richest parts of the world. If skilfully managed, springbok populations can be sustainably harvested at a rate of 30–40 per cent per year.

Domestication, however, is not free from problems. Aggressive territorial defence by males, for example, sets a fixed and rather low limit on population density. Their strategy is to claim a territory rich in resources and then attract the greatest number of females possible—females who are perhaps more attracted by the green grass than by the male's antics. Resource defence polygyny is the technical term for this kind of mating system, where a male attracts several females by serving up tasty titbits. Another disadvantage is that springboks tend to be antisocial, preferring to roam around in small, loosely connected groups with plenty of space between individuals. They cannot be herded about like a flock of sheep. They move in larger crowds only during the big migrations.

It may be possible to address some of these problems through systematic breeding programmes. Such programmes are already underway with the aim of producing meatier springboks with fashionably coloured hides. Nothing stands in the way of selecting for gentle and compliant springboks as well, which in the end might become as manageable as pigs and calves on a European farm— even if this is a long-term aim. As long as there is genetic variation, there are possibilities.

Game management will no doubt provide some hope for a few of Africa's big game species. Far-sighted and enterprising ranch owners in different countries have seen the light, particularly those in South Africa, Namibia, and Zimbabwe. Stricter import regulations in the USA and EU make it more difficult to sell beef in those markets; at the same time an appropriate combination of native herbivores can be managed on the dry savannah earth using its productivity. There are plenty of well-to-do people who are willing to travel from Sundsvall and Milano, Oklahoma City and Dubai and pay large sums of money to help with the harvesting...

Springboks have the impressive ability to survive extreme drought on a diet of the scantiest of plant life. Similar to many other hoofed mammals that are adapted to a way of life where access to resources varies strongly with the seasons, the springbok is a grazer during good seasons and a browser during the bad. It is capable of long migrations if the crisis becomes too severe. Similar to the true gazelles farther north, the springbok has a physiology that is specialized for minimizing water consumption. Since these animals generally spend their time in the most barren grass savannahs, perhaps better described as steppes or deserts, they cannot take shelter in the shade during the hottest part of the day. Their resistance to heat and drought is admirable.

It is impressive to meet these apparently fragile animals in the middle of the land of heat, thirst, and an unforgiving burning sun. I have a particularly strong memory of springboks in the magnificent and barren landscape of the Namib Desert. One early November morning we started off from Swakopmund, driving north along the Namibian coast where, as is so often the case, the morning fog was dense. After stopping at a café in the unlikely seaside resort Hentiesbaai (sandy, damp, foggy, hot, and 12° in the water), shivering and drinking coffee in the raw, damp wind, we steered the car inland through Damaraland and on towards Brandberg, still with the windscreen wipers scraping away at the fog. After exactly 42 minutes we emerged from the fog so suddenly that I could almost hear a 'pop'…

Soon we stopped to warm ourselves up—it took about 30 seconds. Although it was only 9 o'clock the sun was already bombarding the earth with heat. Boundless expanses spread out around us, with low ridges looking like frozen ocean waves, isolated tufts of grass, and a few metre-tall bushes in the depressions. The colours of the ground shifted between black, red, grey, and white, often with sudden transitions. There was life there. The gleam of a black eye revealed first one, then two, and finally three extremely camouflaged larks, which we identified as Gray's larks. They reminded us that the Namib Desert is an old noble desert that has existed so long that species specific only to that area (endemics) have had time to evolve—it is not an upstart like the Sahara. Another bird that attracted our attention was a splendid, almost metre-tall Ludwig's bustard, which with parodic dignity strode along the bottom of a ravine and grazed on grasshoppers, scorpions, or some other delicacies. A couple of geckos let out some squeaks and demonstrated a greater talkativeness than one would expect from reptiles.

We drove on in the rising heat. Twelve o'clock arrived, the sun was almost at its zenith, there were no shadows. Someone pulled a Coca-Cola bottle from the trunk of the car still cool from the previous night and it was more than welcome…

Suddenly the quivering reflections vibrated in an unexpected manner on a nearby slope. We could see with our binoculars that the disturbance was caused by a small herd of springboks—with their beige-coloured backs and legs and their white undersides, they melted in with the background stones, gravel, and dry tufts of grass. If they had not been sporting contrasting black stripes along their sides, we would never have caught sight of them. Alternating between grazing on the scanty tufts of grass and keeping a lookout in all directions, they came nearer and nearer and we could admire their supple movements and graceful build. Suddenly, they all lifted their noses to the wind, testing it intensively and clearly smelling something that wasn't quite right, and with a swish they galloped away down into the next valley and up the next slope, occasionally jumping high into the air. Far off in the distance they again stopped and gazed in all directions, but to us they were again almost as unreal as a mirage.

## MAGNIFICENT DIVERSITY

No one who visits Africa's savannah landscapes can avoid being fascinated by the megafauna living there—the large mammals that humans have decimated or exterminated in all parts of the world into which man has migrated. However, humans are not intruders in Africa—our origins were there. It is on this scene that we have acted a role in the evolutionary drama together with other animals. These other species have had time to adapt their behaviour and thus avoid the fate of extermination at the hand of humans hunting for meat. These adaptations are also how, over millions of years, they have survived and avoided succumbing to sabre-toothed cats, lions, leopards, and other dangerous predators, just as the humans and our ancestors have done. The story was different in other parts of the world: when tribes and clans of efficiently co-operating humans suddenly turned up unannounced, the effect was disastrous for the large eatable or potentially threatening mammalian species. The megafaunas were practically annihilated—humans won on a technical knockout.

In Africa, however, the large tasty mammals evolved adaptations that provided

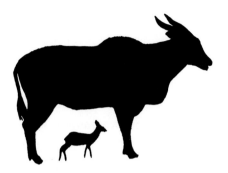

*Figure 15.*
*Antelopes come in all sizes, from the massive eland to the slender dik-dik. Because different species vary so much in size and other ecologically important characteristics, a great many species can co-exist within the same region.*

a certain amount of protection from human predators, similar to the way humans responded to the threat from larger carnivores. Even today there are surprisingly few large mammal species that have become irretrievably extinct on the African continent, even if most have suffered a decrease in numbers or a dramatic reduction of their areas of distribution. In reality, most of Africa's human population has seen as many lions or leopards as most Europeans have seen wolves or bears.

Fortunately, there is still the possibility of visiting African savannahs containing fairly complete sets of large mammal species. Such a visit can lead to a memorable, exhilarating, and aesthetic, experience.

How is it possible that ten, fifteen, twenty, or twenty-five large, herbivorous mammal species permanently co-exist within the same area? Would they not, sooner or later, drive each other out through competition? That several species with similar ways of life co-exist in a certain environment is in reality the rule rather than the exception, whether we are studying herbaceous plants and ants in a Swedish meadow, fish in a coral reef, or trees and birds in a rainforest. But how is it that such systems continue to exist? Why does one species not become lord of the roost? This is a vital question when considering the number of big game species living on the African savannah.

However, this is not simply a case of the peaceful balance of nature—quite the opposite. Chapter 3 described the enormous changes that swept over the Serengeti during the short period of the twentieth century. Dynamics and change are more characteristic qualities of nature than are stability and balance.

One of the most important conditions enabling the enduring co-existence of several species within the same area is that they are at least partially dependent on different resources. In the words of ecologists, there must be enough different niches. If two or more species require niches that overlap too much and therefore have the same resource demands, then sooner or later one of them would gain the upper hand and drive the other away. Accordingly, an animal community must be made up of species that have evolved different specialities. A certain area only has room for one species of zebra and one species of giraffe, for example. Researchers explain that certain 'composition rules' must be followed within animal communities: the building blocks have to be of different shapes and sizes and must fit together in order for the construction to be stable. In part, the composition of animal communities is due to the evolutionary background of the species. Not only individual species, but also different species constellations have their own evolutionary histories.

Living organisms are not rigid and unchanging; they are modifiable, and in many cases can adjust their lives surprisingly quickly to changes in the world around them. They are based on quick modifications, particularly in behaviour and in their way of life rather than adaptations through changes in their genetic compositions that occur over evolutionary time.

Such changes have been studied carefully within the large mammal communities on the African savannah. As early as the 1960s, there were articles about how different herbivore species have different nutritional habits and therefore, as a 'society' could attain and maintain a considerably higher mass per area (kilogram per hectare) than a 'monoculture' of domestic livestock, and this without causing damage due to overgrazing. Since then, many similar studies have been conducted, particularly in the Serengeti region, which have led to significant scientific achievements, both in theory and practice.

The number of individuals of each species is not regulated by biological productivity alone. Both inter-specific competition and intra-specific competition affect an individual's access to resources, reproductive capacity, and chances for survival, and in this manner affect the population dynamics of the various species. Changes in predation pressure, for example when epidemic diseases such as distemper and rabies infect lions and African wild dogs, result in alterations in the competitive relationships between the different herbivore populations. If a certain species, for example wildebeest, for whatever reason increases in numbers, the larger number of wildebeest would—completely unintentionally of course—result in a decrease in the number of zebra or kongoni or topi killed by lions. Predators have the tendency to hunt the prey species that is most abundant. Sometimes certain species like zebras actively seek out large wildebeest herds, as these herds will then act as a living shield for the zebras against lion attacks. When wildebeest leave the short grass savannah in the south-eastern Serengeti and embark on their yearly migration, an unfortunate period begins for the stationary Grant's gazelles, warthogs, waterbucks, and others that are suddenly forced to take the full impact of the lion offensives. On the other hand, it also means bad times ahead for the stationary lions as they sadly watch their main course wandering off towards the west.

The various herbivores also have effects on one another in addition to competition. For example, the effect of one species on vegetation is not necessarily bad for another species; in some cases it is just the opposite. One such case is described by one of the earliest modern wildlife ecologists in East Africa, Desmond Vesey-FitzGerald, based on his experiences from the Rukwa valley in south-western Tanzania. He describes how heavy and abundant animals such as elephants and hippopotamuses as well as eland and zebra literally prepare the ground through their tramping and foraging for more lightweight animals, in this case chiefly puku antelope. In a corresponding manner, the kongoni's grazing on relatively tall grasses results in favourable conditions for wildebeest, which are specialists on short, preferably newly sprouting grasses with a high phosphorous content. Gazelles eat only grass that has been cut down through grazing and grass that is regrowing, thus they avoid areas with tall grasses.

Thus, a complicated web of interspecific relationships exist in which competition, and different kinds of unintentional co-operation, interact with predation to maintain diversity. No single species manages to monopolize resources unfairly.

Interestingly, palaeobiologists who study the life habits of extinct animals based on fossil evidence, have found that approximately the same roles have existed in the savannah drama for millions of years in spite of the fact that the actors have successively been replaced. The roles—the ecological niches—endure, but the species vanish.

Survival requires continual access to a suitable diet. When the time comes for reproduction, the problem of food becomes even more important. Among mammals, the evolutionary process has resulted in females being the sex that invests the most in reproduction. Female mammals are the ones who carry their young around in their bellies for months or even a year, supplying them with large quantities of high quality nutritional substances. And her costs continue after birth: nursing, other kinds of care, defence against predators, defence against murderous males, education of the young, the list goes on.

Education? Well, of course. Cubs and calves are born without the knowledge of which plants are edible or how to kill their prey. A certain amount of education and psychological acclimatization is necessary in order for the young mammal to have any chance of success in life.

A basic requirement for the successful completion of each reproductive project is good access to resources. It is not strange that female mammals prefer to live in areas where there is plenty of food. Neither is it strange that male mammals like to frequent areas where there is a good supply of reproductively receptive females.

The smaller the herbivore, the more dependent it is on certain specific, high quality dietary resources. The dik-dik prefers sodom apples and fallen figs, whereas the elephant fells forests. It is obvious that different kinds of food are distributed throughout the terrain in different patterns, and that the size of the animal influences their ability to travel from one food source to another. In turn, these conditions mean that it can be advantageous for a small animal such as a dik-dik to defend a limited area with stable resources that can feed a nuclear family. Such opportunities do not exist for elephants, which are forced to embark on wide-reaching treks in search of food.

Small mammals have little to gain from gathering in herds as protection against predators. Instead, they trust to camouflage and reclusive behaviour, which require living a quiet life in isolation. A female dik-dik moves solitarily, slinking through the bushes. She would win nothing by going around together with ten just as defenceless female friends. A solitary female buffalo, however, would be much more vulnerable than if she were a member of a herd and her size obviously prevents her from remaining unseen. Consequently, small hoofed mammals live in monogamous relationships or solitarily (with the exception for a female and her young) much more often than their larger relatives. This is interpreted as a solution to two problems: specific dietary requirements and defencelessness against predators.

It is not only among the smaller antelopes such as the dik-dik, but also among the larger antelope, puku and topi for example, that males occupy territories where they attempt to attract one or more females. One study indicated that female puku and topi evaluate the exterior characteristics of males when choosing a mating partner, as well as two territorial characteristics, namely, high resource quality and low predation risk. Other differences between these two species and the dik-dik are that the latter live in thick, bush-covered terrain and are more fussy about their periodically scarce diet, which can prevent males from attempting to attract more than one female. It is hard enough keeping track of *one* female in that kind of dense thicket. Among puku and topi, territories are strictly for mating purposes. A female spends one or more days within a territory where a male territory owner jealously guards her. After she mates, she wanders off and quickly joins up with a herd of other females and their offspring. We have already dismissed the idea that monogamy should occur because males contribute to the offspring's chances for survival. Strictly monogamous antelopes can have males who are just as worthless regarding their contribution to the care of offspring as species with other mating patterns.

The relationships between the spatial and temporal distribution of dietary resources and variation in mating systems, both within and between different hoofed-mammal species are interesting and complicated. Across the entire pattern, the threat of a constantly lurking predator hovers like a dark shadow. In many herbivore populations, the yearly take of predators may reach up to about 25 per cent. Death is a permanent guest in prey species' realities, and a common cause of death is promotion up to the next level of the food chain. Perhaps gazelles graze close to the leopard's lair in paradise—but not for very long. Before you know it the hunt has begun and then the end is near for the slowest.

# 7

## Sapphire in the sand

———————— ❈ ————————

In a mokoro—a canoe made by hollowing out the thick trunk of the sausage tree (*Kigelia africana*)—I glide silently over the still waters somewhere in the Okavango Delta. My guide and gondolier, Royal, a man who during half a century has learned every winding rivulet in this gigantic aquatic labyrinth, steers and poles the mokoro through the delta. The atmosphere brings to mind the Sixth day, or more exactly, the time between *Genesis* 1:26 and 1:27, the siesta hours just before the completion of what we can hope was a carefully considered decision to complete the fauna with one more species, namely, us. My pious daydreams are suddenly interrupted as Royal gently pokes my shoulder with his pole, and with his eyes draws my attention to a sandbank, twenty metres away. A crocodile in the super-heavy weight class lies resting on the shore, with the head and horns of an impala protruding from its gaping mouth. Nearby, two more crocodiles wait, not as big, but twice as greedy as they peer vacantly at the big guy, probably dreaming of a scrap of meat from the yet to be swallowed antelope. When our mokoro drifts nearer, the two smaller crocodiles quickly slip down into the water and disappear, while the giant is not in the least bit disturbed by our presence. We soon realize that the polite and wise thing to do is to leave the well-fed reptile in peace, and with a few apparently effortless pushes of his pole, Royal sends the mokoro into the centre of the river and around the next bend.

Fish of various sizes flash by in the clear water, cobalt blue malachite kingfishers watch the smaller fish with desire, while the white egrets eye the somewhat larger ones and the fish eagles gaze at the largest of all. A flock of pygmy geese rises from a lotus-filled bay and disappears behind the tall screen of papyrus reeds. With a mighty splash, a herd of hippopotamuses throw themselves into the water when they catch sight of us, and a wood sandpiper is so surprised that it bursts into a spring song, reminding me of the mosquito covered bogs and chilly spring evenings back home. 'That was a wood sandpiper, a Swedish bird. It might have been born somewhere in Sweden, where I come from. In six months it will fly back there.' 'I will not follow it', Royal replies. 'I like it better here. Yesterday, you told me of the coldness and darkness in your country. Why doesn't the wood sandpiper stay here? And why don't you stay here?' Well, that is something I really should ask myself.

New impressions and experiences fill every minute spent in the Okavango Delta and time rushes by. For many, the delta offers another taste of paradise, namely water. Although in Scandinavia one can drink clean, fresh water directly from streams and lakes this is not the case on the African savannah. Distances between waterholes are great and the water available is often not fresh, healthy drinking water. In the Okavango Delta, however, the water is clear, cool, and drinkable—like in Sweden. You can even go swimming in it, if you manage to suppress that image of the crocodile with the impala sticking out of its mouth. One can easily see the fish through the clear water as they hurry back and forth in large schools right next to the boat. Do they seek out the shade under the boat because it allows them to see their prey more easily? Because of its superb abundance of fish, the Okavango Delta is home to one of Africa's most dense populations of the magnificent African fish eagle—often called 'Africa's voice' due to its sonorous, ringing call. Fish eagle pairs engage in the most formidable aerial display at the beginning of each new reproductive period. When they become intensely excited, they grip one another's claws and whirl around like a spinning wheel up in the air.

Figure 16.

*African fish eagles displaying their acrobatic skills above the Okavango Delta. Pairs of eagles demonstrate their good qualities to each other performing circus tricks together. In this species both sexes invest equally in reproduction and the pairs remain together throughout their lives.*

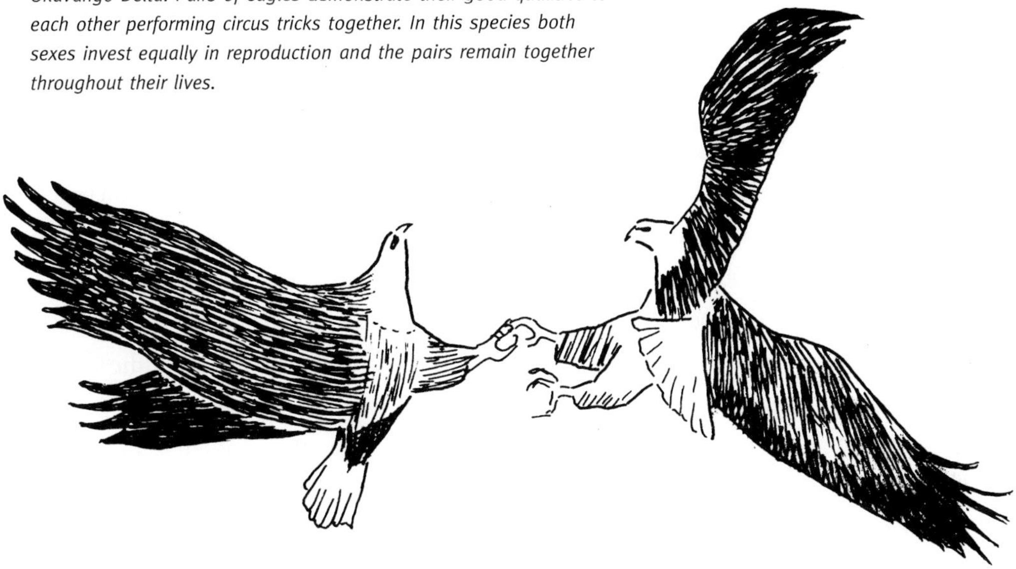

The sapphire in the sand is not only beautiful—it is also generous.

The Okavango Delta is situated on sand that is a gift from the northern reaches of Africa. Erosion wore the mountain cliffs into sand and the sand blew southwards and was deposited when the desert winds abated. This is how the 'Kalahari sand formation' originated. It reaches from the Oranje River in the south through large parts of Namibia, Botswana, Zambia, and Angola, with tongues stretching eastwards into southern Congo (Kinshasa) and northwards into Congo (Brazzaville). Depending on the climate, this Kalahari sand produces everything from 'nothing' (i.e. desert, like in the southern part of the Kalahari, the region that has given the sand formation its name) to woodland savannah and, near the equator, mature rainforests. Forming the northern limits of the Kalahari, the Okavango Delta lies like a blue sapphire—a jewel in the empire of the sand.

But where does all of the water come from? Like the Zambesi, the Okavango River has its origins in Angola's highlands. Its official source is located just east of the city of Huambo, which is situated quite a distance inland, directly east of the large port city of Benguela at $12\frac{1}{2}°$ latitude south. Under the name Cubango, the river runs southwards receiving contributions from innumerable tributaries. It then turns to the south-east and soon after directly east, where it forms the border between Angola and Namibia, and changes its name to Okavango. Finally, it makes a right turn and divides into several arms, releasing its entire contents into the Okavango Delta. It has only followed this route during the last 2 million years. Before that, all the water travelled via the present-day Cunene River and ended up in the Atlantic Ocean—but a disturbance in the earth's crust changed that.

Angola is 'the roof of Africa'. A raindrop that chances to land on this roof can thus end up either in the Atlantic Ocean (via the Cunene, Cunanza, or the Congo Rivers, among others) or in the Indian Ocean (via the Zambesi River). On the other hand, it can proceed directly to the heavens without passing any of the oceans at all, by travelling along the Cubango-Okavango River and evaporating from the inland delta in northern Botswana. Precisely like the sand in the Kalahari, the water of the Okavango Delta is primarily an imported commodity.

These are not small amounts. The average amount of water that is added to the delta after its approximately 1800 km long journey is reported to be around 12 billion cubic metres per year. Since the delta lacks an outlet, this is also the amount that must evaporate.

I treated myself to many thirst-quenching cups of water during that morning together with Royal. The water is filtered through the Kalahari sand so carefully that it is just as healthy as table water taken directly from a spring. (I hope this is true. I have been in the delta three times and have gulped down litres of river water and felt great afterwards. Proof enough for me.)

The size of the Okavango Delta is difficult to assess; estimates vary between 15 000 and 30 000 square kilometres. The boundary between the delta and the surrounding area is poorly defined and, in addition, the water level rises and sinks in conjunction with the seasons. In Angola, the rains fall during the southern hemisphere's summer, that is November to January, but it takes time—about four months—for all the water to complete its journey to the delta. In fact, it isn't until

March or April that the water reaches the delta. Because the local rains in the delta region begin in January, the water level is already on the rise when the 'Angola wave' hits. The situation becomes even more complicated as it takes a long time for the different parts of the delta to receive their ration of water. As elsewhere in Africa, the amount of precipitation in Angola is unpredictable. This is not so important in the actual delta region as there is always plenty of water there, however, it is a different story for the Kalahari.

Although the water flowing in the Okavango River never reaches an ocean, the Zambesi River has another destiny. After a brilliant course including Victoria Falls, the Zambesi flows out into the Indian Ocean. There is a small chance—or was until recently—that a drop of water could be shunted from one or other of the rivers at the last minute. Between the northern sections of the delta and the Linyanti River (a tributary to the Zambesi), there is an 'overflow channel', Selinda Spillway, where during certain wet years water can flow either from the Okavango River to the Linyanti River, or vice versa. The direction of the water is dependent on the relative water levels in the Okavango and Linyanti Rivers. A unique situation? Unfortunately, during the past few decades water levels in both systems have been too low for any water exchange to occur.

Not only does water shuttle between areas—but many of the savannah's large mammals also commute. During the rainy season they spread out across the northern and central regions of the Kalahari, where during the rainy season life is easy for elephants, zebras, wildebeest, and buffaloes. These species undertake the longest treks. During the dry season they gradually draw nearer to the Okavango Delta's permanent water supply. Other species travel only a few kilometres in conjunction with the fluctuation in the water level. July to November is the best time for a visit if you want to see many different big game species. Drought terrorizes the semi-desert regions of the Kalahari during this period, they can barely be called grass savannah, as the only remaining water exists in a few salty waterholes. Only mammals most tolerant of drought and most physiologically economical with water manage to survive on these expanses: oryx, springbok, and those carnivores that are capable of obtaining enough water from their food. The mopane woodlands are nutritionally rich, at least for those animals that can digest dry leaves; but, they are completely lacking in water. Above all, at these times the Okavango Delta is viewed as an earthly paradise. After a long day in the rustling dry mopane woodlands, a human hiker experiences an overwhelming feeling of relief and deliverance when he reaches the green flooded pastures with giant herds of elephants along the horizon and the shimmering lagoons with white and blue lotus flowers and jacanas prancing around on top of the floating leaves. I am sure that thirsty animals must sense relief at this sight as well.

The rainy season in the Okavango also has its advantages and enticements. Herbaceous plants, bushes, and trees burst into leaf and flower, birds sing, build their nests, or transport food to their unfledged young. During the Northern Hemisphere's winter, the bird fauna is boosted by the invasion of numerous migrating birds from Europe and Asia. It is a fantastic experience to observe willow warblers, red-backed shrikes, and spotted flycatchers in this environment, so completely different from their breeding areas. It is hard to ignore the garden warbler over there in the thicket—could it be the same one that was singing so enthusiastically on midsummer's eve back home?

---

One of the most magnificent bird migration experiences I have ever encountered in Africa occurred one January day. Several of us were sitting out on Bobo Island in the Okavango Delta watching as enormous black rain clouds towered up increasingly higher until they became a compact wall of clouds in the north-east. It was one of those years when the rains were very late coming, and a drop had yet to fall where we were camped. The delta region was green and lush, as always, but it was obvious that the vegetation yearned for the absent rains. Our helpers from Botswana worried about their gardens, fields, and livestock and continually gazed up at the sky towards those rain clouds. Please let them come and finally relieve us of this eternal drought! The clouds came and the rains fell. Thunder and lightening heralded an exceptionally torrential rain that continued into the night. By morning however, the rain had stopped and there wasn't a cloud in sight. The sun began evaporating the water from the ground and from the vegetation as we packed up our tents, ate breakfast, and prepared for our departure. We set our course northwards along the sand ridge called Magwikhwe. The sand ridge is covered with low mopane bushes for the most part, but after a few hours we came to an area with taller mopane woodlands alternating with groves of paperbark acacia (*Acacia sieberiana*) and other trees.

Here, all the steppe eagles of the world were gathered for a meeting—or so it seemed. In every tree we drove past sat six, eleven, fifteen, eighteen eagles, and those we saw were only the ones who had chosen to land in the vicinity of the sandy track that passed for a road. Flocks made up of hundreds of birds spiralled over the woodlands. I can only speculate as to how many eagles were actually in the area; a five figure number would probably be a conservative estimate.

Steppe eagles breed in a region stretching from Eastern Europe to the Altai Mountains in Central Asia. They are tremendous travellers that, born on the warm air currents, follow a migration path which runs east of the Black Sea, through Turkey, Israel, and East Africa, down to Zimbabwe and Botswana, and then back again. Large numbers of the eagles pass through Eilat, in southern Israel, during spring and their migration flights have been studied with the help of radar. Depending on the prevailing wind conditions, they travel at between 15 and 100 kilometres per hour and at heights of somewhere between 400 and 1000 metres, sometimes more. Since steppe eagles rarely fly more than six hours per day during migration, they travel only about 300 kilometres per active flight-day. The distance between Karaganda in Kazakhstan and Maun in Botswana, as a bird flies, is approximately 9000 kilometres which would require at least 30 travelling days and as many forced days of rest—back and forth, every year. These eagles must spend almost half of their lives travelling. What tales they could tell us if they could only take up one of their newly dropped wing feathers, dip it in ink, and start writing...

Had all those eagles arrived recently, following the rainstorm as it moved south? Were they attracted to the area by some particularly rich food source, for example swarming termites? We don't know. We know too little about the habits of European and Asiatic migratory birds during their migrations and in their winter resting grounds.

Many herbivores wander out of the mopane woodlands when the drought becomes too severe, and it is generally the periodically flooded fields surrounding the delta that supply them with food on which to graze. These lush fields also have stationary species, or short-distance commuters, that can be observed at any time of the year. The red lechwe is the delta's most abundant species of antelope. It has a modest appearance: pale red-brown hide, tall hindquarters, short muzzle, and backwards-pointing curved horns on the males. Its most characteristic quality, which can hardly be seen in the wild, are its long, splayed hoofs. Their function is to increase the surface area of the hoof and prevent the antelope from sinking down into the mud and mire. The lechwe is a typical wetlands antelope that not only lives out on the open fields, but also in among the reeds and clumps of papyrus. Depending on the water level, they are either invisible in the tall reeds, or easily observed out on the expansive grasslands. They are particularly conspic-uous when, during the mating season, they gather at 'leks' somewhere out on the extensive meadows, commanding good visibility in all directions. The mating system called lekking is one of the few Swedish words that has been adopted within English biological literature.

In the spring, black grouse cocks in Sweden gather at traditional lekking sites, quarrel, fight, and generally raise a commotion as they show-off for the females who arrive at the arena. Females then carefully pick out a partner, mate, and disappear into the forest again. The cock contributes nothing more than a dose of sperm; the hen has to manage everything else on her own.

Red lechwe is an antelope that engages in lek behaviour. The first time I observed a lechwe lek, I was struck by the great similarities with black grouse leks I had seen. Naturally there were differences in the actual behaviour: the lechwe males stood relatively still for example, and were fairly quiet. The males are concentrated in a limited area, fifteen in this case, assuming typical cocky postures and eagerly looking around for females; and a number of indifferent females stand in small groups peeking out of the corner of their eyes at the different males. Similar to black grouse cocks on a lek, the lechwe males were evenly distributed across the arena, each with a small territory, and altercations arose only when one went too close to the boundary between his and his neighbour's lek territory. Despite the apparent lethargic atmosphere, there was tension in the air. All the males wanted to be chosen—and then there were those indecisive, choosy females... Not much more happened on that particular morning when I was watching the lechwe lek; however, the females make their decisions and choose a partner for a very brief liaison.

Similar to black grouse, not all male lechwes are capable of obtaining a lek territory. The younger lechwe males live in envious bachelorhood and are met with threatening behaviour if they approach someone else's territory too closely. Between the males on the lek, there is a clear dominance hierarchy which is stable for long periods. A truce is maintained for the most part via behavioural posturing and calls. Every now and then a real fight occurs, such as when a male decides to challenge one of the others, perhaps a male who is approaching retirement. Certain territories are particularly attractive—as with black grouse leks—and it is over these territories that competition occurs. Territories of lower value surround these attractive territories. Very similar to a meeting hall where a party conference is being held. The heavyweights in the middle, the budding talents surrounding them: concentric distribution patterns steered by the current dominance relationships.

Differences in the value of the various lechwe territories are determined by the degree to which they can attract groups of females. However, it is not easy to determine if it is the territory or its owner that is attractive. One possible difference between territories is their vulnerability to approaching predators. For both lechwe and kob, researchers have established that visibility is important for attracting females. The evolutionary explanation could be that females prefer relatively predator-free territories, males fight and struggle in order to monopolize those territories that attract the most females, and those males who manage to occupy these favourite territories receive more visits by females and higher reproductive success.

In all lekking species studied thus far, male reproductive success is extremely unevenly distributed. One or only a few males on the lek are responsible for about 90 per cent of all copulations. This begs the question, why do all the less dominant males remain at the edge of the lekking arenas instead of moving away and setting up their own territories?

Such a move is disadvantageous for several reasons. One is that the females not only consider the characteristics of the location, but also evaluate male qualities when choosing a mating partner. Even without something to compare with, certain males simply seem unacceptable to females. In addition, it seems as though these special areas where females can compare a number of males facilitate their choice of partner. For less qualified males, whether it is due to youth or some other shortcoming, there is simply no other alternative than to come to the traditional lekking area, bide their time, build up their bodies, their ornaments, their status, and perhaps occasionally have the opportunity to mate with some absent-minded female on her way to the location manager. This is exactly how male topis (another antelope) organize leks.

The male who succeeds in occupying a territory favoured by females is well off in many ways. His copulation frequency increases, as females of both lechwe and kob are very traditional; when rut begins, they visit the same territory time after time, as well as copying one another's mating choice. Particularly among kob, a female who is in the process of joining a lek prefers to go to a territory where there are already several females. This saves time and maintains quality since inexperienced females copy the choices of other females. For the males: he who has plenty shall have more...

The Okavango Delta is one of the most important drought refuges for wildlife in an area that includes enormous regions of savannah in Botswana, Namibia, Zimbabwe, Zambia, and Angola. These five countries almost touch in the region of the fantastic Victoria Falls and are together responsible for a large part of the pristine remnants of Africa's savannah and savannah animal life. Just imagine if the leaders of these countries, making their place in history, were to guarantee the conservation of this priceless natural heritage for the growth and development of their own countries as well as for the rest of the world.

At the beginning of the twenty-first century, this region still has an elephant population of at least 100 000 individuals, which live an almost natural life. They undertake annual treks along traditional routes and they behave in a manner that can best be described as non-aggressive towards humans, neither panicky and shy, nor friendly and trusting, but almost respectful. Mutual respect is a desirable and appropriate relationship between elephants and humans.

———— ❂ ————

That is what it felt like one September night on one of the small islands in the delta with the full moon at its zenith and the air full of wonderful and peculiar sounds. A spotted hyena sang a melancholy solo with an unusually clear alto voice, occasionally accompanied by the impressive snorting and grunting of a group of hippopotamuses in a lotus bay. Fiery-necked nightjars repeatedly called out their entreaty 'Good Lord, deliver us', and the wood owl's rhythmic hooting could be heard from the lofty mopane forest. Neither did the African night's most persistent voice let us down, the call of the Scops owl. As an exotic inflection, we recognized the call of a pair of greenshanks as they flew south. We sat around a fire enjoying ourselves, chatting, celebrating a birthday by having a drink of…

…when without warning, the trembling of a borassus palm broke the peace, shaking so that its leaves rustled and a number of fruits fell and thudded to the ground. Then everything became still again until a minute later when the tree shook again. Visiting elephants, of course. During the after-

*Figure 17.*
*Borassus palms, with their strange swollen trunks, are a prominent component of the landscape in the Okavango Delta. Elephants consider their fruits delicacies.*

noon, we had seen a patrol of eight males, about 15 to 20 years old and around 2½ tons, enjoying a mud-bath orgy in a pool not far from our camp-site. Naturally, the moonlit night was perfect for a late supper of borassus palm fruits—one of their favourites in the Okavango Delta.

Suddenly, two elephants stood in a clearing, at the most fifteen metres from our table. Where did they come from? Their metre-long tusks gleamed in the moonlight. Then they took a few silent footsteps into the shadows, and a minute later a fever-berry tree fell with a mighty crash until a leaning date palm trunk slowed down its progress. Now we glimpsed not just two, but four elephants standing close together near the fallen tree, breaking off branches and stuffing them into their mouths. Crackling and crunching could be heard from the demolishing of the tree, but not a sound could be heard from the culprits. The atmosphere was magical: trembling palms, fruits thudding to the ground, falling trees, crunching branches—but by whom? We knew, but those doing the job were quieter than mice.

The hours of the night passed. Silent giants suddenly obscured a part of the starry sky. A blocked moonbeam. The shimmer of a tusk. Falling palm fruits. The elephants rummaged about in the vegetation for several hours. The camp-site's little bar remained open extra late that night. Sleep was out of the question.

Someone lost patience and tried shooing the elephants away with a loud expletive in French and a wave of a towel. The elephant who was the target of this pygmy attack pulled itself to its full height, turned towards the irritant, folded out his enormous ears, raised his trunk and let out a powerful trumpeting call. The nervous Frenchman refrained from replying as he crawled into his tent and made no further fuss.

Mutual respect.

# 8

## Masculine mothers in moderate collusion

THE SONG OF THE HYENA is one of the most magical of all the nightly sounds on the savannah. 'Song' is not an exaggeration, as hyenas can sing wonderful arias with clear, full alto voices and poignant expressiveness. Occasionally, these hyena songs are reminiscent of Mozart's Queen of the Night.

However, musical virtuoso performances are not the only vocal exercises included in the spotted hyena's repertoire. Frequently, a vibrating call that gradually increases in strength and pitch is audible from up to five or six kilometres away on still nights. Most often, wandering males are the ones that perform this song and it acts primarily as a contact call: I'm here, where are you? Another well-known sound is the hysterical, giggling laugh that is usually heard from startled, fleeing hyenas. For communication at closer distances, these talkative carnivores engage in diverse grunting, hissing, and growling, which can be heard near their lair or when they gather around a larger kill.

This chapter describes only one of the world's four hyena species, the spotted hyena. The spotted hyena is significantly larger, more numerous and easier to observe than the brown hyena, the striped hyena, or the aardwolf.

The word 'hyena' has come to be used as a symbol of an individual whose liveli-hood is the corruption and death of others. However, when ecological field research began gathering momentum in Africa during the 1960s, it was discovered that the spotted hyena was not the cowardly and despicable pursuer of the miserable remains of others, which was its traditional image. Instead, they were revealed to be skilful hunters that killed from 50 to 95 per cent of all the animals they consumed. In many ways, they are fascinating animals that, because of their successful manner of coping with life on the savannah, deserve the same respect as all the other savannah species.

The out-dated picture of a majestic lion amiably dining on a newly slain zebra with a greedy, drooling band of nervously giggling hyenas circling has had to be revised. In many areas lions are more often guilty of stealing a hyena kill than vice versa. Human 'hyenas' earn their livings as parasites on the misfortunes of others to a much greater degree than their zoological models.

Perhaps their looks have given spotted hyenas their bad reputation. All hyenas have disproportionately large heads and forequarters compared with their sloping hindquarters (although to a lesser degree in aardwolves), and they look extremely clumsy. When they run, they jolt about in a stiff, awkward, and ungainly manner. They often allow their mouths to hang half-open in what appears to be an insecure and slightly silly sneer. It is not unusual for them to be covered in mud and dust, and sometimes their noses or their entire faces are completely encrusted with dried blood from their last dinner. The spotted hyena does not have feline suppleness, rippling muscles, or elegance. However, it does have many other gifts and has every reason to claim that it is the most successful of the African savannah's carnivorous mammals.

---

The terrain is so open in Etosha in northern Namibia that you can gaze across kilometres in all directions from only a low ridge or the roof of a car. If you manage to locate a small pool of water in the dry season, you will definitely be rewarded if you stop and keep your eyes and ears open. One afternoon we stopped at a lookout point near such a pool. Thirsty birds of many different species flew in to drink from that cloudy water, only to fly away again as quickly as possible, as the water also attracted several hungry predatory birds. A tiny little sparrowhawk snatched a social weaver from right in front of our eyes. All of a sudden an elegant guest from a faraway land flew gracefully, low over the dry grassland—a male pallid harrier that made a sudden cast and managed to snare a bird—a greybacked finchlark. A pair of blue cranes—the male dramatically larger than the female—walked about slowly in the distance pecking at grasshoppers and other insects. Flock after flock of Namaqua sandgrouse flew in from different directions, landing on the bare slope just above the water's edge and then, fussily nodding like doves, walked down to the water and drank from the life-giving liquid. Springboks were everywhere, a herd of oryx stood ruminating underneath some small trees, and the hours passed peacefully, interspersed with interesting observations and experiences.

Our attention was drawn to a medium-sized animal that suddenly appeared on a sandy slope a good distance away. Soon there was another: two spotted hyenas, who tested the wind and peered out over the plains where, in all directions, scattered herds of springbok could be seen. After a minute or two, the two hyenas began moving in a swift but unhurried tempo across the sparsely covered grassy plains on a course directed towards us. They quickly switched to their characteristic jolting run, which looks so ungainly and awkward but quickly covers the ground. Both of the hyenas passed only a couple of hundred metres from solitary as well as small groups of springboks, and even closer to a lazy tail-swishing and ruminating herd of oryx. There was no reaction by either the hyenas or the antelopes. A pair of crowned plovers flew up in commotion over the hyenas. The plovers probably had eggs or chicks somewhere in that desolate landscape.

When the hyenas were about 300 metres from us, a third and then a fourth hyena appeared apparently out of nowhere, probably from a hole in the ground, following the first two. About a hundred springboks were grazing in a shallow depression a few kilometres away—males, females, and several quite small calves—and we presumed that this herd of springboks was the hyenas' ultimate goal. Eventually, several of the springboks nearby began worriedly looking in the direction the hyenas had taken, apparently feeling that the situation was a bit uncomfortable, and without panic they quickly began moving away. The hyenas—three of them anyway, the fourth seemed to have tired of the whole idea—jogged laboriously onwards. The hyenas as well as the springboks soon disappeared from sight and, since the sun stood low over the horizon, it was time for us to return to our field hotel, Okaukuejo.

What we had witnessed that evening was the very undramatic prelude to a routine hyena hunt. Spotted hyenas live in clans (groups with strong kinship ties) that usually include between 40 and 100 individuals; however, they do not hunt in such large groups. What we had seen was a typical episode, because hyenas usually hunt alone or in small groups. A large hyena group is hardly ever observed together as a unit.

Similar to wild dogs but unlike felines, spotted hyenas hunt without using wily ambush tactics. Their strategy is to search through the herds of herbivores until they discover an individual that seems an easy catch. Newborn calves and foals as well as very pregnant females are naturally tempting quarry. Animals are good observers. Predators have the amazing ability to identify individuals with small defects, a functional affliction, or a handicap, whereas prey species have been forced to evolve comparative skills in determining if they are in the danger zone when a predator arrives on the scene. Our observations of how the hyenas began this particular hunt shed some light on the prey species' nonchalant behaviour. The springboks and the oryxes paid no particular notice to the hyenas—until a herd of springboks understood that they were the likely goal of the hunt and felt the need to depart before it was too late.

What the hyena lacks in ability to sneak up unawares on its prey, it compensates for by having exceptional endurance. They often pursue their quarry over many, many kilometres—relentlessly like fate itself, jogging along after the unfortunate animal they have decided on making into their dinner. If it is a large animal, such as a zebra, several more clan members may join in and the hunt begins to appear more organized; however, hyena clans are not generally closely-knit hunting teams.

Like all hunts, hyena hunts result in one of two possible outcomes. In two-thirds of all hunting attempts, it turns out that the quarry has more endurance, is tougher, or more able to defend itself than the hyenas had imagined, in which case they are forced to give up the chase. Panting heavily, they lie down and perhaps lament over their failure. Or they catch up with the quarry and kill it. If it is a small animal, then the process is quick: the victim dies almost instantly when the hyenas crush its backbone and tear open its abdomen. Sometimes a larger animal that fights back manages to defend itself so well that the hyenas are forced to retreat and wait for more clan members to notice their predicament and arrive with reinforcements. A zebra stallion defending his herd is not one to be played with. The conclusion of a hunt may be drawn out and extremely painful. Wildebeest, zebras, waterbucks, or any large animal can literally be devoured alive. After the long chase the quarry is most likely (and hopefully) in such a state of exhaustion and shock that it feels little of the grisly torture. This may, however, be wishful thinking. The condition of the prey animal during the last stages of the hunt has not been studied on the savannah. In the United Kingdom, when red deer, which are hunted by groups on horseback finally give up, they are in such a state of shock that they would probably die anyway without the final gunshot that ends their misery.

Spotted hyenas kill and eat noisily and the noise attracts other clan members to the meal. In the end, the dead animal is covered with a noisy mass of hyenas that growl, hiss, and snarl at each other, but almost never cause each other any serious bodily harm. A hyena that manages to tear loose a jaw, a part of a leg, or a section of intestines withdraws from the tumult to eat in peace. It would make sense to be a little quieter since other animals such as lions and jackals often hear the commotion and come to seize their portion of the fresh kill.

Hyenas are the most efficient at using up the complete carcass. Whether they kill the animal or whether they find a cadaver—the plate is always licked clean at the end of the meal. Hyenas eat all but the horns and hoofs of buffalo and other large animals, and sometimes they also turn their noses up at the undigested stomach contents. They consume and digest the skeleton as well as the teeth of their prey. Some of the more resistant material comes up again, and the overabundance of calcium the hyenas ingest via the crushing and eating of bones comes out in their excrement. Because of this, hyena faeces are a distinctive white colour and disintegrate into powdery calcium gravel. When the opportunity arises, spotted hyenas also eat human cadavers and human refuse. However, the greater part of their diet is obtained in their natural habitat via the skilful hunting of animals that can weigh up to three or four times their own body weight.

Spotted hyenas live in clans, which are composed of a number of related females and their young as well as a number of unrelated immigrant males. These clans live in demarcated and mutually patrolled and defended territories. Both the size of the territory and the number of clan members vary from region to region. The greater the access is to game, the larger the hyena population. Some spotted hyenas live a solitary existence, particularly in agricultural areas with a dense human population. Here, they are hunted by humans and become dependent on garbage for their livelihood. In their natural habitat, they live in large groups within a territory that is demarcated by smelly glandular secretions and by howling. They engage in fights only when necessary.

In the Serengeti however, hyenas as well as other large predators have a serious problem. Every now and then their food just gets up and walks away. An area that is teeming with food in the form of thousands of wildebeest, zebras, and Thomson's gazelles during one part of the year is almost depopulated during another season. So the hyenas have to adopt a completely different tactic—they turn into long distance commuters. They embark on hunting expeditions that usually last three or four days for nursing females with young, and up to ten days for other individuals. On average, nursing females make about 45 such excursions each year, which means that they trot back and forth across 3500 kilometres of savannah annually. Other hyenas take an average of 15 hunting trips each year covering about 1200 kilometres. Amazing animals. The young can survive several days without nursing as the females provide milk that is extremely rich in fat—richer than any other carnivore studied thus far.

In most cases, solitary hyenas or small groups embark on these extended excursions—not the entire clan. The wandering hyenas are able to pass through other hyena territories relatively unmolested or bothered. When a certain territory contains a large number of prey animals, commuters have permission to 'guest hunt' in those territories. It seems as though hyenas have the ability to discern between harmless hunting patrols and threatening invasion forces. This tolerance ends if a larger group invades a new territory with the intention of taking it over. Horrible battles can occur between these powerfully armed beasts. The largest group wins.

When prey is scarce, spotted hyenas may attain a significantly higher biomass (live weight) than other carnivores that have not evolved the ability to seek provisions outside their own territories. Therefore, it is only natural to consider why territory owners allow strangers to pass through their territory, and in some cases take food from them. It is conceivable that because of the hyenas' powerful weaponry and generally high levels of aggression, real fights between hyenas could easily escalate and result in great losses for both sides. Consequently, both sides win by clearly signalling their intentions and by mutually following certain rules of the game. 'No more than three in a group and passage only through certain corridors'—is the type of rule the Serengeti hyenas seem to follow. These corridors are usually placed along the edges of the territories, avoiding the central regions.

Within their clans, hyenas live in strict dominance hierarchies and are actually in continual competition with one another. Females are primarily dominant over males, who weigh on average 10 to 20 per cent less than the females. Also, there is a strict hierarchy within the female collective as well as the male collective. Being located high in the dominance order is of enormous significance for an individual's survival and reproduction, as this means priority both at the dinner table and in mating opportunities. Females remain in their birth clans throughout their lives whereas males emigrate. The higher the rank a male has, the longer he can remain in the security of his birth clan, and when he finally emigrates to another clan, he is larger and has a higher competitive ability.

One of the factors that greatly affects a male's status in his home clan is his mother's social position—a high ranking mother can give her sons an important advantage in the form of high status and delayed emigration. This causes bitter competition over status among females: their reproductive success, measured as the number of grandchildren, greatly increases if they manage to send a number of powerful and competitive sons out into the world. Mating opportunities are extremely skewed among the males in a group and the alpha male is responsible for most of the matings. A female that manages to produce four splendid sons who then move to four different hyena clans can succeed in being grandmother to scores of grandchildren. The fierce competition over status that takes place in a spotted hyena clan has led to several curious adaptations.

Aggression is generally caused by male sex hormones (androgens) of which testosterone is the best known. Within most mammalian species, testosterone levels in male fetuses are significantly higher than in female fetuses; however, in the spotted hyena the levels are surprisingly similar in both sexes. This mechanism is what causes young female hyenas to become aggressive and ready for conflicts—they become masculinized.

The high androgen levels in hyenas affect not only their temperament, but also their physical construction. An important component in the competition for dominance among spotted hyenas is the exhibition of a magnificently erect penis. This might pose a problem for females one might think, but not insoluble... The external sexual genitalia of female spotted hyenas have evolved to bear an amazing resemblance to a male penis. The clitoris can stiffen and swell up, looking deceptively like an erect male penis. The labia have grown together and been filled with a fatty tissue so that they resemble testicles. The truth is that even an expert observer of hyenas, at a distance, cannot determine the sex of a spotted hyena.

This thorough reconstruction of the external female genitalia with the sexual opening passing through the elongated clitoris results in serious complications. However, the clitoris can be withdrawn into the hyena's body via special muscles so that her vagina is located on the surface of her abdomen. The male's erect penis is long and upwardly curved. The male assumes an almost sitting posture at the outset of copulation, which makes it possible for penetration via the female's retracted clitoral opening. It is hardly surprising that inexperienced hyenas have a few practical 'love-making problems'.

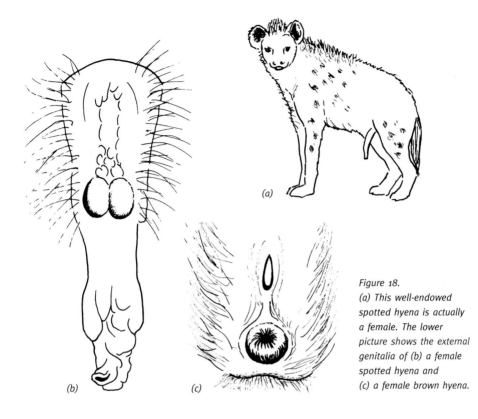

Figure 18.
(a) This well-endowed
spotted hyena is actually
a female. The lower
picture shows the external
genitalia of (b) a female
spotted hyena and
(c) a female brown hyena.

Additional problems arise as parturition is due to occur after 110 days. The canal the young pass through during delivery goes through the narrow clitoris (a little over 2 centimetres in diameter). Consequently, it is not only humans who are doomed to painful childbirth, but also spotted hyenas. The clitoris often ruptures during the birth of a usual two cubs, whose heads measure 6–7 centimetres in diameter and who weigh up to 1700 grams, resulting in serious inflammations particularly in first-time mothers. Female hyena mortality rate is higher in the first year they give birth than it is during either the previous or the following years. Masculinization definitely has its price. Becoming an alpha female must be worth the cost.

The spotted hyena cubs are proportionally larger and more developed than the young of other carnivores, which doesn't make delivery any easier. Why must they carry this weight on top of an already heavy burden? Presumably it is vital for a hyena to be aggressive and ready to fight from the outset. A bitter struggle begins between the newborn siblings shortly after birth. The mother generally gives birth in the open just outside her private den, which is commonly an abandoned aardvark hole. She carries her offspring into the den directly after delivery. The one who is largest and fiercest begins at once to maul its brother or sister as well as trying to prevent him or her from reaching their mother, who prefers to nurse the young outside the entrance to the den. The net result is that one of the offspring generally dies within the first week. Contrary to the young of other carnivores, and as an additional expression of their aggressive tendencies, spotted hyena young arrive in the world with bared teeth: their canine teeth are over a half a centimetre long. They are good weapons to have during sibling rivalry. The young are also unusually well developed in other respects: their eyes are open and their movements well co-ordinated.

If the young are twins of opposite sexes, they have an increased chance of survival. A little female hyena that kills her sister rids herself of a future competitor within the clan, and a little male hyena eliminates a rival for his mother's tender, social care. The siblings are not lacking in motives for their deeds.

Female hyenas remain in their home clans their entire lives. In a clan that has been decimated by disease or human persecution and has fewer members in relation to the availability of resources, it is advantageous for females to give birth to daughters, who in turn will produce daughters. However, a female that lives in a clan with a long history of successful growth and therefore an incipient resource problem, wins by producing sons who leave the clan and provide her with grand-children without 'economically' burdening herself. Their ability to adjust the proportion of daughters and sons comes in handy in increasing the chances for a nearly decimated population to make a comeback.

A study in the Masai Mara region in southern Kenya has shown that in a clan with many individuals, more males than females were born. The opposite was the case after the clan was divided into two, becoming less dense and thus having better access to food. (This of course was the entire idea behind dividing the clan.) One deplorable reason why there are fewer hyenas within a certain region than abundant resources would suggest is that they are decimated through active control, often in the form of poison. This threat to hyena populations is extremely serious.

It would be interesting to know how a female hyena makes her strategic decision to invest in more sons or more daughters. (Although the male's sperm determines the sex of the offspring, no one believes that he is the one that tampers with the sex ratio among the offspring.) Also, what happened when the two divided populations mentioned above reached full size? Did the females return to producing more sons than daughters? If the theory is true, this is what we would expect. Spotted hyenas are not unique when it comes to the ability to manipulate the sex ratio among their offspring. This has been observed in several different species of birds and mammals, not to mention bees and other hymenopterans, who are real professionals at regulating the sex ratio of offspring. Evidence that such so-called adaptive variation of the sex ratio also occurs in our own species has also been published. Where reproductive success is concerned, it is better to produce sons if the current population has a surplus of females or vice versa. Because of this, one can explain why more boys than girls are born in a population that has a shortage of men due to the ravages of war.

Although the spotted hyena is undoubtedly a highly social animal, many aspects of its way of life require each individual to fend for itself. A female keeps her young in her private den for just over a week, before moving them over to a communal nursery where every mother nurses her own offspring. There is no mutual care. Hunting takes place either alone or in small groups, although the spoils are often shared by many more.

This way of life enables a number of related females to secure complete control over a certain land area with all its resources. Group behaviour provides an advantage in competition with other carnivores, whether it is in stealing food from others or defending food that the hyenas have brought down themselves.

Female hyenas rarely run the risk of strange males killing off their young as often occurs among lions and many primates. The male spotted hyenas are much too submissive towards females to dream of such an action. Perhaps female hyenas prefer to place their cubs in small, tight holes where adult hyenas can hardly enter as an extra security measure.

The spotted hyena may be so successful that it is negatively affecting the precarious population of African wild dogs. In a comparison of several regions, researchers found that there were fewer wild dogs in areas with a higher spotted hyena density. Because the wild dogs' hunting methods are extremely demanding, the loss of only a small portion of their kills to thieving hyenas means that they cannot maintain their energy balance between expenditure and intake. The only areas where wild dogs are surviving reasonably well are Selous in southern Tanzania and Kruger Park in north-eastern South Africa, which have tall grass and generally dense vegetation. There, the dogs are able to hide their quarry from the sharp eyes, alert ears, and sniffing noses of hungry hyenas.

# 9

# *Lion prides—nursery schools and death patrols*

———————— ⦻ ————————

It is early afternoon in the Masai Mara. The view is fantastic. Because of the severe drought on the short grass plains, a large portion of the Serengeti's herbivore herds are gathered here. The grass is lush in the Masai Mara and rivers and waterholes provide abundant water. There are grazing herds of wildebeest in all directions and the zebra's bark can be heard all around. As usual, the zebras look plump, healthy, spirited, and trim.

We decide to stop on a hill with a sweeping view. A slight breeze blows over the grass, causing it to wave like a field of grain. Far in the distance we hear the cry of a fish eagle, answered shortly by its partner. A bateleur eagle whizzes by directly above us, causing a thrill of excitement among the observers: what inspirational design by the Great Creator. A long line of guinea fowl comes running out of some bushes, steering towards a nearby thicket. What can have scared them?

A muddy waterhole attracts many of the savannah inhabitants to its shores just below our lookout hill. A steady stream of laughing doves and Cape turtledoves flies back and forth from the pool. A sparkling green and white little bird lands at the pool's edge but rises again almost immediately as if realizing that it had come to the wrong address: an emerald cuckoo. Seven spotted hyenas lie dead still in the mud and water, a couple of them sporting bloody muzzles, and all with bulging bellies. Clearly they have eaten a fine lunch, which required a long siesta. A blacksmith plover mistook one of the hyenas for a muddy bank and landed on its hip: the hyena twitched, the plover shrieked in terror and flew a few metres away. Short episodes, tranquil tempo, withering hot sun.

On the other side of the shallow valley, the ground rises to a low ridge. Suddenly, we sensed a movement in the grass on the crown of the ridge. A lioness sat up, gave a monumental yawn, and then fell to the ground again.

Off towards our right and down in the valley a small herd of wildebeest slowly approached. Someone pointed out that if they kept their course they would pass between the lion and us. Would something interesting happen?

The lioness over on the hillside was obviously asking herself the same question as she raised her head, sniffed, and looked towards the wildebeest. Much to our surprise another lion head popped up out of the grass, and then another, and another... There were five in all and they gazed towards the wildebeest meandering in the valley, clearly unaware of danger.

Three of the lionesses stood up and then, as if a silent command had been given, crouched low to the ground and moved along the ridge towards the wildbeest herd, which was still half a kilometre away. One after the other they lay down in the grass about a hundred metres apart, concentrating intensely on the herd. At times they were invisible; sometimes we could just make out their ears or heads. They were positioned for the perfect ambush.

We sat spellbound. Perhaps we would see a genuine hunt. We had seen many lion prides during the previous weeks, but since lions do nothing for 20 or 22 hours of the day, they had all been resting. Lion watching can be very contemplative. Might this be our lucky break...?

Oh no! Three topi antelope come careering out from a small grove of acacias and gallop down towards the wildebeest. Warned by the topi, they turn around and jog off through the valley together.

One by one the lions stand up, shake off the dust and grass, and stroll back to the place where we had first seen them and where two members of the pride had remained the entire time.

This was a typical episode: most predator hunts fail. The lions didn't seem to put much effort into this particular episode. During this period, the area was full of prey and their hunger was therefore probably not too severe. Most lion encounters are significantly less eventful than this. Generally, the entire lion pride lies spread out on the ground, some on their backs, others on their sides, and all looking as lazy as cats. Craig Packer and Anne Pusey who have studied lions for many years, write: 'The lion is extremely adapted for doing nothing. To the series of inactive noble gases krypton, argon, and neon, we would like to add the lion.' However, if there are young cubs in the pride there is usually a little more activity: one wants a swig of milk and searches out a distended lioness teat, another one tries to catch an irritating fly or bite the black tuft of hair at the end of some adult's tail. The idyllic atmosphere seems perfect, but for the most part it is an illusion. Lion prides can appear lazy, but often their inactivity is forced. Often enough, hunger tears at their stomachs, cub mortality due to starvation and other factors is high, and neighbouring prides constitute a continual and deadly threat. There is plenty to worry about if you are a lion.

Lions are the only genuinely social cats. A typical pride numbers anywhere from a pair up to twenty or so adult females, from one to nine adult males, and a varying number of cubs (under two years old). The largest pride I have seen was in Tsavo: three males, sixteen females, and thirteen cubs of various ages. However, most prides are considerably smaller than this—between five and ten individuals. In addition to the more or less stationary prides, some lions wander about, either alone or in groups of two or three individuals.

As with so many other mammals, the framework of the lion social group is made up of a number of closely related females. The lionesses in a pride are all mothers, daughters, granddaughters, nieces, and cousins. Sometimes the males in a pride are related to each other, often brothers, and may be unrelated, but they are almost never related to the females in the pride so that in normal situations lions do not run the risk of inbreeding.

Lion prides effectively divide their area into territories, and within a particular region these territories can have the same borders year after year as a result of being inherited along maternal lines. If reproduction is successful and enough daughters are born, the survival of the territory and pride is guaranteed. Males come and go, but females remain in the pride in which they were born throughout their lives.

A solitary lioness lives a miserable life. Threatened on all sides, she is forced to sneak around in the narrow corridors of no man's land that exist between established territories. She can hunt if she is healthy and full-grown; however, she is unlikely to reproduce. Even if she is visited by a willing male during one of her receptive periods and becomes pregnant, her cubs will most likely die soon after birth. She would be forced to leave them for long periods of time to go hunting, and even if the cubs were well hidden, they would be defenceless against jackals, hyenas, and above all, other lions. Infanticide is very common in the lion's world.

There are various speculations as to why lions have evolved their social way of life. Presumably their ancestors were solitary beasts since this is the normal strategy for all other felines. However, for some reason, the bodies of the lion's ancestors increased in size. This would have allowed them to kill larger prey and also to survive long periods of starvation. A lioness can actually go for weeks without eating and for months on very meagre rations. The lion's large size also makes it capable of travelling greater distances than the smaller felines can manage. Gradually it must have become less profitable for lions to be nomadic rather than to remain stationary. By monopolizing resources within a certain region they would be guaranteed access to food, thus improving their reproductive success. So lions established the habit of defending a territory.

What would a lion do if it found that the entire area was already occupied and it could not manage to secure a territory for itself? Build a coalition. Two against one increases the chances for success during competition. Who does the lion build a coalition with? With a relative, of course. As we have mentioned in other sections, relatives share a genetic interest. An individual can increase the frequency of his or her own genes in future generations through not only his or her own reproduction (although this is the most effective way), but also by helping close relatives in their reproductive efforts. Increasingly larger coalitions could have been built to conquer and defend the territories needed for living and reproducing in a kind of arms race. Success would result in many cubs, increased crowding and competition, and co-operation within the group becoming increasingly important.

Do males and females have similar interests in this respect? Probably not. Female success is primarily dependent on reliable and rich dietary resources, whereas male success is dependent on fertilizing the greatest number of females. It is easy to imagine that sociality first appeared among female lions, while the males, in the usual mammalian manner, wandered around searching for receptive females. Only later did solitary males or brothers join up with a group of females, together defending them from other males. The basic rule is familiar: females settle where the ecological conditions (often access to resources) are best; males settle where access to females is greatest.

As a result of this difference in the territory's significance for males and females, when outsiders threaten the territory females defend it against other females, whereas males, sometimes with the help of females, defend it from other males. Understandably, females are unwilling to share their territory's resources with unrelated females. Territories are inherited along the matrilineal line so invading females are met by a large patrol of amazons ready to fight for home and hearth. If the number of defending females is greater than the number of attackers, then the home team will surely win. Roaring and threatening behaviour are generally enough to turn back enemies. However, terrible battles occur if the teams are more or less equal. Frenzied fighting is not a masculine speciality.

Male lions expend an enormous amount of energy in marking out their territories. One of the greatest experiences during an African night is their roaring duels, which literally cause the cool nights to tremble. Their voices are so deep that you feel rather than hear their gurgling roars. Other animals become silent; people move a little closer to the campfire.

Sooner or later however, the moment of truth arrives for the males in a territory. Another group of males, four brothers perhaps, appear at the territory's edge and strike a course towards the centre of the territory with its greatest attraction: females. The territorial males roar and advance threateningly on the intruders. The scene could be taken from a classic western, with four desperados arriving in a little town on the prairie with the aim of taking over and then being met at the town's border by the sheriff and his deputies.

Fights between male lions are formidable. Often, more than one of the participants receives life-threatening wounds during the fight. Sometimes the attack is repelled, but if the newcomers are stronger in number and motivated enough, then a change of ownership takes place. A male or a group of males seldom maintains control over a territory for more than two or three years.

The first thing the new males do is to kill all the cubs in the pride that are younger than about nine months old. Older youngsters are driven off to an almost certain death. As a result, the victims' mothers soon come into heat and, in time, give birth to the new males' sons and daughters. If within two years these males are also defeated and chased away by a new group of males, then the new gang of males will kill all their young. It is important for the males to remain as long as they possibly can. The stakes in the battles between male lions are great; the fights mean much more than simply life or death. They result in either a genetic fiasco or a genetic success.

Don't the females care that the newcomers brutally murder their cubs? A closely-knit male coalition does not accept any opposition. Male lions are much larger than lionesses: where would a lioness run to if she was able to rescue her cubs? Some strong lionesses do actually try to take their cubs and escape from the murderous males, and in some cases they succeed. In general however, a shift in territory ownership means death for the young of the defeated male or males.

Thanks to their co-operative behaviour, lionesses are often able to defend their young from solitary wandering male lions as well as from other animals that might kill young lion cubs for food (primarily hyenas). That lionesses have evolved the habit of living in co-operative prides is most likely a result of the fact that they can then take turns in keeping a lookout for bloodthirsty male lions and hungry hyenas. One of the functions of the pride is to act as a kind of nursery for the young.

Many years of research, primarily in the Serengeti, has led to the conclusion that the most important driving force behind the evolution of the pronounced sociality of female lions is the chance, to a certain extent, of being able to protect their young. In turn, males have been driven towards their own form of social co-operation in that females are concentrated in established groups that can be conquered and defended if the males co-operate.

It is not good for a pride of lions to become exceedingly large. Too many lions within a limited area would lead to a scarcity of food resources. If reproduction is particularly successful and a pride becomes too numerous, then it divides and some of the females set off to establish a new territory. It is to their advantage if they remain within earshot of their old territory because if they should be invaded by wandering males, their roaring would be able to be heard in their 'old home'. Since the males from the original pride still have a share in the young, they can be expected to join in and help keep out the invaders.

The males in a pride are often, but not always, related to one another. Even if they are not related but have met and formed coalitions later in life, they are loyal comrades until death. This fact has been discovered through a series of interesting playback experiments. Researchers have taken advantage of the fact that most lion communication is acoustic. They have recorded the roars of different individuals and then with the help of powerful loudspeakers, played back the recorded calls in different situations. They can tamper with the playback roars and simulate different kinds of threatening situations to see how the animals react. When a male lion hears roaring from approaching, unknown lions, he goes out to meet the enemy with complete disregard of the danger, which is quite impressive. He is usually not alone but is a member of a small group of males who together own or think they own a group of females. Whether or not they are related, they stick together and fight to the end when the enemy stands outside the gate. Even when researchers playback an extremely dangerous situation in the form of a superior number of attackers, there is no hesitation: the 'musketeers' stick together. They know that their days are finished if they lose. When a solitary, ageing male goes out against such a superior force, he goes towards his last battle rather like a Japanese kamikaze pilot.

With the aid of modern techniques in molecular biology, researchers have shown that the social relationships between males in a coalition are dependent on both the number of individuals and how they are related. The greater the number of males, the more unequal paternity is among the cubs in the pride. This explains why large coalitions are almost always composed of related males, whereas smaller coalitions may be composed of unrelated companions. Those males that live together with their brothers can accept low reproductive success: they share an indirect success in that their brothers pass on their genes. Such tolerance does not occur between unrelated males, where victory for one is unavoidably a loss for the other.

These experiments have also demonstrated that lions can count. If researchers play the roars of a single female and the home pride is composed of one female, then she will go out to meet the virtual enemy. If the researchers play back the roars of three females, the home pride female remains crouched where she is. If the home pride is composed of two females, they go out unhesitatingly to meet the loudspeaker that represents a single female. They go out somewhat more slowly against a speaker that sounds like two females, and only reluctantly and uncertainly against speakers that sound like three females. Such is not the case for males: they go into battle regardless of how many opponents there are. They have less choice than the females.

All lions are not equally brave. Different members of a pride behave in different ways when the moment of danger arrives. For example, it is usually one or two females who take the point position in a battle patrol and thus assume greater risks, the others follow at a safe distance. The leading lioness often glances back towards her straggling companions, but does not punish them in any way. If the researchers increase the threat by adding an additional speaker, some of the cowards pull themselves together and come up beside the leader, while others do just the opposite and become more cautious, falling further and further behind. They seem to freeload off the more daring females' willingness to defend them. Why should one fight for companions that are unwilling to contribute to the cost of defence? Why tolerate a burden of parasites?

These are the kinds of questions raised by any lion researcher who is familiar with evolutionary theory. Currently, there are no satisfactory explanations to this skewed risk-taking behaviour in lion prides. For the moment, we must be satisfied with discussing several different possibilities.

A lion's life is filled with dangers and often ends in violent death. In spite of this, most of their days are occupied by hunting for food and caring for their cubs without any border battles or fights. Since every displacement of males in a pride leads to litters of cubs being killed and new young being conceived, several of the lionesses have cubs of the same age. All these cubs spend their time in a communal day care centre, where females take turns in watching them. The young are allowed to nurse from any female that has milk, although in times of food shortages mothers will give priority to their own cubs. Could it be that the cowardly females assume a more prominent role in domestic chores? No one knows for sure, however, observations indicate that this is unlikely.

One factor that influences the females' behaviour in both defensive roles and hunting is their age. From weaning at about eight months, up to between three and four years old, a lion's willingness to participate in defence against invaders to the territory gradually increases. In some situations, a cowardly lion may be a novice that would throw away its life needlessly if it were to participate in the battle.

Members of a lion pride also contribute to hunting to different degrees. Hunting is also a dangerous activity since not only giants such as buffaloes and giraffes, but also smaller prey animals such as warthogs, zebras, wildebeest, and ostriches are strong, quick, and armed with dangerous weapons. Some lionesses participate in hunts less frequently than others, particularly if the quarry is only a smaller- or medium-sized prey animal. However, they come trotting up to share in the meal after a successful hunt. You would think that lionesses that let their companions down in defensive situations might compensate by being energetic and effective when it came to hunting. Sadly there is no convincing evidence for this alternative either.

It is presumed that those lionesses that seem to sponge off their co-sisters do reciprocate in some manner, even if it has not yet been identified. Are they perhaps excellent caregivers to the cubs and exceptional at providing milk? No one knows. Undeniably, they increase the numerical strength of the pride. Researchers have found that three females roaring in unison can ward off wandering males with murderous inclinations, while the roaring of a solitary lioness doesn't have the same deterring effect. Perhaps the function of the cowardly lion is to cause the pride's defensive and attacking abilities to seem more formidable than they actually are.

Those lions that avoid risky hunts and dangerous battles ought to live longer and produce more offspring compared with those that are more daring. However, courage and enterprise often bring advantages to an individual in some diffuse way or other. It might be of vital importance to be high in the social hierarchy of the pride when the crucial moment arises. So, how does one attain such a position? Chiefly, through showing off. In species after species, researchers have found that apparently foolhardy acts sooner or later pay off via enhanced status with its accompanying advantages or priority regarding individual reproduction. Thus, an evolutionarily acceptable reason for certain lions bravely volunteering and fearlessly attacking murderous enemies and sharp-horned and hard-kicking prey animals may one day be found.

The most thorough study of the lion's hunting methods was conducted in Etosha in northern Namibia, an area very different from the Serengeti. Based on detailed observations of almost 500 hunting episodes, researchers concluded that female lions actually have a very complicated hunting system that depends on different individuals co-operating in a flexible manner. Lion prides living in the barren environment of northern Namibia were generally small and on average included only six females. Various females tended to prefer different roles in the co-operative ambush and chase hunts conducted by the pride. When the quarry was identified, the lionesses began moving to surround the prey: two of the lionesses moved off to the left and two around the right side of the proposed quarry, which in Etosha was often a springbok, zebra, or wildebeest, or sometimes an oryx, giraffe, or ostrich. One or two females remained in their original positions. If everything went according to plan, the lions on each flank would drive the quarry in the direction of the lioness or lionesses that stayed in the middle, well hidden in the grass, and who for the most part executed the final attack—grabbing hold of the prey's throat, and pulling it down. The other lionesses would then come running at top speed and often begin eating even before the animal was dead. Lions usually kill their prey by strangulation.

Even though there was a clear division of labour during most hunts, individual females were quite flexible and adapted to how the prey reacted. Lion prides in Etosha were less stable than those in the Serengeti and the females could be organized in different groupings from day to day. They adjusted their tactical roles depending on the composition of the hunting team. The strongest and most experienced lionesses tended to take the central position to capture and kill the quarry. There are many and sometimes quite amusing observations as to how younger and inexperienced lions have spoiled what would otherwise have been a successful hunt. They may be too impatient and attack from too far away. Similar to other felines, lions have fantastic acceleration abilities, but are only short distance sprinters. Attacking from too far away simply sets the stage for failure.

What about the male lions? They don't bother with hunting when they are with a pride of females. Male adult lions are the epitome of laziness. However, after the prey has been brought down they come trotting up to take their lion's share. Customs vary from place to place. Males were never seen participating in hunts in Etosha, whereas in the Serengeti, males helped out when the quarry was large game such as buffalo, an important prey species during the seasons when wildebeest and zebras migrate to the Masai Mara region.

Even solitary lions, both male or female, will find enough food to survive. Although the largest prey animals are not attainable, smaller prey such as warthog sows and their piglets are enough to satisfy a solitary lion. In addition, lions steal food from cheetah, leopard, and wild dog kills. Thus, improved success in hunting is unlikely to be the primary reason behind the evolution of lion sociality. Rather, their extreme sociality has developed from the females' need for co-operation in the defence of their young from killer males. In turn, female groups make up a concentrated resource that males—alone or in coalitions—have the possibility of defending against competitors. As a by-product of the females' day care programme for the young, male death patrols were created.

Does the lion behaviour in Etosha help to explain the cowards who sponge off others in the Serengeti lion prides? There are hardly any spongers in Etosha, possibly a reflection that Etosha is a much more arid environment than the Serengeti. There is no room for living off the hunting success of others in Etosha. Population density is much lower in Etosha, territoriality much less pronounced, and the exchange of pride members more extensive. Ecological differences seem to provide a hint as to why the lion's way of life is so different in the relatively lush Serengeti compared with the considerably more barren Etosha.

The lion's hunting team is highly effective, even though about two thirds of all hunting attempts end in failure. The more fragile and vulnerable carnivore populations such as the cheetah and wild dog populations can still be decimated or completely eliminated by a flourishing lion population. Lions are superior competitors for food and, in addition, kill wild dogs and cheetahs as well as other meat-eaters whenever they get the chance. Lions tend to be the most active and conduct their hunts at night. Their hunting success is influenced by the level of darkness: lions prefer to hunt in open terrain without the hindrance of moonlight. If it is too light, they retreat into dense thickets or woodlands where it is easy to hide.

However, the lions living in those territories located within the Serengeti's most open areas have poor reproductive success and would actually cease to exist if it weren't for the surrounding bush and woodland savannah's continual export of lions onto the plains. Most animal species have different productivity in different environments in the same geographical region. Certain populations produce an abundance of offspring that go to export; other populations are completely dependent on continual immigration from other areas in order to survive. This insight is of extreme importance for practical conservation work: imagine what would happen if you made the decision to preserve a few places that were nothing more than black holes.

Certain carnivores (and birds of prey) may specialize in particular kinds of prey species. This has also been observed among lions. In Savuti in northern Botswana, a group of three lionesses exclusively hunted young elephants. If young elephants wandered too far away from their mothers, the lions took their chance. Some of the elephant hunts had lengthy and gruesome conclusions. The lion's technique of seizing their prey by the throat or biting the nose so that their quarry suffocates is not as successful with elephants, who breathe through their long trunks. In one case, researchers were eyewitnesses to some gruesome scenes as an elephant lived for over an hour and a half while the lions tore at its abdomen and dined on its muscles and entrails.

It was early morning on the shore of the Chobe River along the border between Botswana and Namibia. A partially eaten giraffe bull lay on the barren ground and the most magnificent of male lions sat guard at its head. The lion had an enormous mane surrounding his head and neck, black with yellowish-gold locks, side-whiskers that were blown back by the fresh morning breeze, and a chalk-white beard that decorated his chin. His eyes were like amber, his posture prouder than a lion on a coat of arms.

Twenty metres away, the pride he belonged to lay under some scanty bushes—four females, of which two were only adolescents, and six cubs. We had seen them all at a nearby waterhole the previous night. Their chests rose and fell in quick rhythm, almost panting, and their tails flicked listlessly. It is hard work digesting a feast… The grand male got up, looked towards the river, and ponderously walked towards the shore. Before he got more than ten metres a pair of black-backed jackals that had been crouching behind some tufts of grass with greedy looks in their eyes dashed up and began tearing at the giraffe's entrails hanging from its open abdomen. Quick as lightning the lion turned, took a few steps towards them, showed his formidable fangs, and produced a malicious guttural sound. His heraldic dignity was gone and he became the image of stinginess pushed to the limit which bound him to the giraffe cadaver swarming with flies despite the fact that thirst was tearing at his throat and the glittering water was only a stone's throw away.

# 10

## Baboon thoughts

The sun sets quickly in the tropics; the transition from bright daylight to complete darkness takes only a few minutes. An orange-yellow sun floated some distance above the horizon in the west as we drove along the gravel road to the frail raft that would transport us across the Nile; however, the clock indicated that sunset would soon be upon us. We hurried onto the small raft, tied down our Land Rover, and with the help of a winch, transported it across the river. This short crossing landed us in Murchison Falls National Park in western Uganda.

A couple of hundred metres from our landing site a baboon sat in the top of a tall, flat-crowned acacia. His eyes were fixed on the sinking sun. His thick mane showed that he was a male, his body size and stocky build that he was in the prime of his life, and his stillness that he felt safe and satisfied. He sat as motionless as a statue, as if he had been on the lookout for days and was completely lost in his own thoughts, or simply captivated by the gorgeous sunset. What was he feeling? What was he thinking about?

I have seen the same sight on many occasions: an old male baboon sitting motionless in the top of a tree or on a cliff, staring out into the sunset wearing an almost devout expression. Meanwhile, other members of his troop continue with their daily activities: fussing and quarrelling, grooming one another, playing, and chasing one another. The sight of such old grey-haired men, apparently deep in meditation, can be quite poignant. Why do they behave in this manner? You would expect that each behaviour would have a function in an individual's life. Why do they retreat to these perches and do nothing rather than stuffing themselves with tasty morsels before bedtime?

This is the savannah baboon. Savannah baboons are abundant and successful, and they are divided into several diffusely delineated geographical races inhabiting a large part of Africa south of the Sahara with the exception of the larger regions of continuous rainforest.

Primates are extremely sociable: they each have a distinct personality, continually interact with other members of their troop and never voluntarily wander about on their own.

Whilst working near Mtera in the heart of Tanzania I had a glimpse of baboon troop life. My Tanzanian assistant and I had arrived and made our camp late in the day and had not seen what the area looked like except that it was a grove of tall yellow-trunked fever acacias. We put up the tent and soon had the fire crackling; supper tasted delicious, and, as always on the African savannah, the night was full of sounds. We frequently heard worried barks from a herd of zebras, perhaps disturbed by a leopard or lion; soon after we had retired to our tent we heard, or rather felt the vibrations from a pair of bellowing lions. A herd of elephants was snorting and splashing as they took their evening bath in the nearby river. A Scops owl seemed to measure the passing of time with its rhythmic raspy call, a pair of crowned plovers woke up every now and then and protested, and in the distance a pair of tree hyraxes were engaging in an intensive territorial dispute.

I was awake before dawn, listening to all the sounds. Gradually, I noticed that every now and then small twigs or pieces of bark were falling on the tent. As there were so many other sounds demanding my attention, I didn't take much notice. Lions had apparently made a kill nearby and were conducting a noisy conversation around the breakfast table. Far off in the distance I could hear the most magnificent of all the African sounds—the elephant's signal, so difficult to describe, half trumpet, half bass saxophone, a greeting from the Power and Glory…

At first light I crawled out of the tent and blew some life into the fire. The rustling in the trees over my head made me realize that I had shared a camp-site with a troop of savannah baboons—though they had spent the night in the attic flat whilst I was on the ground floor.

Neither the baboons nor I were in a hurry. For a long time we sat quietly, shivering in the cool morning temperature, occasionally looking at one another. Only after the sun had climbed above the horizon did several of the baboons carefully and stiffly begin climbing down from the trees, and with their characteristic hobbling walk began spreading out across the area. These were the younger members of the group, equivalent to human teenagers but in fact only two or three years old, coming down from the trees, lively and awake. They amused themselves by playing chase, grooming one another, and smelling and tasting things they picked up from the ground.

After a few more minutes the rest of the baboons climbed down from the trees and slowly spread across the surrounding open land. It was the middle of the dry season and they seemed most interested in digging up roots, which were both nutritious and had a high water content. They seemed to appreciate the seeds and pods from the acacias as extra treats. They had probably dropped many of these pods from the trees and it was thus their own hard-earned food they were devouring; however, a herd of impala antelope—males of various ages—were also taking advantage of the fallen acacia seeds. It was enjoyable, listening to the sound of crunching by both baboons and impalas—two species that seem to get on well with one another.

It was starting to get warm and pleasant now, and the stiffness and slowness in the baboons' movements had disappeared. As I looked out over the troop it was easy to see that individuals were not just randomly positioned. Quite the opposite, as many of them sat in small groups, munching and occasionally engaging in frenetic bouts of grooming. Every individual kept a continuous check on what everyone else was doing. In a few places, tight groups of three or four females sat with their young—from small black-haired babies with anxiously wrinkled faces and ears that were too large, to adolescents who had clearly begun to feel somewhat tied down and were making short expeditions in different directions in order to wrestle with their friends. Stout males sat interspersed throughout the group. I counted five males, each with a couple of females, who sat with them grooming them in characteristic monkey-manner, ridding them of skin parasites and dried skin. It is said that baboons are unusually clean animals.

At the far edge of the glade sat a solitary large male baboon that looked like a nervous person waiting for an important job interview. No-one behaved aggressively towards him, but all the same, his facial expression was one of expectancy and caution. It was quite obvious that he wanted to create a good impression and be accepted into the troop.

No human harassment of baboons occurred in this region and they were relatively relaxed, even if they cast a cautious glance my way every now and then. It was easy to observe them at close range. Many small dramas were acted out. A group of young rascals competing over who would dare go the farthest out on a branch—until one of them suddenly won but tumbled to the ground. A female sat holding a very small baby baboon, perhaps only a few days old. She was the centre of a group of females, both with and without their own young, all wanting to touch her baby and preferably hold it in their arms. The mother was a bit cautious and reserved when suddenly a very large male approached—one of the biggest in the troop—and pushed most of the females away. Submissively, they moved aside—and to my astonishment the mother stretched out her arms and literally handed the baby over to the male. He smacked his lips in a friendly manner, sat down with the baby 'in his lap', and began to groom the mother's neck! An idyllic family atmosphere.

The situation was a little less peaceful in a different part of the glade. There, one of the females was in heat, which could be seen quite clearly from her grotesquely swollen, red buttocks, and she had formed a relationship with one of the large males in the troop. Only a moment ago, I had seen them copulating. Another male watched the couple with undisguised envy without daring to contest. Behind him sat a third male and they began frenetically grooming one another. This is an alliance in the making: these two subordinate males have worked out that the only way to de-throne the male who is together with the female is to gang up on him.

After several hours of baboon watching, other duties called us away. The baboons departed for some other place with more food or perhaps towards the river, which contained water despite the drought, at least where the elephants had dug down into the riverbed.

These morning hours near Mtera were were filled with interesting insights into the social life of savannah baboons. The troop comprised about forty individuals: five stout adult males, fifteen or so adult females, and about twenty young baboons of both sexes. They all knew each other, and had different reciprocal relationships. The females behaved fairly peacefully towards one another as they were probably all related to each other. As with most other primate species, the females constitute the framework of the group via their internal family ties, whereas the males are included in the band for a limited time and do not develop such firm social relations as the older females. Some of the females in this troop showed great intimacy; in one case they all climbed down from the same tree where they had clearly spent the night together close to one another. Detailed studies have revealed that such groups of females are often grandmother, mother, and daughter, thus closely related to each other. Perhaps even more interesting are the special relationships established between certain males and certain females. When the female handed her baby over to one of the large males, there is no doubt that these two baboons were 'friends'; that is they had a long-term, special relationship with one another. Similar to humans, friendships between baboons are often expressed by searching one another out and enjoying closeness. Baboon friends spend quite a bit of time mutually grooming, while human friends usually do not pick at each other's hair, but instead pat one another on the back or hug. Friendships result in distinct advantages for both parties (as does all co-operative behaviour). When necessary, the male acts as protector for his friend and her offspring, primarily against other baboons but also against predators. The female clearly profits by having one or two powerful males as her friends. In return, males profit from a friendship with a female by often—but not always—being given priority when she comes into heat. When this occasion arises, competition occurs between the adult males over which one she will choose for her companion during the critical few days when fertilization is possible. The male who has perhaps been her faithful friend and protector for several years is in a good position to be selected as father of her offspring—but sometimes she arbitrarily chooses a completely different paramour. When her receptive period is over, she returns to the companionship of her faithful friend without her escapade resulting in any serious or lasting disturbance in their relationship. In the same manner, a male will sometimes leave his female friend and enthusiastically compete to be chosen as mating companion to another female outside his usual circle of friends. Being friends with an influential female in the troop is of such importance for a male's own social rank that it is worth a lot of sacrifices, even if he may not win any sexual advantages when that time comes. If a crisis occurs in his social life, then support from a dominant female and her relatives can be of great importance for him.

Although males compete fiercely for the attentions of females in heat, the females make the final choice. A male who tries to force himself on an unwilling female seldom repeats that mistake. Her distress cry brings her female relatives running, and perhaps one or two muscular friends (or those who want to be her friend), and they hurl themselves on the perpetrator with a tremendous fury. Rules of conduct in a group can be upheld only if those who violate them are punished.

Two males are sometimes friends with the same female. If she chooses one of these males as her special companion during her receptive period, then the other one does not make much of a fuss. Perhaps next time it will be his turn, and two males that establish an alliance clearly have much to gain in the long run by sustaining their relationship, and they do not let the fickleness of a female get in the way of their friendship.

Female baboons spend their entire lives in the troop into which they were born. Males on the other hand leave their birth-troops when they reach sexual maturity. In most animals, the disposition to leave one's relatives is greater in one sex than in the other, probably because they avoid mating with close relatives. An individual that moves to another troop reduces the risk of the negative effects of inbreeding occuring in his or her offspring. In most primate species, males are often the ones that disperse while females remain in their home groups. However, it is difficult for a male baboon to be accepted into another group. He is literally forced to sit in the waiting room where he tries to make contact with a female, preferably one who is high on the social ranking scale, and then get invited to be her friend. If he manages to succeed in this endeavour, he is almost immediately accepted as a full member of the troop. Females are programmed to reduce the risk of inbreeding by avoiding mating with their fathers, brothers, or sons, and they are often attracted to strangers. When they choose a male other than one of their friends as a companion during their mating period, it may well be a newly recruited male who is chosen.

Savannah baboons live in troops, which in some areas can reach numbers of over a hundred individuals. These troops live nomadic lives and use different nutritional resources as they become available. They are not particularly territorial since different troops often cross paths without engaging in battle. However, savannah baboons don't all live in peaceful and exemplary neighbourliness. On the contrary, violent conflicts may occur between different clans, and both injury and death can result from these bitter battles. Shrieking and roaring can be heard everywhere. An irritated or threatened baboon male is an extremely terrifying sight. The troop's adult males are the fighters. There is an especially high risk of conflict if one of the two troops that meet contains a female in heat. Naturally, she presents a powerful temptation to the males in both groups. The males in her own group do not voluntarily give away such an important resource, but instead display their weapons—their long and sharp canine teeth. Sometimes these mutual threats are sufficient and the troops continue on their way without a fight.

The female baboons hardly participate in these inter-troop controversies. They

Figure 19.
The canine teeth of male baboons are much larger than females' and they act as signalling devices or weapons if needed! Male baboons' pupils contract when they find themselves in threatening situations, which gives them a peculiar staring expression. A male baboon is a formidable opponent for both competitors and predators.

might hoot and cry out threateningly and dart about trying to look involved to show where their sympathies lie, but for the most part, they wisely keep themselves far from any combat. Among savannah baboons, adult males are almost twice as large and much more heavily armed than females, so females don't stand a chance in any real fight. In addition, females have no reason to fight—they are the resources being fought over. The outcome of the struggle doesn't change the females' situation in any significant manner.

The savannah baboon and the vervet monkey live side by side in many places and border conflicts are common among vervet monkeys. A border conflict usually begins with the exchange of threats and invectives between groups. Normally both groups move away from the area in an orderly manner. Sometimes however, too much is at stake and real fights break out between both males and females. Why the differences between these two species? There are two convenient explanations. First, vervet monkeys live in defended territories, territories whose nutritional resources are just as important for females as they are for males. Second, the size difference between the sexes in vervet monkeys is insignificant, so a female actually has a chance in a fight against a male.

An atmosphere of apparent indifference exists between troops of savannah baboons. Yet, violent battles may shatter this atmosphere. However, many other emotions are shared between baboon individuals from different troops—romance for example. In one instance a female in one troop became attracted to a male in a neighbouring troop, and she almost literally seduced him so that he left his own troop and joined her group. Such acute love affairs not only affect adolescent baboons, but also high ranking adult males who can change groups several times in their lives.

A male with many faithful female friends is able to borrow their babies when he needs them. And when does a male need to borrow a baby? When he ends up in conflict with other males. All the baboons in a troop care for babies with solicitous tenderness. In addition, all the females are related and have mutual interests in all the babies; thus, the males have a very good reason not to end up on the wrong side of a female. When two males get into a serious dispute that threatens to escalate into a fight, the male who feels a bit unsure or more subordinate quickly grabs one of his girlfriend's babies and holds it in front of him—and the mother does not oppose this apparently risky 'use' of her darling baby. With the sight of a little baby in the arms of his opponent, even the angriest male baboon loses a greater part of his fighting spirit, especially since he becomes the focus of critical looks from the female collective. The threatening feud is thus resolved without either of the combatants losing face.

Every baboon—male or female, young or old—has their own credentials and their own special situation. Therefore, every individual must behave in such a way that maximizes the probability for that individual's reproductive success. Although a baboon troop appears to be woven together by hundreds of ties, it is still about the success of individuals. No baboon stays longer in any group than is advantageous for his or her reproductive success. Heaven forbid that one should talk about sacrifices for the good of the group. All parties must profit from group living—otherwise the group is blown apart by individualistic behaviour. The interests of other individuals limit the different lifestyles one individual can pursue. This is true for all species. Everyone tries, but few succeed.

What is most significant for the evolution of group living among savannah baboons? Why do they not live alone, in pairs, or in small family groups? When baboons left their original environment (which was probably the rainforest) and began living on the open savannah, they became increasingly vulnerable to predation by ground-dwelling carnivores. This favoured the evolution of increasingly larger groups composed of related females and their offspring. Eventually, groups became so large that one single male could not control all the females and thus 'multi-male groups' evolved. These multi-male groups are typical of baboons as well as many other primates. The larger the groups became, the more important it was to have a clearly signalled—but continually tested—hierarchy, which minimized the social stress that would otherwise reduce everyone's reproductive success. Both the threat of predators as well as the fact that the baboons were forced to make longer treks in order to meet their nutritional needs led to their increase in body size. Sexual competition also increased in those groups with several males, which led to an increase in male size. In other words: sexual dimorphism increased.

These ideas are supported by comparisons between savannah baboons and both of the other baboon species found in Africa. The hamadryas baboon is closely related to the savannah baboon. It lives in comparatively more dry and desolate regions, which means that predation pressures are less. The scarcity of food and the lack of predators cause the hamadryas baboon to live in small groups composed of only one dominant male and a few females with their offspring. Since females are so few in number, one male can manage to control and defend his harem from solitary males. In their natural environment the male behaves like a shepherd for his small flock. Ecological factors have thus led the social lives of hamadryas and savannah baboons to look quite different.

Similarly, the gelada's distinct social life can be interpreted as being a result of special ecological conditions. This species, which is placed in a different genus from the two other baboon species, lives solely on grass—a plentiful nutritional resource in the mountain fields of the Ethiopian highlands, the gelada's habitat. Although grass occurs abundantly it is an energy-poor food that has led to a reduction in the gelada's body size, increasing their vulnerability to predators. Thus they live in enormous groups, often including hundreds of individuals. In such numbers, social stress might become a serious problem, but among these primates smaller groups of closely related females constitute the framework of a complicated social structure which maintains peace.

I wonder if it is their psychosocial environment and relationship problems that male baboons are thinking about as they sit in the tops of the umbrella acacias as the sun sets and night approaches? Hardly—but do not underestimate them! The person who looks deeply into a savannah baboon's hazel eyes may catch a glimpse of a psyche whose depths no human has yet fathomed.

# 11

## *War and peace, crime and punishment in chimpanzee society*

In the hope of gaining an audience with a group of chimpanzees, we left Mweya, in the Queen Elizabeth National Park, Uganda, early one morning. Our route took us through a region of dry bush savannah and we saw very little of interest—a few solitary buffaloes and a couple of warthog families. We paid little attention to which species of birds darted back and forth across the road before disappearing into the dew-covered foliage. However, a pale bird of prey sitting in the highest reaches of a candelabra euphorbia caused us to screech to a halt: was it a pallid or a Montagu's harrier? On this occasion, it was a pallid harrier—a winter visitor from somewhere in south-east Europe or Asia.

Then we came to open plains covered with lush grass and occasionally interspersed with a dense copse of bushes around a termite mound. Magnificent euphorbias and caper bushes (*Capparis*) dominated the dense thickets. Apart from the plentiful and elegant kob antelopes there was little big game to be seen. This did not look like typical chimpanzee habitat. I glanced sceptically towards my travelling companion even though he usually knew where he was going.

Gradually we saw what looked like a dark streak in the grass, which on closer inspection was the top of a long row of large trees. Clearly there was a ravine in the distance, with a completely different kind of vegetation from the open grass savannah. The Chambura Gorge is a couple of hundred metres deep with very steep, tree-covered slopes and a fresh, flowing stream at the bottom. It was the crowns of these trees that we could see.

Two National Park attendants met us and guided us along the steep and slippery path into the gorge. They were excellent hosts and proud to show us what the gorge had to offer. One of them carried a rather dilapidated Kalashnikov rifle. At the bottom of the valley we began walking alongside the river. We caught sight of a troop of elegant black-and-white colobus monkeys almost immediately: they moved so that their long fur and long tails swayed elegantly around them resembling fashion models with expressionless faces showing off a new fur coat.

After an hour or so one of the group saw something big and black up in a tall *Pterygota* tree on the other side of the valley, perhaps 150 metres away. There he sat, the old one in a tree, a huge male chimpanzee with a greyish back, a coal-black face, and hazel eyes—eyes that had seen it all and were now fixed on us. We each sank down on a tree stump or log—awestruck—with a sense of respect as for an older relative that one has heard much about, but never met. I will never forget the look in his eyes. What control, what thoughtful composure. He stared at us for long periods. Behind him in the tree, we caught a glimpse of another, considerably smaller chimpanzee that clambered up and down in the branches obviously finishing off breakfast. Every now and then the large male would slowly extend his arm and pick a piece of fruit, which he would carefully inspect with his nose and eyes before popping it into his mouth. The other chimpanzee climbed higher in the tree to reach some tempting fruits. It was a young adult female, also large, even though she looked small and slender compared to the old one.

Our guides told us that we were watching the dominant alpha-male and one of his lady friends from the local group of chimpanzees. The troop was probably on its way to a new feeding location in the long ravine and these two were bringing up the rear. Our guides also told us that the Chambura group had recently expanded when two young females had turned up, perhaps from the Maramagambo forest in Queen Elizabeth National Park. Evidently some contact remains between the different chimpanzee populations in Uganda despite being separated by roads, settlements, and cultivated fields—a fact we were glad to hear.

After an hour or so, the old one decided that it was siesta time. With a few graceful movements he climbed a couple of metres higher in the tree up to where there seemed to be a previously tested resting place in a large fork in the branches. There, he made himself comfortable, leaned his head forward on his arms, and arranged himself for a good, long nap. There was no doubt in our minds that the audience was over and we carefully retreated so as not to disturb him. There was an abundance of old and recent chimpanzee droppings on the path, full of undigested seeds, some larger than hazelnuts from *Pseudospondias microcarpa* and *Sterculia dawei*.

When we arrived back at the camp-site the sun was directly overhead, sweat was dripping, and we needed a cool drink. Finally, we realized why the old AK47 is so popular and is carried with enthusiasm by thieves, police, and ordinary citizens in so many countries around the world. If you pull out the magazine, the top edge is equipped with a seam that acts as an excellent bottle opener. The Cold War is over and we celebrated this by opening our Coca-Cola bottles with the magazine from an old Russian automatic rifle.

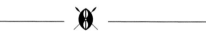

War is enduring—only the antagonists change. Sadly this has been true throughout history. The twentieth century had its fair share of bloody wars and genocide. Earlier centuries also had their periods of ruthlessness, suffering, destruction, and death, although the methods may have been more primitive. Conflicts were probably only avoided where some kind of environmental factor kept the population density at such low levels that different groups of people generally had little contact with each other, or at least didn't need to compete over resources.

Are wars between tribes or nations unique to humans? Is there an inclination for war in human nature? The answer to the first question is 'no' and to the second question 'yes', at least judging from recent research on the biological evolution of human behaviour during the past few million years. Comparisons with our nearest relatives in the animal kingdom are particularly important, and among these relatives we can count both species of chimpanzee. Chimpanzees, bonobos, and humans have such genetic similarity that we could be classified as three species within the same genus. The separation of the lineage that led to chimpanzees and bonobos, and the lineage that led to us, occurred as recently as 5–7 million years ago. Until that time, there were no chimpanzees or humans, only a common relative. Natural selection assisted the transformation of that mutual relative into the present-day separate species in both cases, through adaptations to the demands and opportunities of the surrounding world. Thus, behavioural comparisons should be most favourable between us and those species with which we are most closely related. Why else do we prefer to use apes and monkeys over other animals when we test new medicines or vaccines?

It was this insight into the close relationship between humans and these apes (often called 'anthropoid apes') that prompted a series of long-term research projects focusing on chimpanzees which began in the 1960s and early 1970s. The most famous and successful of these projects was initiated in 1960 by Jane Goodall in Tanzania and focused on the chimpanzees in the Gombe region on the eastern shore of Lake Tanganyika. Despite many serious problems and incidents, this exceedingly successful and significant research project continues today.

The Mahale Mountains including Kungwe, the highest peak, are located farther to the south along the shore of Lake Tanganyika. In this region, a Japanese research group led by Toshisada Nishida began a chimpanzee research project a few years after the start of the Gombe project. My presentation of the life and habits of chimpanzees is based largely on the results of the Gombe and Mahale studies. Both these regions are characterized by expansive miombo forests in extremely hilly terrain, with gallery forests in the valleys, fragments of mountainous rainforests on some of the hills, and open meadows on the heights. Chimpanzees spend almost their entire lives on the ground in this kind of environment. More recently, the Swiss biologist Christophe Boesch has made significant contributions by studying the lives of chimpanzees in a completely different environment—the lowland rainforests of the Ivory Coast. Research has also been conducted on chimpanzees in captivity, for example by Frans de Waal, who has studied the large chimpanzee colony in Arnhem Zoo, in The Netherlands. Although experimental methods can be used to a greater extent in zoological parks it is an artificial environment, and results that cannot be substantiated from observations in the wild should be treated with a certain amount of scepticism.

One criterion for a good study of animal behaviour is that the study objects should be individually identifiable. Individuality is especially notable among primates, which share great psychological similarities with humans. Generally, the individuals in a group look so different from each other that researchers have no problem recognizing them, just like their human friends. Primatologists (biologists who study primates) almost always end up having personal relationships with their study objects. The researchers give each individual a name to distinguish them during conversation and also in their reports. This is especially true for the Gombe and Mahale projects, where despite all the scientific methods and critical analyses, the researchers' reports are like a family saga.

The chimpanzees in Gombe and Mahale live their lives in very complicated societies where several cohesive sub-groups are discernible. However, the composition of these groups varies from hour to hour. When a chimpanzee suddenly appears from behind a bush, you don't know if he is alone or if he has a gang of friends tagging along. The only individuals that always remain together are mothers and their young. Chimpanzees live in a 'fusion-fission' society. Members of the society are free to spend their days however they please: a solitary walk along a stream, throwing a party for adolescents in a fig tree full of fruit, a quiet day together with mamma and other siblings. Or, large gatherings with energetic social interactions throughout the entire community.

It sounds like an idyllic existence. However, chimpanzees (with the exception of the very small, young ones) must constantly guard against danger and try to solve problems in order to survive and maximize their reproductive success. Chimpanzees engage in both domestic and foreign conflicts, their societies live in alternating states of war and peace, and the results of the various conflicts are of extensive significance for the destiny of each individual.

Solitary chimpanzees or groups of chimpanzees roam about freely—but only within the boundaries of their own community's territory. Beyond their territory are other communities, and even if the boundaries are indistinct, the risk of attack from neighbours is greater the closer one comes to the boundaries. Sometimes solitary adult male chimpanzees or, more often, groups of two but up to fifteen or twenty make attacks in these outlying zones. Males spend a considerable amount of time patrolling the border zones of the group territory, as well as conducting raids into neighbouring territories. The nucleus of a chimpanzee society is made up of a large group of males who are closely related to one another: fathers, sons, brothers, and cousins. It is these males, united by blood ties, that defend the territory against intruders and that also conduct attacks on the neighbouring communities.

Territories and territorial struggles are common in many animals—birds, fish, and mammals. A single male is the actual territory owner, and he has such a strong incentive to defend his established territory that he is virtually unbeatable when he has the home advantage. Chimpanzees, however, do not follow this general rule. Among chimpanzees, home ground does not bring an advantage, the outcome of a conflict is determined by the number of individuals in the groups. If five male chimpanzees are out on a raid in a neighbouring territory and they encounter a group of two, they attack immediately, and the defenders are wise if they flee, head over heels. Fights between chimpanzees are ferocious events, where the defeated may lose an eye, finger, toe, testicle, and lots of blood. It is not uncommon that one or more males receive such serious wounds that they soon die of complications from the battle. If a group of patrolling chimpanzees encounter a neighbouring group of approximately the same size, an acoustic war breaks out that can be heard from a great distance and may continue for several hours. Eventually, one group or the other begins to feel inferior or less motivated and retreats. After a few additional threats, the loud barking cries become silent and peace returns to the forest.

Certain tactical principles are followed in these border conflicts between chimpanzee societies. If the enemy is greater in number, run for your life. If the enemy is fewer in number than your own group, attack and injure or kill as many of your opponents as possible. If you encounter a strange female chimpanzee, treat her according to her civil status: if she is a young female that has yet to produce offspring, show her only a limited amount of aggression, or even treat her in a chivalrous manner. Such a female should be lured over to one's own group since she would then represent a strengthening of the group's reproductive capacity. If she already has offspring, she should be violently attacked (frequently causing serious wounds) and driven away. If she fails to protect her young, as often happens, they will fall into the hands of the attacking males and come to a ruthless end: killed in a (sometimes) surprisingly long, drawn-out manner and sometimes eaten. As far as is known, this is the only situation where chimpanzees commit cannibalistic acts.

There is a built-in counterbalance in this system. The more males there are in a group, the greater military potential it has. However, at the same time, competition increases between males over mating opportunities. It is the compromise between these conflicting demands that results in chimpanzee societies never becoming too big. When a group contains about twenty sexually mature adult males, a division often occurs, where one group of males accompanied by a few females (especially their mothers) establishes a new territory next to the original one. This is not a painless process. There isn't always a suitable empty territory near the old one and the emigrating individuals change from allies to enemies overnight. Soon after the separation, bitter wars can erupt between those who remained and those who emigrated. All old friendships are gone with the wind. He who is not with us is against us.

The framework of a chimpanzee community comprises several closely related males. Females, on the other hand, come from surrounding communities. Inbreeding, which can have negative consequences for offspring, is avoided as only one sex disperses from its birth group. The males in a community usually extend a 'friendly' welcome to new females; but these newcomers are often met with a certain amount of aggression from the community's resident females. If a chimpanzee community doesn't keep its numbers up, it becomes increasingly subject to raids from neighbouring communities and eventually can't take the pressure. The community's original females start disappearing and too few new ones are recruited. The territory shrinks in size, food runs out, defensive abilities decrease—and one day the community no longer exists. Its domain is taken over by one or more of the surrounding communities.

Although chimpanzees are not organized and armed, they do have several warlike qualities and behaviours. They are exceptionally hostile towards outsiders. When defending their territory against enemies or conducting raids in the neighbouring territory, the males of one group settle their internal differences. They don't hesitate for a second when it comes to fighting, injuring, and killing their opponents. There are differences in fighting techniques between controversies arising within a community and war between individuals from different communities. In the first case, a certain degree of restraint is shown and serious injuries or deaths are relatively rare, although they do occur. Individuals from other communities, however, are treated like the animals, such as baboons, colobus, or antelope young, that chimpanzees hunt and capture for food: they are torn apart, alive. Enemies are not seen as 'other chimpanzees', but as 'other species'.

Fights and competition between different groups force males to stick together in order to defend their domains, their females, and their offspring and are probably one of the most important reasons for the special social structure of the chimpanzees. Without effective defensive forces, a chimpanzee community is doomed to failure. The easiest form of co-operation is between close relatives, who have common genetic interests. Thus, male relatives join together and defend those resources that are of vital importance for their own reproductive chances.

Jane Goodall wrote about the chimpanzees at Gombe. She ended her chapter on territories and territorial conflicts with the following words: 'The chimpanzee, as a result of a unique combination of strong affiliative bonds between adult males on the one hand and an unusually hostile and violently aggressive attitude toward nongroup individuals on the other, has clearly reached a stage where he stands at the very threshold of human achievement in destruction, cruelty, and planned intergroup conflict. If he ever develops the power of language—and he stands close to that threshold, too—might he not push open the door and wage war with the best of us?'

Chimpanzees, particularly the males within the community, have much to win through unified and tactically co-ordinated actions against hostile groups of chimpanzees; consequently, it is hardly surprising that they support one another when war threatens.

However, every individual male chimpanzee also has his own private ambitions, and among these, maximum reproductive success always has the highest priority. Since all males have this ambition, competition over females naturally occurs. Females are generally the resources that limit the reproductive success of males. Even if blood is thicker than water, and a male chimpanzee doesn't lose as much when he refrains from breeding to the advantage of his father, son, or brother as he does to an unrelated individual—he still wins the most by siring as many offspring as possible himself. Why, then, do incessant, violent fights between males not occur in a chimpanzee community?

The promiscuous sexual behaviour of female chimpanzees may have evolved in order to prevent extreme and violent jealousy among males. Since the females need the protection of a numerically strong group of fit and healthy males it is to their advantage to reduce the frequency and violence of male fights and prevent unnecessary injury. When a female chimpanzee comes into heat, she therefore signals as clearly as she can—the skin around her genitals swells and turns red or pink, and she presumably also emits a most alluring odour. During the days when she is in this condition, she diligently copulates with almost all the males in the community, often in rapid succession and in full view. So that no one misses what is going on, she also cries out with a loud mating call during copulation.

Her generosity towards the males has an element of unfairness in it. The alpha male of the group (the most dominant male) is given priority on those days when she ovulates (is ready for fertilization). This behaviour increases the chances that the alpha male will be the father of her next offspring, but her sexual generosity doesn't preclude another male from winning the prize in this round of life's lottery. For this reason males engage in desperate struggles to become the dominant male. However, challenging the chief is not recommended for one male alone; he is ready to fight with vehemence to keep his coveted position. What can an envious male chimpanzee do to reach the desired role of leader? He makes an alliance with another male, one who is equally greedy but who doesn't dare attack the leader on his own. Two can beat one...

Thus, domestic policy among male chimpanzees is based on building alliances with influential companions, breaking these off when something better comes along, preventing your worst opposition from building coalitions and through those gaining powerful positions that threaten your own ambitions... A political manoeuvring that is thought to be one of the most significant factors behind the evolution of the animal world's most competent brain (next to our own).

Various chimpanzee researchers have described hundreds, if not thousands of episodes that illustrate the rules of conduct for chimpanzees: do unto others what they do unto you, and if he or she does not—sooner or later—pay back your favours, immediately stop all collaboration. Keep an eye on the pattern of social relationships. Obtain and keep friends that are in debt to you. Punish deserters.

Time and time again, both in the wild and in captivity, chimpanzees who do not 'return favours' have been turned away from feasts on newly killed animals, and in addition, have often become objects of direct aggression. Tit for tat. An eye for an eye and a tooth for a tooth. He that mischief hatches, mischief catches. Language is full of ancient proverbs that are about just this: crime is followed by punishment—eventually. A gift must be followed by a gift in return—sooner or later.

Even for those who are familiar with the ground rules of social relationships within a chimpanzee community, it can be difficult to keep up with all the details of the complicated games between individuals. Among primates in general, and perhaps chimpanzees in particular, memory abilities are so good that a long period of time can pass between a favour and the return favour. In some cases, chimpanzees are willing to give loans to one another with long payback times. However, the partner must also be dependable. Previous transactions must have left positive memories.

To make the situation even more complicated, revenge is sometimes taken out on a completely innocent relative of the guilty party both in chimpanzees and other primates. The parallel with today's instances of blood feuds is obvious. The social lives of primates have clearly reached an astounding level of complexity.

Chimpanzees customarily share the food they find. Frans de Waal, the Dutch chimpanzee researcher, has studied what rules the chimpanzees follow during this act of generosity. Among many other things, he found that a chimpanzee offers food almost only to those individuals who have recently groomed his fur and, in this chimp-manner expressed their friendly intentions. Other individuals however, will be brusquely dismissed when they beg for food. Thus, one way of obtaining food is to groom assiduously a companion who often has something good to share. Being groomed by many individuals in the community is a sign of high status in the group. Consequently, it is profitable to give away a little food in exchange for another bout of grooming—some individuals buy their high social prestige with bits of food as payments. de Waal compares a chimpanzee group with a market, where merchandise and services change hands between the different individuals. Even sex can be obtained at the markets. The exchange rates for food, grooming, and sex fluctuate depending on who the partners are and what their needs are.

Chimpanzee adult males make up the nucleus of the community. They favour a large company and in times of prosperity, this group of males may include up to twenty muscular and ready-to-fight warriors. Chimpanzee females, however, prefer to spend their time in the company of one or a few best friends. Life-long friendships may occur between some females, who usually sit or travel together, engage in long bouts of mutual grooming, and support one another when conflicts flare up. Since young females for the most part leave their birth communities, these friends are seldom mother and daughter. On the other hand, two sisters, or two unrelated females who have left their birth community simultaneously, can maintain special friendships for years in the new group. You can almost imagine how they might sit and dwell on the fact that everything was better in their childhood homes.

Another important link in chimpanzee societies is that sons maintain a lengthy and special relationship with their mothers, sometimes lasting their entire lives. When they have been out on patrol with the chaps and return home, an emotional reunion is often enacted between mother and son. However, during the days when the mother is in heat and is the centre of frequent mating orgies, the son keeps his distance. Matings between closely related individuals very rarely occur among chimpanzees. Neither does there seem to be any unwilling copulation on the females' part. Rape is not documented for any primate species other than humans.

That female chimpanzees mate with almost every male in the community, from the youngest to the oldest, reduces the risk of discord and fights, which would otherwise bring about diminished fighting effectiveness by the army. It also reduces the temptation for males to abuse or kill the small babies in the group. If each of the males has good reason to believe that he is the father of every young chimpanzee in the group, then they should of course refrain from infanticide. On the other hand, if a male were to realize that he was not the father of a certain young chimp, he might be tempted to kill the young one, wait for the mother to come into heat again, and then try to become father to her next offspring. This kind of behaviour occurs regularly in several other primate species so that males can have the chance of being father to the next offspring. Infanticide occurs for the same reason among other animal groups besides primates, for example lion prides and even such apparently peaceful animals as barn swallows, camels, and dolphins.

Infanticide may well have played an important role in the design of group living among primates. Why, for example, doesn't a group of chimpanzees comprise one male with some females and their offspring? Wouldn't it be easier to get rid of the mob of hungry and troublesome males? If females rejected all but the alpha male, then the others would leave and search for female groups without a male and this would avoid competition over resources, which is one of a group's unavoidable disadvantages.

However, females gain an advantage in gathering a powerful group of body-guards around them. Using their promiscuous sexual behaviour, females convince males that it is also to their advantage to remain with the group. Once the males have decided to remain, they are more or less forced to enrol in the army and defend the females and their young. What would happen if they didn't and a group of strange males invaded the territory? All the young would be killed, both male and female (if they are not sexually mature). A solitary male would have no chance against two or more males who joined in an alliance.

Chimpanzees seem to be firmly established in an extremely social way of life. Living alone makes individuals much too vulnerable, especially females. Travel-ling in patrol groups has many advantages in the hard life on the savannah.

Some of the more fascinating observations reported by chimpanzee resear-chers are about the resolution of conflicts and reconciliation within groups. One of the most important and probably most difficult tasks for an alpha male is trying to prevent violent fights among the lower ranking males. In many cases, an intense stern look is enough, at other times a forceful vocal rebuke is issued, and in the worst cases, the alpha male is forced to take hold of the one(s) causing trouble and clobber him/them. There are several behaviours and vocalizations—

Figure 20.
Some chimpanzees prop up the stone anvil they use to crush nuts by wedging an appropriately shaped stone beneath it. However, they don't learn this trick until they are mature and are able to copy other adults. Such culturally determined behaviours are very localized, and the habit of stabilizing an unstable platform has only been observed in the rainforest chimpanzees of the Ivory Coast.

words, if you will—that chimpanzees use to make up with each other after the conclusion of a conflict. A friendly group—everyone's best life insurance policy.

Females also show a great interest in keeping order in the group and they sometimes act as a peacekeepers. There are some hilarious stories of how one or two stout old chimpanzee aunts together have used their strength to put cocky and rowdy males in their places. In some chimpanzee populations, cultures have arisen where males fight with weapons such as sticks and stones. On one occasion, one of the group's dominant females went up and simply took the weapons from two angry males before they had the chance to start using them: 'Well boys, if you must fight then at least do it without weapons!'

We know that humans who have been wronged or have 'lost face' have ill feelings and a lust for revenge towards their surrounding social sphere. Such atmospheres are not conducive to co-operation and unity. Several behaviours in chimpanzee society are used to force a kind of reconciliation between the previous antagonists or to provide the losers with a smidgen of satisfaction. The dominant males and females of the group are the ones who, alone or in united force take on the function of a crisis group; all to keep the community in good shape before the ever-threatening chance of attack from other groups in the region.

In a society such as the chimpanzees have, a male who wants to climb in status and insure himself a long life with many young cannot achieve this on his own. By acting alone a chimpanzee can cause an alliance of competitors to turn against him; and no support in conflict situations, together with low popularity among the females when it is time for sex, leads to an empty and frustrating life.

Successful chimpanzees attain a 'good reputation' in the community through their behaviour. Those without friends in the group have serious problems as shown by this episode from a zoo. Two males joined together to dethrone the alpha male, and after a few attempts, they defeated him in a fight. The defeated male hobbled away from the scene of the battle with his head bowed and blood dripping from various body parts. However, when the two males prepared to enjoy the sweet taste of victory, they received the surprise of their lives. The female

*Figure 21.*
*This 'ethnobotanizing'*
*chimpanzee is infected by*
*worms and is curing himself*
*by eating leaves from*
Aspilia mossambicensis,
*a plant in the composite*
*family. Humans in many*
*parts of Africa also exploit*
*its medicinal qualities.*

chimpanzees definitely did not approve of the shift in leadership and they fixed the new power holders with cold stares, negative gestures, and unfriendly abuse. Three weeks later, the dethroned king was back on his throne.

Just because male chimpanzees are violent and physically stronger than females doesn't mean that they always have the last word—generally the opposite happens. All males mate with the females—but never without the female's consent, and in the end, it is the females who prioritize among the prospective fathers during the critical days when they are fertile and sex is not simply sex but sex plus fertilization. It is mostly males who build coalitions, who quarrel and fight, and who are dominant over females—but it is the ladies club who decides who sits and basks in the glory on the alpha throne.

All politicians know that an external enemy is the best inducer of internal harmony. However, this rule has its roots in the deep past: this dictate of social living was carved in our genes before human and chimpanzee predecessors separated millions of years ago. The success of the entire primate order is built on what one researcher has described as 'obligate sociality'.

The advanced sociality of primates, based on solidarity and unity in external affairs and selfishness in internal affairs, has required the evolution of behavioural rules or 'ethics'. These behavioural rules order individuals to commit acts that, at least in the short term, are unprofitable. The individual who fights bravely for the group when the enemy attacks, who shares needed food, who administers peace between clashing wills, and who contributes to reconciliation at the end of conflicts takes risks, loses food, and sacrifices time; but will also increase the probability that his or her own reproduction will be successful. On condition that group members reward such short-term unselfish acts in some way, especially through increased reproductive opportunities, it will become even more advantageous to concentrate on characteristics such as bravery in war, generosity in peacetime, and interest for social harmony. Thus, these characteristics spread and become building blocks in the species' nature.

On the other hand, the individual who deserts family and friends when danger lurks, who does not share resources, who does not care about the well-being of others in the group, and who does not return favours, risks ending up on the losing side and being forced to watch as the others multiply and fill the earth. A group where everyone acts in their own short-term interest quickly goes under in competition with other groups where individuals make a long-term investment and accept that repayment may not come until far in the future.

These ethical principles are deeply rooted in the nature of primates and evolved because they improved the chances of reproductive success in individuals obeying them. Along the way cognitive capacities arose that enable us to evaluate and judge the behaviour of others. Admiration and rewards await those who save a fellow-being from sure death in the flames, who give money to charity, or who are willing to sacrifice their life for their country.

If chimpanzees had a language and could write, some of them, just like some of us, could write novels such as *War and Peace* or *Crime and Punishment*. Such episodes exist in their world as well. However, as far as we can see, they cannot discuss them and definitely cannot write novels about them. On the other hand, neither could we humans do these things until just recently—and how many of us can manage them today?

# 12

## *Bonobos: 'make love, not war'*

IN THE 1930s it was realized that Africa was home to two species of chimpanzee. *Pan troglodytes* is distributed from Guinea in the west to Uganda and Tanzania in the east and was discussed in Chapter 11. In a considerably more limited area south of the Congo River lives another species—the bonobo, *Pan paniscus*, previously called pygmy chimpanzee. Since this species is not much smaller than the 'regular' chimpanzee its name was changed to bonobo. Bonobos are more slender and have slightly longer arms than chimpanzees and, in addition, have distinctive cranial characteristics. Young chimpanzees have pink faces at birth whereas young bonobos have black faces. One clear feature that differentiates these two species is the pitch of their voices: bonobo calls are much higher in pitch, and sound 'childish' compared to chimpanzee voices. The most recent common ancestor of chimpanzees and bonobos lived 2–2.5 million years ago, which is half the time that the human lineage has been separated from the combined chimpanzee–bonobo lineage.

In comparisons of the species, it is primarily the bonobo's social behaviour that has been of interest. Bonobos live in relatively large groups that always remain together, whereas chimpanzee communities are generally divided into several smaller groups that live isolated from one another for days or weeks. Bonobos have diffuse, if any, territorial boundaries, the relationships between group members are significantly more relaxed, and the dominance hierarchy more flexible, sometimes even difficult to discern at all. Females rather than males set the tone of the group's social life. Males compete intensively over attaining the highest dominance position, and mothers play an important role in the outcome of this competition. A young male who has a high-ranking mother succeeds much better in his attempts at social climbing. One similarity between the two species is that it is the young females who leave their birth groups to set out in search of homes in neighbouring groups.

Human interest in sex has transformed the bonobo into a much talked about, if not admired, primate. It has been called 'the erotic primate' in some accounts. Indeed the bonobo could claim copyright on the expression 'make love, not war', as their daily life is full of explicit sexual behaviours—not necessarily connected with fertilization and reproduction. These agile primates are very creative when it comes to discovering new ways to copulate, masturbate, rub, poke, lick, and sniff their own as well as the genitals of others. Preferably several at the same time, young and old, all possible combinations—everyone keeps at it for all they are worth. This industrious sexual, or rather genital activity is used in many social situations that are not dealt with using genitalia in other animals, including chimpanzees. Bonobos have developed this behaviour more than any other species. Dominance displays, conflicts, peace mediations, alliance formation— in these and many other situations, the bonobos use their genitals as signals or instruments.

Although it is not surprising that the chimpanzees and bonobos have different habits, it is interesting to consider what environmental factors have contributed to the evolution of different behavioural patterns in our two closest relatives during the short period of 2 million years.

We don't yet know enough about the bonobo in its secluded rainforests of southern Congo (formerly Zaire) to do more than speculate. The rainforest is relatively rich and reliable in dietary resources. There are plenty of fruit-bearing trees where even a large group can gorge themselves with food. Accordingly, there is little reason to defend a territory from neighbouring groups, and even less reason to begin consuming meat. The entire group can remain together without needing to fight over food. Without the need for military service or hunting, the relationship between the sexes has perhaps become more equal among bonobos than among chimpanzees. It seems that the abundance and distribution of important resources such as food is the most important underlying reason for the differences between patterns of social behaviour in various closely related species. In the end, we worry most about our daily bread. We only turn our minds to other things when our stomachs are full.

Bonobos, like chimpanzees, are not ancestors to humans. However, these two species are undoubtedly our closest relatives. Their behaviour and way of life can therefore provide us with some ideas and suggestions about how our own ancestors lived and what were the most important contributing factors to our own evolution. Perhaps bonobos can supply us with some pointers about how our mutual ancestors lived before they left the rainforests, and perhaps chimpanzees in the forest savannahs of western Tanzania can illustrate some of the difficulties these ancestors met on the road from the rainforest to the savannah.

# 13

## Humans—marked for life

### Down from the Family Tree

All life on earth has a common origin, and from this perspective, all living things are related. Human origins, just as those of all other species, go back to the origin of life approximately 4 billion years ago. Many of our most significant refinements of construction are much older than the human species. Moreover, these refinements evolved by natural selection in a very different world. Our feet, stomachs, kidneys, and brains are firmly characterized by what has occurred during these millions of years of evolutionary history. Our genetic formula is based on the same chemical elements—nucleic acids—as are found in the bacteria that lived billions of years ago. Genetic material was packaged in chromosomes by single-celled protists (protozoans) some 2 billion years ago, and no other alternative has surpassed the effectiveness of this construction. Our bodies are organized so that labour is divided between specialized cells that are grouped into tissues and organs—a tried and tested solution about a billion years old. An internal skeleton, four limbs, sexual reproduction, mammary glands and suckling, as well as extremely social behaviour are other useful components that evolved long before our own species' recent origins. We also share these characteristics with many of the earth's other living organisms in a historical (phylogenetic) perspective.

It is difficult to think of bacteria and yeast as our ancestors. The origin of mammals might be an easier starting point for own species' family history, that is, towards the end of the Triassic period, about 210 million years ago. The earliest organisms that researchers have undoubtedly determined to be mammals lived during this time. These organisms, Morganucodontidae, were small shrew-like creatures that evolved from a group of early reptiles but were different in several significant respects. Their brains were proportionally larger and their spines more flexible, giving greater agility and perhaps the ability to climb. Their teeth were differentiated for particular tasks and their jaw articulation was completely reconstructed. Instead of disappearing, the old reptilian articulation became a superb acoustic structure in the ear allowing us to enjoy Brahms, the Beatles, and chaffinch song. Suckling was probably an early and important mammalian adaptation and it provided the zoological class name for mammals, Mammalia, from the Latin *mamma*—female breast.

During the enormous period of time (three-quarters of mammalian history) between the origin of mammals and the global catastrophe that resulted in, among other things, the extinction of the dinosaurs, mammals were forced to play a subordinate role in the evolutionary drama. Eventually, however, their moment of glory arrived. Perhaps a meteorite extinguished the previous main characters. There have even been speculations that the small nocturnal mammals became adapted to a predatory lifestyle, developed an appetite for dinosaur eggs and young, and eventually caused the dinosaurs' downfall. We have all been small and vulnerable at one time, even *Tyrannosaurus rex*. Was the extinction of dinosaurs the result of a biological catastrophe and not a cosmic one?

Whatever caused the extinction of the dinosaurs, this event provided mammals with their opportunity. There was a period of explosive adaptation during the first few million years after the demise of the dinosaurs. A multitude of ecological niches had suddenly become vacant, there was space for all kinds of new lifestyles, and it was definitely a good time to be a mammal.

Primates were one of the fastest mammalian orders to appear on the dinosaur-free scene. These first mammals were a group called Archonta, whose success

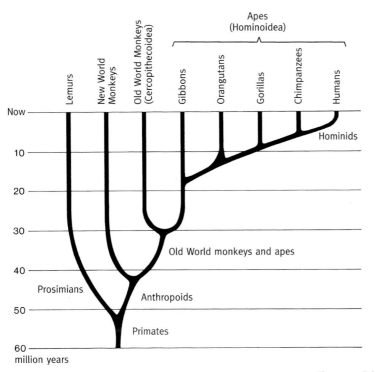

*Figure 22. Primate family tree.*

was primarily due to a refinement in vision. Today, the descendents of this group make up two well-known and comparatively species-rich orders, namely Primates, with almost 200 species, and bats (Chiroptera), with at least 1000 species, in addition to two species-poor and relatively unknown orders, tree shrews (Scandentia), with 18 species, and colugos or flying lemurs (Dermoptera), with 2 species. The two latter orders are limited to the rainforests of South-East Asia.

Within the primate order are some relatively primitive groups or 'half-apes'; lemurs and galagos (bushbabies) are some of the more familiar species of these animals. The rest of the primates, about 150 existing species, are designated as anthropoids ('human-like'), and they are characterized by their anterior-directed eyes and their relatively large brains. These evolutionary developments have influenced the characteristic shape of the primate skull with its large, anterior-directed eye sockets encircled by bone and a more or less dome-shaped and spacious cranium.

The anthropoids—the 'true' primates—are usually divided into two primary groups: New World monkeys (Platyrrhini) and Old World monkeys (Catarrhini). The most recent common ancestor shared by these two groups lived during the time when primates first originated and began evolving as a separate evolutionary lineage. Approximately 30 million years ago, a division occurred within the Old World monkeys that gave rise to monkeys (Cercopithecoidea) and tailless apes (Hominoidea). The latter are often called anthropoid apes.

Initially, it seems that the apes had the advantage; however, in terms of the number of species and geographic distribution, monkeys eventually surpassed them. Today, apes include the orangutan (*Pongo pygmaeus*) and ten species of gibbons (*Hylobates*) in South-East Asia as well as the gorilla (*Gorilla gorilla*), chimpanzee (*Pan troglodytes*), and bonobo (*Pan paniscus*) in Africa and, of course, the cosmopolitan human (*Homo sapiens*).

## Enter Humans

Humans have not evolved from any of the company of apes mentioned. On the other hand, since we were united with them more recently than with any other animal species they are our nearest relatives. Recently? The rate of evolutionary processes is always slow in relation to our own perception of time. The history of life must be considered in a time-scale of millions of years. The primate considered by many to be the most recent common ancestor of monkeys and apes, *Aegyptipithecus*, lived 30–35 million years ago in Egypt. Indeed, Africa is our original home in an even more profound sense than we usually realize. Long after *Aegyptipithecus*, somewhere in Africa, a population of apes divided in two. One of those groups gave rise to the chimpanzees, and the other to our own evolutionary line, which has remained separate from all other evolutionary lineages since then. This division of one population into two somewhere in Africa occurred as 'recently' as 5–7 million years ago.

New species generally originate (speciation) when a population of one species divides into two. If these two groups remain isolated and are unable to exchange genetic material, the different environmental factors in their respective areas of distribution will drive evolution in different directions. After some time, they become so different that they are no longer able to mate with one another if they meet again, or if they did mate, they would not produce fertile offspring. They have become 'true species'. This is how species diversity or biodiversity increases on our planet.

How do two populations actually divide? There are various causes, for example: a change in climate can divide previously continuous rainforest into two or more fragments separated by corridors of vegetation that rainforest animals refrain from, or can't cross; an ice age might extend a glacier or tundra, fragmenting a previously continuous forested area; islands and mountaintops can act as isolated areas where, given enough time, populations can slowly evolve into new species.

Speciation can occur particularly fast if the separated population contains few individuals. Chance may lead to an otherwise rare gene becoming over-represented and successful. If one out of five females in a founder population has a certain genetically-induced physical characteristic and she reproduces excep-tionally well, she will become the mother of a large part of the new, expanding population, which will carry her special physical characteristic. Such a founder's effect can provide speciation with a flying start.

Another factor that influences speciation is the degree of difference between the (environmental) conditions in the area of original distribution and the colonized area. If the founder population finds itself in an environment with dras-tically different conditions compared to their original area, natural selection may rapidly lead to extensive changes.

Our final independence occurred about 7 million years ago. At that time, there was a species of ape that lived somewhere in eastern Africa whose population

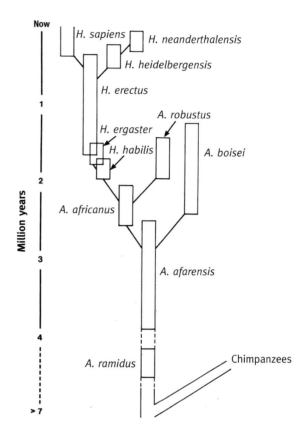

Figure 23.
One version of the hominid
family tree. The hunt for
fossils continues. We all
want to discover our
origins...

became divided. One of the populations became the starting point for the evolutionary line that after many twists and turns led to chimpanzees and bonobos—
the present-day species belonging to the genus *Pan*. The other population became
ancestors to the evolutionary line that after even more variations and thorough
reconstructions produced only one species that exists today, namely humans,
*Homo sapiens*. This evolutionary lineage is known as the *hominid lineage*, and its
members as *hominids*.

What did this African primate, the common ancestor to chimpanzees,
bonobos, and humans, look like 5, 6, or 7 million years ago? We can only speculate. Most evidence indicates that this ancestor shared many similarities with

present-day chimpanzees. It was undoubtedly arboreal with four limbs resembling those of today's chimpanzees or bonobos. It probably lived in the rainforest or perhaps along the edge of the rainforest and the surrounding woodland savannah with strips of gallery forest following watercourses. During that time, the climate became drier with greater seasonal variations (Chapter 3) causing Africa's savannahs to expand quickly at the cost of the rainforests. On the periodically tinder-dry savannahs there were green areas of great ecological significance due to their supply of leaves, fruits, and other juicy foods during all or a greater part of the year. Today, most chimpanzees live in rainforests, although there are two or three extensively studied populations in Gombe and Mahale, both on the eastern shore of lake Tanganyika in Tanzania, that live in mosaics of woodland savannah, gallery forest, and mountain rainforest. Bonobos, however, live exclusively in lowland rainforests. Both these species are expert tree climbers and always spend the night in a secure nest in the treetops. They are extremely well adapted for an arboreal life; they are not so graceful when they move about on the ground, walking with the help of their knuckled fists. Bonobos–chimpanzees–hominids: they represent an ecological, but not phylogenetic sequence, from the rainforest via different mosaic landscapes to the savannah. A similar sequence may have been followed during the evolution of the hominid lineage.

There is still a gap in the fossil record between 5 and 7 million years ago when the population of our missing or unidentified ancestors divided and the time when the first hominid species appear in the fossil record. Did this division occur at all, and if so, when?

The answer to this can be found by comparing the DNA in our own cells with that in the cells of chimpanzees. DNA, deoxyribonucleic acid, is the genetic recipe for the manufacture of living organisms—dung beetles, ostriches, baboons, humans, or whatever. Over time, DNA molecules change via mutations that occur at a low, but consistent frequency. This means that the time since two populations were last united can be calculated by measuring how different the DNA molecules are in the two populations living today. The longer the time since they separated, the more differences will have accumulated. Accordingly, we shouldn't be surprised that there are fewer differences between human DNA and ostrich DNA than there are between human DNA and that of the aurora butterfly—the differences between ourselves and baboons are even fewer, and between humans and chimpanzees, only 2 per cent. This 2 per cent difference in our DNA molecules is equivalent to a separation time of at most 7 million years. Consequently, molecular biological methods allow us to identify both chimpanzee species as our closest living relatives, as well as delimiting the period of time that has past since we shared a common ancestor between 5 and 7 million years ago. As would be expected, the degree of similarity in the DNA between chimpanzees and bonobos is even greater than the correspondence of human DNA with either of them.

Thanks to an intensive and successful search for fossils, the gap between the chimpanzee and the first fossil hominid lineage has decreased significantly. The oldest known hominid species was uncovered in southern Ethiopia, dating back to about 4.5 million years ago, and received the name *Ardipithecus ramidus*. The species name is taken from an Ethiopian word for 'root', referring to the position of the species on the hominid family tree. However, the species *Australopithecus anamensis*, whose fossil remains have been found in Ethiopia and Kenya, is also over 4 million years old. The competition between these forms over who was first on the scene has yet to be decided.

What special characteristics do these hominids have? On what criteria are decisions based as to whether a certain species should be assigned a place in the hominid lineage or in the chimpanzee lineage?

Walking on two legs is the most basic invention of the hominid line. Even the fragmentary fossils, in particular the construction of the base of their skulls, show that both *anamensis* and *ramidus* had already begun to walk upright and on two legs. The base of the skull is formed differently in organisms that hold their heads in vertical line with the body, as in humans. In, for example, dogs and chimpanzees, powerful muscles hold the head in front of the body, and prevent it from sinking to the ground. Hominids developed relatively small canine teeth but

several characteristics that are more similar to chimpanzees reveal their phylogenetic origins, particularly that their brain volume was not of any impressive size.
However, they fulfil the most rigorous criteria for being the 'missing links'.

The next hominid form, *Australopithecus afarensis*, evolved about 4 million
years ago in the sunny valleys of the expanding East African savannahs. Again,
Ethiopian territory is the home of this fossil find.

While the earlier forms were hardly recognizable as individual beings, *Australopithecus afarensis* has a face and thus a personality, which makes it much more
real than its probable predecessors—*ramidus* and *anamensis*. Almost half a
complete skeleton of *A. afarensis* has been found. The discoverer of the fossil-find

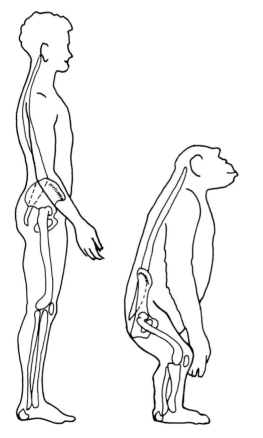

Figure 24.
Walking upright on two legs is
the most significant hominid
characteristic. The remodelling
of our bodies to accommodate
it is incomplete and is borne
out by our bad backs, worn
knees and miscellaneous
skeletal aches and pains.

named this female 'Lucy', after the popular song 'Lucy in the sky with diamonds'. In addition to Lucy—the 'First Lady' of the hominid lineage—several more *A. afarensis* individuals have been discovered and from these, we know a little about how they looked. Lucy had long arms and short legs as well as hands and fingers indicating that although she walked on two legs, she was also an accomplished tree climber. From trees they have come, to trees they shall return— whenever danger threatens. The brain of *A. afarensis* was similar in size to that of chimpanzees and their aptitude was presumably similar. Lucy probably didn't try to solve differential equations nor was she bothered by existential questions.

The sexes were very different in size among *A. afarensis*. Men reached an average height of 145 centimetres, whereas women barely reached a metre. Weight differences were even greater: about 65 kilogrammes for men (the size of a featherweight wrestler) and 30–35 kilogrammes for women. Such extreme sexual dimorphism indicates a furious competition between men over access to women and powerful sexual selection to the advantage of large men. Thus, it is easy to imagine that *A. afarensis* lived in polygynous constellations. One can dream about the 'First Family', how they might have sat under the shade of an acacia with a large, rough man in the middle surrounded by a small harem of petite women and their tiny babies. He probably looked around uneasily, irritated by the increasingly daring approaches of his rivals, and on guard against the huge hyenas he noticed on the nearby slope. Maybe he checked that the trees were climber-friendly.

The oldest *A. afarensis* find has been dated at 4 million years; however, the youngest finds are only 2.5 million years old. Somewhat earlier than the youngest *A. afarensis* fossils, however, a new hominid turns up in East Africa—*Australopithecus* (or *Paranthropus*) *boisei*. This hominid is most well known from the Olduvai gorge, located between Ngorongoro and the Serengeti in northern Tanzania. *A. boisei* had a heavier build than *A. afarensis*, huge jaws with large teeth and powerful chewing muscles (thus its nickname of 'the nutcracker man'), as well as a pronounced sagittal comb stretching from the forehead to the neck along the skull. This bony comb may have provided a place of attachment for powerful jaw muscles, but it might also have acted as an ornament, evolving as a result of sexual selection. The larger the comb, the better looking the man—or so the *A. boisei* girls might have thought.

Olduvai has become world famous thanks to the abundant fossil hominids chiselled from the cliffs or sifted from the gravel along the slopes or at the bottom of the gorge. Several generations of the Leakey family have worked on this and other fossil-hunting projects in East Africa. Visiting the Olduvai gorge is a powerful experience. One feels a great admiration for the Leakey family and all their Tanzanian and other associates who, year in and year out, have literally cooked for their research in the scorching hot gorge. One can easily imagine their joy when something new, something really important is uncovered. Even more however, one is captured by those beings who long, long ago lived in the Olduvai gorge and on the surrounding plains. They experienced times of starvation and times of abundance, pain and fear, joy and celebration. They survived, and one feels a degree of pride in one's ancestors.

Evidence indicates that for a period, *A. afarensis* and *A. boisei* lived at the same time and in the same place in Africa. They were built so differently that in all likelihood they occupied different ecological niches and experienced little competition from each other. Two similar contemporary hominids, apparently the ecological equivalents of the two East African species, have been discovered in South Africa where the lighter species is named *Australopithecus africanus* and the heavier one *A. robustus*.

Did any of these *Australopithecus* species give rise to the first *Homo* species? Most likely. As *A. afarensis* disappeared (Lucy and her companions), a new species with a much larger brain appeared. This new form was identified from a higher and younger stratum of the Olduvai gorge. Leakey's report on this fossil discovery was followed by an enormous scientific uproar: was it really a new species that had been discovered, or was it simply a deviation from the *A. boisei* hominids? Not until additional finds were made at Lake Turkana in northern Kenya was Leakey's proposal taken seriously, and now, their new Olduvai species is completely accepted. Both the construction of the jaw and the larger brain volume (although the variation is great) propose the inclusion of this species within the genus *Homo*, with the species name of *habilis*, which can mean 'handy'. This species name was chosen because these beings were the first to make extremely simple stone tools. However, doubt continues as to whether *H. habilis* evolved directly from *A. afarensis* or whether *A. boisei* or perhaps *A. africanus* (which has a strong following) were links in the chain.

Whether *H. habilis* were the first toolmakers is also uncertain, since finds of 2.5 million-year-old stone tools have been made in layers that seem to be older than the oldest *H. habilis* individuals at Olduvai and Koobi Fora (at Lake Turkana). We don't know which hominid species fabricated these tools. Was it *A. boisei* or an earlier *Homo* species? A possible key figure and transition form in the hominid family tree is *Homo ergaster*—a figure we would like to know more about.

About 1.8 million years ago, another impressive figure appeared, *Homo erectus*, the 'upright walking' human (an unfortunate name since *H. erectus* was certainly not the first hominid to walk upright). This species may have lived across most of Africa, although the fossil finds are generally limited to Tanzania, Kenya, and Ethiopia. *H. erectus* probably originated in East Africa evolving from *H. habilis*. The most complete *H. erectus* fossil is of a tall, young man who has been called the Nariokotome boy, after the place near Lake Turkana where his remains were found. He would appear to have been tall and well built even by today's standards, at a height of 190 cm. It is an interesting thought that first *A. boisei*, then *H. habilis*, and finally *H. erectus* had successively lived at Olduvai before humans arrived on the scene. In other localities, hominid history is even longer and encompasses the entire series from *anamensis* and *ramidus* via *afarensis* to *sapiens*. And we think that Stonehenge and rune stones are old!

*Homo erectus* had three notable characteristics. Physically, they were tall and slender (similar to modern savannah inhabitants), they had low but long and spacious skulls with a volume almost as large as present day inhabitants (up to 1000 cubic centimetres), and some individuals had prominent eyebrow ridges. Below the neck *H. erectus* was for the most part a modern human. Secondly, *H. erectus* people were more advanced toolmakers than their predecessors. The desire for meat in their diets may have prompted the invention of tools for cutting and preparing it. *H. erectus* fossils are commonly found with fossil antelopes, swine, hippopotamuses, buffaloes, and elephants, and it has been assumed that *H. erectus* included more meat in their diet than their predecessors. Perhaps they hunted actively or even stole kills from larger predators. Whatever the case, the new tools would have opened new opportunities for survival. Sharp-edged, stone tools could cut open the bodies of dead animals allowing access to more of the available meat. In addition to their stone tools, *H. erectus* probably also made tools made from wood, horn, teeth, fish bones, and porcupine quills; however, none of these have been preserved.

The third characteristic of *H. erectus* was their tendency to lead nomadic lives and colonize new areas. Not only did they populate their own continent from Morocco to South Africa, they also became the first hominids to march out of Africa. From about a million years ago, perhaps even earlier, *H. erectus* has been found in China as well as Indonesia—travelling to some of these locations indicates good seamanship. It is possible that they reached southern Europe, or arrived there shortly afterwards. With such a wide distribution across different environments, physical characteristics vary greatly between different populations of *H. erectus*. Such regional differences in appearance are called geographic racial variations and also occur in many other animal species.

In many respects, *H. erectus* stands out as an exceptionally successful model human and his existence for 2 million years attests to this. He left behind a lasting memory—*Homo sapiens*. However, this didn't occur as a simple succession where one form suddenly replaces the other. It seems that a population of *H. erectus* in Africa became isolated and quickly underwent such complete evolutionary change that they maintained their distinctive characters when they came into contact with other populations of *H. erectus*, preventing interbreeding. Thus, a new species had evolved, which some authors call 'archaic' *Homo sapiens*, or *Homo heidelbergensis*. This being had an even larger brain than *H. erectus* and some individuals had brains larger than those of modern humans. Their temporal regions had expanded, their foreheads had become higher, their eyebrow ridges smaller, and the shape of their faces had come to be more like yours or mine. In turn, at least two additional species evolved from this diffusely defined species—modern *Homo sapiens* and Neanderthals (*Homo neanderthalensis*).

The question of when these forms evolved is a matter for lively debate. The transition from one species to another is a slow and gradual process that is often interrupted when incompletely genetically isolated populations re-establish contact and begin hybridizing. The Neanderthals had an independent history stretching back over a half a million years and must have evolved from a *H. erectus* or *H. heidelbergensis* population. Thus although the Neanderthals share a common ancestor with *H. sapiens*, they are definitely not our ancestors.

The prelude to the most recent and ongoing act in the hominid drama occurred a few hundred thousand years ago in Africa. (Maybe even a million years ago.) One population of humans, perhaps the transition form between *H. erectus* and *H. heidelbergensis*, was in serious trouble and had decreased in number to only a few thousand individuals. In such circumstances, large amounts of genetic variation are lost so that the population is genetically more uniform after the bottleneck than it was before. In addition, rapid evolutionary changes and innovations can occur in such small, isolated populations. Chance can result in certain previously rare characteristics increasing in frequency and eventually becoming completely dominant. Fundamental evolutionary innovations may develop preferentially in small and isolated populations that have landed in new and stressful situations. Since many populations of hominids have been small, perhaps only a few thousand individuals during long periods of time, their population sizes would be similar to the numbers of apes today. Naturally, a small, isolated population that ends up in a foreign environment, runs a greater risk of dying out; but if they survive they may have useful innovations in their adaptive arsenal.

In this case, the population survived and came out of the ordeal literally as a new people, the true *Homo sapiens*. They were superior to other *Homo* populations in many respects and about 100 000 years ago they began a global conquest, which signified the end for all other hominids, including the Neanderthals.

When *H. sapiens* invade a new area, it is bad news for the indigenous inhabitants whether Neanderthals, other *H. erectus* descendants, or the large and edible animals, the so-called megafauna. The take-over continues today as we force our way in and selfishly transform and exploit every corner of the world's many ecosystems. *H. sapiens* is undeniably an ecological success. Just how durable this model is the future will reveal. So far, we have existed only 10 per cent of the time that *H. erectus* walked on the earth.

The great interest that biologists have for the evolutionary history of our own species has not resulted in the elucidation of hominid phylogeny (evolutionary history), systematics (systematic internal relationships), or taxonomy (demarcation between different divisions and their correct designations). In fact opinions differ in many questions of detail but the overall picture is gradually becoming clearer.

One example of the uncertainty regarding the phylogeny of hominids is that there isn't even agreement as to the time of such an important event as the separation of the chimpanzee and the hominid lineages. Although most scientists believe that 7 million years is a reliable date, the geneticist Ulfur Arnason and his research group at Lund University have caused uproar by claiming that this event should be pushed back to about 13.5 million years ago. If they are correct, the mutation frequency in the DNA of hominids must be much slower than in comparable animals. Only the future will reveal if there is something fishy buried among all the hominid fossils and DNA molecules.

## FLIGHT FROM THE RAINFOREST

There is disagreement on how many species of hominids have existed between the first staggering but independent steps were taken by the first hominids, and the present and probably last stop for the lineage, where only one hominid exists. Some suggest that at least twenty or so hominid forms have existed, all of which should be considered as separate species and given a scientific name since they were genetically isolated from other contemporary species. How many of these hominid species should be included in phylogenetic ancestry that has led to *Homo sapiens* and how many are dead ends? A simple provisional hypothesis is that a chain of species comprised *ramidus/anamensis—afarensis—boisei* and/or *habilis—erectus—heidelbergensis—sapiens*. But what roles do *Australopithecus africanus* and *Homo ergaster* play? More information will gradually be uncovered from the soil and cliffs of the African savannahs, filling in the details of hominid evolution.

Thus, evolutionary change proceeded from the rainforests out onto a more open wooded or mosaic savannah with patches of everything from rainforest to open areas. No doubt, wetlands, lakes, and rivers attracted the emigrants from the deep rainforest. That the common ancestor of chimpanzees and hominids came from the rainforest is also highly likely. The phrase 'out of Africa' is certainly familiar and can be complemented with 'out of the rainforest'.

All the Asian apes live in rainforests. Orangutans and the ten species of gibbons are all tree-dwellers, sharing the ability to swing between trees using their long arms. (The technical term for this is 'brachiation'). In Africa, however, the hominids gradually abandoned the rainforest and began to live a terrestrial life, in a more open terrain. In some regions, modern chimpanzees are tending to inhabit increasingly open areas—and chimpanzees, bonobos and gorillas all spend a great deal of time on the ground. This enables us to make comparisons between these, our closest relatives, and ourselves.

One vital question is: what drove or lured the early hominid species out onto the savannah? The rainforest certainly has advantages as a habitat. It is the most species-rich biome on the Earth. It is warm—counteracting the high heating costs of warm-blooded (homoiothermic) animals. There is no burning sun or desiccating wind to draw moisture out of the body's tissues. Water is plentiful and is always available. There are 12 hours of day and 12 hours of night throughout the year. The really large carnivores are confined to the ground, at least when they are hunting, and can be avoided by climbing up the nearest tree which is usually no more than a couple of metres away. There is some annual variation in temperature and precipitation and thus in the production of buds and fruits, but not enough to cause shortages in vegetable matter in the treetops, on the ground in the glades, or along forest edges.

Naturally, we don't know what caused a tailless primate—a predecessor of *Ardipithecus ramidus*—to withdraw from its dependence on the rainforest. Did the competition with monkeys for fruits and berries become too difficult? Monkeys have certain adaptations in their digestive systems that allow them to digest unripe fruit and consume a greater variety of foods than the apes do. However, there may be completely different reasons for leaving home than competition with other species. One's own home may become too crowded; population pressures and within-species competition can be trying. Increasing population density and the beginning of resource scarcity may have driven some pioneers from the tailless primates out of the rainforest and onto the savannah. Why do people live in Sweden? The first group of immigrants probably moved to that barren land 12 000 years ago because times had become so difficult in their previous home regions that emigration was preferable. It was only when children were starving in southern Sweden that the emigration waves to the USA began.

Like all pioneers, the earliest savannah hominids experienced difficult times. For many thousands of years their reproduction may not have been successful enough to counteract mortality—but they remained. New emigrants would have trickled out of the rainforest and onto the mosaic savannahs, maintaining populations of humans in a landscape to which they were poorly adapted. A similar pattern exists among many species of animals today: certain locations are highly productive and produce more individuals than can be supported, some of them are therefore forced to leave and search out new locations in which to live. Despite poor living conditions at the new site, it may be marginally better than their original home region.

In such compulsorily exported populations in extreme environments where a large portion of individuals can't reproduce at all, any genetic variation that provides an individual with a slightly better chance of survival and reproduction is of great importance. Natural selection works hard in new environments. Gradually, the savannah-colonizing hominids adapted to solve the problems that they encountered in their new environment—it was no longer a threatening and dangerous outlying expanse, but a secure and friendly home.

The savannah pioneers had the future ahead of them. Dramatic climatic changes during the last five or six million years, among other things, have resulted in the expansion of the savannah and the shrinking of the rainforests. These climatic changes have been accentuated on the African continent by the growth of the Rift Valley mountains that screen off eastern Africa from the rain clouds that originate over the Atlantic Ocean. The hominids evolved in the dry, savannah-like region east of the Rift Valley. This is 'East Side Story'—the cover name for the evolutionary processes leading to our own species' origins, which all evidence indicates occurred in east Africa: from Ethiopia in the north to Transvaal in the south.

There were three main difficulties that the early hominid pioneers encountered out on the savannah. Individuals had to travel much greater distances. Fruit and nut-bearing trees occur only sparsely on the savannah and it was necessary to travel long distances to find them, especially if they produced fruit only periodically. Neither could they count on the same source year after year. A herd of elephants might have come through destroying everything in its wake. Searching and roaming became never-ending activities.

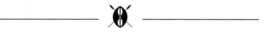

Hide behind a bush near a fruiting fig tree, perhaps, at the edge of a dried-up riverbed that winds across the savannah. Sit completely still, keep watch, and you will see a lively drama. Hornbills, starlings, cuckoos, bulbuls, louries, and other birds arrive at the breakfast table from all directions. A gang of vervet monkeys are so busy with their fig orgy that, surprisingly enough, they refrain from their usual pestering and quarrelling. And what is that moving along the edge of the high grass over there? Two male baboons stare towards the fig tree, checking that the area is leopard-free. A few minutes later, they signal to the rest of the troop that the coast is clear and the whole gang marches out from the grass and up to the fig tree, which they climb quickly. The chief himself and a couple of his girlfriends remain on the ground in the hope that some of the goodies will fall down from the wild party up in the tree. A heavily-laden fig tree is a three-star restaurant that merits a substantial trek for fruit-loving primates. Well-worth remembering and returning to in future years.

Waterholes on the savannah are distributed sparsely and attract visitors from near and far. Another unevenly distributed resource is meat. Meat became an increasingly important resource for hominids inhabiting the savannah, and regardless of how they acquired it, it required speedy and lengthy treks.

The cartoon portrayal of the rainforest in the *Jungle Book* as a place where you can sit down, wait a while, and a delicious fruit will eventually fall into your outstretched hand, is of course not true. However, such a gift from above is even less likely to occur on the savannah. There, you must be quick on your feet to avoid dying of thirst or hunger.

The tropical sun is a relentless enemy, especially in combination with wind and the lack of water in the open savannah environment. Almost all savannah organisms have evolved structural, physiological, and behavioural adaptations to increase their resistance to heat and dehydration. A few of the more common tricks are to seek out shade when available, to limit activity to mornings and evenings, to become exclusively nocturnal, or bury oneself in the ground. Grant's gazelle, oryx, and ostrich are examples of animals that manage to survive in near desert-like conditions by making the most of the moisture in their food. Plants and insects also exhibit many examples of extreme adaptations evolved as aids in maintaining their balance of liquids in the glaring sunshine of the open savannah or semi-deserts.

For the hominid that aspired to settle on the savannah, there was also the threat from large carnivores. Although carnivores, such as leopards and large snakes, in the rainforest consider primates as delicious additions to their diets, most primates are exceptionally skilled climbers and are far less vulnerable to predators when they are up in the trees. Out on the savannah there are more predators:

wild dogs, hyenas, cheetahs, and lions supplement the leopards and snakes. Climbing a tree would provide some protection—but this solution is not always available.

The openness of the landscape and the behaviour of savannah carnivores increase the vulnerability of primates to predation. Three of the savannah's larger carnivores—spotted hyenas, wild dogs, and lions—live and hunt in co-operative groups and thus pose a serious threat to their prey species. What can a helpless little hominid do against such formidable predators?

The facts suggest that the earliest hominid migrations from the rainforest were forced. Leaving an environment to which one has become specifically adapted over millions of years is an extremely bad idea. There may be different climatic conditions, fierce competitors, taxing parasites, and hungry predators. Only if conditions at home are terrible should an individual leave to search for other grazing or hunting grounds. However, there is rarely a choice and individuals have to make the most of a difficult situation.

The first savannah pioneers, the ones who make up the root of the hominid family tree, may have been 'economic refugees' from misery and failure in their previous home territories. Perhaps they weren't driven from paradise, but into paradise instead—the African savannah.

## FOOTPRINTS AT LAETOLI

One day, about 3.7 million years ago, something very dramatic occurred at Laetoli not far from Ngorongoro (which had not yet been created). Sadiman, one of the many volcanoes in the region, erupted and expelled a great deal of fine ash which covered the surrounding area. The rains came shortly afterwards, transforming the ashy powder to a thick paste. Before it had time to dry and harden many different kinds of animals visited the area and, like guests in a guest book, left elegantly pressed footprints: hares and guinea fowl, buffalo, giraffe, rhinoceros, and elephant. In September 1976 as two young researchers walked through this area looking for a sliver of bone that would reveal some important fossil, one of them picked up a bit of dried elephant dung and threw it at the other. As he ducked, he caught sight of some human footprints, just like on a wet, sandy beach, only this was cast in cement that was millions of years old.

Two years later, Mary Leakey—the grand old lady of palaeoanthropology—found more footprints in the solidified volcanic cement at Laetoli—of an adult and a child, who had walked together approximately 3.7 million years ago.

Were they Lucy's friends? They belonged to the species *Australopithecus afarensis*.

When I went to Laetoli and saw these footprints, my imagination ran away with me and took me back to the same place, millenia before. I saw my ancestors, whose lives and deaths have influenced me, wandering together on the savannah, long ago. Perhaps it was a similar day with a coolness settling in at the end of a hot day, a fresh afternoon breeze rustling through the tops of the fever acacias, and birds emerging from the shadows to search for food. Perhaps a father (the larger footprints are so large that they presumably belonged to a man) allowed his child to accompany him on a hike. They may have been on their way to harvest the bee hive he had found earlier in the day with the aid of the guiding antics and chirps of a honeyguide, or to tear off a piece of meat from the buffalo killed by carnivores and take it home to their own small flock. They walked in silence, for they almost certainly had no spoken language, but they undoubtedly communicated using glances and gestures.—'Can I eat this kind of berry?'—'No, leave those alone.' They walked hand-in-hand and were surely quite fond of one another.

The footprints in Laetoli prove convincingly that 3.7 million years ago hominids already walked upright on two legs and although not straight and tall with a springy step like a modern athlete, they didn't jolt along like chimpanzees. Hominids began walking upright on two legs long before they became quick-witted. These creatures were probably no more quick-witted than today's chimpanzees or bonobos. Hominids can actually be defined as tailless primates that walk upright, and this attribute has characterized their, and our, anatomies. Powerful selective forces have worked on this million-year-old programme.

Those individuals possessing the improved ability to walk on two legs gained great advantages over their clumsier companions.

The closest relatives to hominids, the two species of chimpanzees, walk using all four limbs, placing the knuckles of their hands on the ground as they walk. Similar to other primates, with or without tails, they can walk or run for short distances on their hind legs. Sixty per cent of their body weight is supported by their hind legs, which differentiates them from other four-legged creatures such as horses or dogs who bear only 40 per cent of their body weight on their hind legs. This extra weight on their posterior extremities must have led to the transition to bipedalism. There is also a division of labour between their front limbs and their back. Even gorillas, orangutans, baboons, and vervet monkeys do some things only with their hands and others only with their feet.

One of the problems with leaving the dense rainforest and entering the more open and mosaic savannah landscape was the need for a larger individual action radius and an improved ability to travel. The hominid lineage unquestionably evolved from a pronounced arboreally adapted animal—it is climbing that has created the heavy back-end in primates. If a tree-dwelling animal is reconstructed to become terrestrial, able to travel long distances, is it preferable to make it 'truly four-legged', like a dog or a horse, or 'truly two-legged', like an ostrich or a human?

The scamper of a chimpanzee seems clumsy when compared with the more efficient walk or run of a human—surely bipedalism and upright posture are a great improvement. However, humans walking or running across the wide-open savannah appear mediocre compared with the sleek antelopes in the same weight class. One weakness of humans is that we use significantly more energy per distance run than an antelope of similar size. For humans, standing upright requires far more energy than lying down; for an antelope the difference is significantly smaller. We are forced to use energy to remain balanced, whereas an antelope can relax while it stands on four legs. Sadly, not even our world record-holding athletes are particularly fast when compared to many of our four-legged friends. The world records for men for 100, 800, and 10 000 metres are equivalent to speeds of 10, 8, and 6 metres per second respectively. A trotting-horse reaches speeds of up to 16 metres per second over an English mile, and a greyhound maintains similar speeds over 500 metres.

From an agility point of view, it was probably an improvement that the 'original hominid' raised itself onto its back legs; however, from a functional point of view, it would have been even better to shift the body weight forward and reconstruct it on a similar plan to that of a dog or gazelle. The 'original hominids', adapted to climbing, were built in a manner that made it easier to stand up on their back legs than to fall forward and become true four-legged creatures. For certain tasks, two legs and two arms may be more useful than four similar legs. All primates can keep track of and divide labour between manipulating hands and walking feet; hominids have taken this division of labour to the extreme. The extra height gained by standing up raised our eyes higher above ground level and increased the range of vision—a significant advantage in the early discovery of predators.

As I moved to get up from my chair after writing these lines, a pain shot through my back. It was lumbago reminding me of its existence and the price so many of us pay for our incomplete construction. Upright posture and walking on two legs demanded a thorough alteration in the construction of our bodies, and the painful twinge in my back is a reminder that this process has yet to be finished. 'Give the monkey in me a chance?' I don't have anything against that—but does it have to happen in the form of lumbago?

## BY THE SWEAT OF ONE'S BROW

We had just arrived at a small village after hiking in the burning hot sun for a few hours. The temperature was 36°, our clothes were soaked with sweat, and our thirst was enormous. At the simple village bar, an ordinary can of Coca-Cola cost three

American dollars, which led me to mutter something unprintable (in Swedish) about the low ethics of the man behind the counter who could take advantage of thirsty, dehydrated hikers. My companion interrupted me and hissed: Fifty dollars wouldn't have been too much! Despite the fairly short hike, our bodies were literally aching for liquids.

Our species shows that at some time during our history we have gone through a period of intense temperature stress. The clearest indication of this is our lack of hair which enables our bodies to cool down when air comes into direct contact with our skin. When we begin to overheat, our bodies react in two ways. An increased amount of blood is directed into the peripheral blood vessels in the skin where part of the heat escapes via dissipation from the surface of the skin. In addition, approximately 1.5 million sweat glands start producing sweat, which evaporates directly from the naked skin and cools the body down. In intense heat, a human can lose up to 1.5 litres of liquid per hour. The human body must have access to an abundant water supply for our cooling system to function. Naturally, humans also reduce the risk of overheating (heat stroke) by engaging in appropriate behaviours. A lengthy siesta in the shade of a mango or cashew tree is a prudent and enjoyable custom during warm weather.

Humans may have been forced onto their hind legs to lessen the surface area exposed to the burning rays of the sun. An added advantage would be that more of the body is located higher up in the wind currents, which improves the evaporation of sweat. Compared with genuinely desert-adapted animals, humans are not particularly good at enduring heat and drought. Our abilities for adaptation are clearly limited in this respect—it is not so easy to turn a rainforest animal into a desert animal.

The lack of hair on humans may possibly have a parallel among whales and other aquatic mammals, in which case our evolutionary line must have passed through an aquatic stage. However, most scientists dismiss this hypothesis and maintain that the lack of hair among whales and humans evolved for completely different reasons. Whales probably lost their fur to reduce friction and become more streamlined. However, to keep warm in often ice-cold water, they instead acquired a layer of insulating fat. Even humans have a layer of subcutaneous fat, although sadly it doesn't give us a streamlined shape; on the contrary, it increases the curvature of the body—sometimes in a very attractive manner. There is actually no evidence that our ancestors went through an aquatic stage, splashing around in tropical lagoons encircled by coral reefs and enjoying regular shellfish dinners on the beach—no matter how nice it sounds!

On the sun-exposed savannah the intense solar radiation may have lead to sunburn with accompanying inflammation. The skin's outer layer of cells contain a pigment called melanin which provides protection from solar radiation. The less pigment a person has, the greater their risk of damage from ultraviolet radiation. Thus people who live in sunny regions have adapted to produce a large amount of skin pigment to minimize this problem. However, ultraviolet light is required for the manufacture of crucial vitamin D and this may be why people living in regions with very little sun have lost much of their pigmentation. In addition, pigment is costly to produce, and natural selection encourages the body not to produce more of a susbtance than is absolutely necessary.

We naked primates have some hair remaining. The hair on women's heads and men's beards have probably persisted as a result of sexual selective forces, while pubic hair and the 'embarrassing' hair under our arms retain odours that may be important in mate selection and sexual customs. Relatively new research indicates that olfactory and chemical signals generally play a much greater and more intricate role in our sexual choices than we perhaps realize. The perfume industry was obviously aware of this long before today's behavioural biologists.

## The Most Important Thing

Living alone does not make an animal strong—on the contrary, it actually makes it weaker and more helpless. This explains why we see flocks, herds, and groups of the most diverse animal species, at least during some part of their lives. The advantages of group living greatly surpass the disadvantages, such as competition over important resources, risk of infection with different diseases, and other negative results of being together with other individuals. Most importantly, it reduces an individual's risk of falling prey to a predator. Death in the jaws of a predator—a lion, an eagle, or a snake—is a common end for creatures living in the wild. As a member of a group, there is a surrounding, living shield against attack from a pack of wild dogs, for example. The shield is particularly effective if there are other individuals in the group or herd that are slower or that can be bullied to remain towards the outside of the group thus minimizing vulnerability in the centre. In addition, an individual in a group can reduce the time spent watching out for predators. Each individual must spend some time on the lookout, even if it reduces their feeding time. The more animals there are in a group, the less time each individual must spend on the lookout. Although tempting to neglect lookout duty completely and instead gorge themselves with food, it can be costly to cheat as the status of cheaters drops. Demonstrating that one can manage lookout duty and remain in good condition increases one's prestige. Individuals must continually optimize their behaviour by comparison with other members in the group.

As a member of a group an individual can take advantage of other individuals' knowledge of current food availability. Particularly among animals with long life spans, there is an important transfer of knowledge from older individuals to younger individuals. Local populations have traditions and culture in the form of collective knowledge which is transferred from generation to generation, not in the form of genes, but as memories, reaction norms, and knowledge.

The threat of predation would have been a significant influence for early hominids. This threat may have laid the groundwork for our present social behaviour. A solitary little *afarensis* who encounters a group of hungry hyenas—what do they do if there is no easy-to-climb tree nearby? The more impressive hominids have also had every reason to avoid eye-to-eye encounters with a lioness ready to attack. Even the tall *erectus*—the young man from Nariokotome (with or without a weapon)—would certainly shudder at the thought of such an experience, as would a solitary *sapiens* on his way to the pub in the next village. However, within a group many pairs of eyes have a greater chance of discovering approaching predators. With sufficient warning there is time to climb a tree and, if discovered, the predator is unlikely to attack since it doesn't want to sacrifice time and energy on a futile hunt. Commonly, predators become confused when there are several prey animals from which to choose; a co-ordinated group can actively defend themselves against their enemy. As long as you aren't the slowest member of the group, then someone else will probably fall prey to the predator.

Unfortunately, if the pride of lions is large in number, co-ordinated, and hungry, then neither early warnings nor waving sticks will help. Hundreds of thousands of hominids have probably been devoured by savannah predators. However, group behaviour has certainly helped. Individuals with the propensity to join others have, on average, lived longer and produced more offspring than those who have lived alone. Many researchers believe that this is how group living originated in hominids. External threats have amplified the tendency to live in groups.

Group living existed long before both humans and our hominid predecessors. At the time of the separation from the half-apes (prosimians) 30–35 million years ago, anthropoid apes had already begun following the 'social path'. This characteristic is of fundamental significance to most primates. Our sociality has become much more complicated, particularly since average group size probably increased when certain primates climbed down from the trees and became more terrestrial. Primate species that live in open environments tend to organize themselves into larger groups than those that live in more densely vegetated environments—although the rainforest bonobos live in very large groups (Chapter 12).

It is difficult to keep track of everyone else's shifting social positions and relationships in a large group of individuals. Joining a group certainly doesn't mean abandonment of one's own highly egotistical ambitions. The group exists for the individual, not the other way around. It is of vital importance for each individual's success that a skilful compromise is struck between the selfish programme of a maximum number of mates and offspring as quickly as possible at the lowest price and with the fewest risks, and the social programme prescribes behaviour that grants continued membership in a group of just the right size and composition. It is now generally accepted that humans evolved large brains to cope with the problems that life in a large and complicated group entail. Accordingly, the most important thing is our social intelligence.

So why don't the wildebeest, springboks, or the hosts of starlings, swallows, and cormorants have brains the size of footballs? Although antelopes live in groups, they do it without being 'personally acquainted' with each other. They have short-term internal dealings: a buck flirting with a female, two bucks fighting, a mother doing her utmost to protect her calf from hungry hyenas and jackals, but these social interactions are short-lived. Males don't usually participate in the care of young; the calves soon become independent and leave their mothers; no family relationship lasts more than two generations, and on the whole, one can conclude that a herd of antelope, with a slight exaggeration, can be described as an unstructured group of anonymous singletons.

Not so for primates. Only a short time spent observing them clearly reveals that individuals in a group of primates have intensive, individual, and complicated relationships with one another. I hope that my accounts of baboons, chimpanzees, and bonobos (Chapters 10, 11, and 12) have convinced the reader that a group of primates is definitely a tightly woven group—a circle of acquaintances—on a completely different level to a herd of wildebeest or a flock of starlings. It is the social complexity of the group that has necessitated increased brain capacity in primates in general and hominids in particular. In this respect, antelopes and birds do not seem to have the same pressures as primates.

There are actually a number of other animal species that have a similar level of individuality and complexity of social systems, for example elephants, lions, and perhaps some of the other larger carnivores, as well as certain dolphin species. Probably because we ourselves are primates it is easier for us to understand the social attitude of other primate species than it is to understand what it is like to be an elephant, a lion, or a dolphin.

Enlarging the brain, however, is not without cost. Within most evolutionary lines, high costs have probably been the primary obstruction to a pronounced increase in brain size. First-rate raw materials are needed in order to construct the most complicated of the body's organs, and a continual and abundant supply of first-class nourishment is necessary to keep it going. Although the brain of a modern human weighs no more than 2 per cent of the total body mass, it demands up to 20 per cent of the total energy consumption. It is expensive being clever. Extremely powerful selective pressures must have driven the tripling in size of hominid brain volume during the past 5 million years. In terms of reproductive success, it has been highly profitable to have a larger brain than one's companions. Knowledge and craftiness have granted status, power, and attractiveness. On average, this has clearly granted more offspring when examined from an evolutionary perspective.

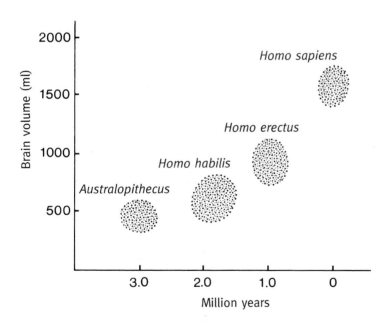

Figure 25. Hominid survival and our own species' jackpot in life's lottery are primarily a product of our cunning; its adaptive value has been the driving force behind the evolution of our over-sized brains. Maintaining a large and well-furnished head is costly—but has obviously been profitable.

During the course of evolution however, not all parts of the brain have grown proportionately the same. Human brains have a more highly developed cerebral cortex (neocortex), particularly the frontal lobes. This area of the brain is where cognitive functions take place, which give us the abilities to think, talk, and handle complicated information.

The evolution of an increasingly large brain and cerebral cortex in hominids has occurred through a relatively simple mechanism. Changes in the size and proportion of the brain have been accomplished chiefly through changes in the timetable for embryonic growth. An increasing number of brain cells have been given an increasingly longer time during which to grow, enabling the acquisition of more sophisticated structures and functions. In addition, the entire organism has had a longer period of time before development ceases. The result is that we have an 'over-developed' brain, which in numerous respects surpasses all other biological constructions.

An alternative explanation is just the opposite: that the brain has prematurely stopped developing and retained several childlike (neotenic) characteristics, which would explain the exceptional learning ability of hominids. This argument is based on the fact that a child's brain seems to have greater flexibility and learning ability than the brain of an adult. Those who support this argument also usually point out that humans resemble the young of apes more than they do the adults as the skulls of young primates are rounded and the jaws receded. Recently however, it seems that this argument has lost many of its followers. Adults are not large children. The development of our brains does not cease prematurely, but continues longer than in other comparable animal species. The outer physical appearance of humans has no significance for the manner in which the brain functions.

Comparative studies of contemporary species of monkeys and apes have demonstrated a close statistical relationship between brain size in proportion to body mass and cerebral cortex size in relation to brain volume on the one hand, and average group size within the various species on the other. The larger the social group, the larger the brain. A positive relationship also exists between group size and the time spent in that most social of all primate activities—grooming. The larger the group, the more intensive the social interactions.

A simple calculation demonstrates how quickly social complications can grow with increasing group sizes. Every individual in a group has an 'outgoing' and an 'incoming' relationship with every other individual. For example, Carl does not like Lisa, but Lisa likes Carl; both Carl and Lisa are simultaneously subject and object in their internal relationships. If the group contains 10 individuals, Carl has $9 \times 2 = 18$ relationships, and Lisa has the same. The social network of the entire group will accordingly include $10 \times 18 = 180$ strands. Do Carl or Lisa have to worry about those $180 - 18 = 162$ relationships in which they themselves are not involved?

Absolutely. Relationships between other individuals can greatly influence their own positions and their own future prospects within the group. If Dan and Larry gang up against Carl, then it is important for Carl to discover this in time so that he can gain support from Allan and Fred. On the other hand, Sue is backbiting about Carl to Lisa, which causes Lisa's sympathies for Carl to diminish and instead, she begins having a more positive attitude towards Eric, something that influences Carl in more ways than one. Eric's mother is a very important person who can make life difficult for anyone she has reason to oppose. Thus we could continue endlessly.

These problems become infinitely more complicated with an increasing number of group members. If the group size doubles from 10 to 20 individuals, Carl has 38 outgoing and incoming relationships, and the group's entire network contains 760 strands. At group sizes of 100 or 500 individuals, every individual will have 198 or 998 relationships respectively, and the entire network will contain 19 800 or 499 000 strands. The human brain seems to be adapted to handle a group size of 150 individuals at the most.

Thus hominids evolved over millions of years on the savannahs. Characteristics such as two legs, lack of hair, and the disproportionately large brain with its specially enlarged cerebral cortex were favoured by natural selection, as they helped Lucy and those who came after her to solve several of the most difficult problems that rainforest inhabitants encountered as they began their lives on the savannah. The long distances travelled, climatic trials and tribulations, and the threat of savannah predators, transformed a furry, acrobatic creature with four limbs and average intelligence into a naked being with two legs and two arms who became a wise wanderer on the expansive savannahs.

## THE GROUP: INDIVIDUAL LIFE INSURANCE

The fundamental purpose of group behaviour was probably to improve protection of individuals from predators, however, there are many factors that affect group size, behaviour, and composition among different animal species. Group behaviour in a number of savannah species, excluding *Homo sapiens*, has already been outlined to show how a species' social lifestyle is influenced partly by current ecological conditions (primarily the distribution of food resources), and partly by relationships between the sexes and between generations and the reproductive systems of those species. The higher primates that left the dense rainforests and travelled out onto the more open savannah landscape developed an advanced strategy of teamwork.

With the exception of humans, no modern primate species occurs in groups that are larger than one or two hundred animals. Individuals obviously have a tendency to seek out and remain in the company of others—but only up to a certain group size. Above that limit, losses become greater than the number of births and immigrations and group size stagnates or shrinks. Often, large groups simply divide into two separate parts.

Robin Dunbar, a prominent primatologist, has pursued the concept of 'smallest acceptable group size' primarily by studying savannah and gelada baboons—the latter is a species that lives in large groups on the grassy open mountain meadows in the Ethiopian highlands. Dunbar argues that minimum group size is controlled by the risk of predation. He has collected data on savannah baboons from various regions of Africa that indicates a clear relationship between the nature of the terrain and the intensity in which the baboons scan the area and exhibit restless behaviour. The denser the bushy vegetation and the greater the distance between trees, the greater the nervousness and the larger the group size. Dense bushy vegetation provides predators with better opportunities to sneak up on baboons, while a greater distance between trees reduced the baboons chance of quickly climbing to safety. Since group size is limited by these factors there must be areas where baboons can't live because predation risk necessitates a group size that is larger than the available food supply would allow. Consequently, within their area of distribution baboons are limited to environments where they can survive in groups larger than the minimum acceptable group size but which provide them with adequate protection from predators.

For a baboon—just as for any other living creature—the most favourable predation risk is zero. What prevents a baboon troop from becoming so large that the predation risk of each individual member diminishes further? Dunbar maintains that, in addition to access to resources, the growth limit for a troop of baboons is the activity budget of individuals. A larger troop must move quickly through an area due to the foraging constraints similar to those for impalas that we covered in Chapter 6. With increasing group size, eating and travelling takes up a greater part of the day. This, in turn, means the shorter the working day, the smaller the maximum group size. Climate, among other things, determines the length of the working day. Primates tend not to be very good at living in intensely hot or extremely dry conditions and therefore need a proper siesta in or under a shady tree—the warmer it is, the longer the siesta. In addition, they are typical daytime (diurnal) animals that can't work the nightshift. Since their working day, particularly in dry and hot climates, is relatively short, it influences their maximum group size. Dunbar found that this relationship between climatic variables (precipitation, temperature) and group size held in savannah baboons except for four populations where the baboons lived in larger troops than would be expected from the climatic variables. Three of these 'erroneous' baboon populations have since experienced population crashes, namely those in Amboseli (southern Kenya), Mikumi (southern Tanzania), and certain parts of the Namib desert (Namibia). Their lifestyles were clearly not stable in the long run.

In addition to marching, eating, and sleeping, baboons need to attend to their social relationships. A primate troop is a network with a structure which surpasses that of most other animals in its level of complexity. An individual's entire life, from birth to death, takes place within a group of individuals of which many are relatives. A solitary wildebeest or a solitary hippopotamus is undoubtedly very alone—but a solitary baboon or chimpanzee is nearly unthinkable. The lifestyle of a hermit causes astonishment among we humans.

Despite many memorable encounters, I shall never forget the one and only time I saw a completely solitary savannah baboon. It was in the forest near Lake Nakuru in Kenya—particularly famous for its amazing numbers of flamingos. The solitary baboon was an adult, though rather young female, and what we first noticed was her unusual stillness. We stopped and trained our binoculars on her. She had an expression in her eyes that I have never forgotten over all these years: forlornness and despondency. Was she sick or injured? We climbed out of the car and took a few steps towards her. She gave a start as if she had been deep in thought, retreated reluctantly a few metres, and then disappeared into the dense bushes. There was something on the ground where she had been sitting. It was a dead baby baboon, perhaps two or three weeks old, with a terrible gash or bite on the side of its head. What was that female baboon thinking just then? Are grief and sorrow modern human inventions?

All this complicated, intensive sociality requires time and mental energy. The advantages an individual gains from social living decrease if he or she does not manage his or her relationships in an appropriate manner. Every baboon must continually maintain or, preferably, increase his or her status or prestige in the

*Plate 15. Cheetah – the terror of springboks, gazelles, hares, and guinea fowl. The cause of the significant decline in cheetah populations in many areas is so far unknown. Chobe, Botswana.* PHOTO TOMAS JOHANSSON.

Plate 16. (left) Thomson's gazelle – tsetse flies and all. Where these serious cattle disease vectors are abundant, land cannot be used as pasture for stock and may instead be used as a national park or game reserve. *Masai Mara, Kenya.* PHOTO BO TALLMARK.

Plate 17. (above) River banks and lake shores in many parts of Africa are still home to huge crocodiles – ancient creatures designed for the heyday of giant reptiles more than a hundred million years ago. *Samburu River, Kenya.* PHOTO ALLAN CARLSON.

*Plate 18. (above) Why swim in the crystal-clear waters of the nearby Okavango Delta when you can have such a great mudbath here? Moremi, Botswana.* PHOTO TOMAS JOHANSSON.

*Plate 19. (top left opposite) Spotted hyenas finish off the remains of a wildebeest while surrounded by several vultures. Amboseli, Kenya.* PHOTO ALLAN CARLSON.

*Plate 20. (bottom left opposite) The spotted hyena is number one among carnivores for sociality. Masai Mara, Kenya.* PHOTO BO TALLMARK.

*Plate 21. (top) An idyllic scene of lionesses and cubs playing and cuddling each other on a comfortable rock. But not far away male lions may be lurking with murderous plans for the cubs... Masai Mara, Kenya.* PHOTO BO G. SVENSSON.

*Plate 22. (bottom) With greed in his amber eyes this handsome lion is defending this rotting giraffe carcass against potential scavengers. For him the carcass represents a full stomach and several days' leisure. Chobe, Botswana.* PHOTO TOMAS JOHANSSON.

*Plate 23. (top) Speed trap? This male savannah baboon seems to be taking a break to watch passing safari vehicles. Tsavo, Kenya.* PHOTO BO G. SVENSSON.

*Plate 24. (bottom) As in most primates, the bonds between mother and young last a long time in savannah baboons. A young monkey has plenty to learn before being able to lead an independent life.* PHOTO ALLAN CARLSON.

*Plate 25. Vervet monkeys grooming each other in typical
primate fashion. While this may remove a number of
parasites, its primary function is as a vehicle for social
interactions.* PHOTO ALLAN CARLSON.

group—only then are his or her profits maximized by sociality. This requires carefully and constantly updated information about one's own relationship to all the other members of the group. Not only that, but it is also advantageous to have current information concerning the internal relationships between all, or at least certain, other members of the group.

Keeping track of all these relationships is a prerequisite for building alliances. If primate B cannot get what he wants because primate A is too dominant, then B can try to attain his goal by building an alliance with primate C. Perhaps B + C can manage to dethrone A by acting together. However, if this happens, a troublesome rivalry is created between B and C. Perhaps C tries to win this new conflict by becoming friends with his old rival A? Not this time. A has already initiated a promising alliance with D and E and dismisses the invitation by C. One only needs to observe a troop of savannah baboons for a short time to realize the political games played within the troop. Even primates who spend their depauperate lives in zoological parks have still kept their talent for cheating and other such monkey business.

An increasing amount of energy and time is required to keep on top of, and participate in, the constant changes within the social patterns as the group expands. Dunbar maintains that an individual's ability for social cognition about him- or herself and others, as well as all the relationships that exist or could exist, sets the limits for how large a group of primates can be. This limit is often lower than the maximum acceptable group size prescribed by the external environmental conditions. The cerebral cortex is not large enough, and this sets a limit for the number of social activities an individual can deal with.

What about humans though? Can we calculate the group size our brain is adapted for? Robin Dunbar and his co-workers reckon that our cerebral cortex can tolerate group sizes of about 150 people. This figure seems absurdly low when you think about cities such as London, Bangkok, or Chicago. Additionally, many people consider themselves members of a social network that includes far more than only 150 people.

Think about your own situation however: with how many people do you have a truly social relationship? Naturally, most of us 'know' many people; perhaps we know their names and professions and say hello to them when we meet them in the stairwell or at the food market. However, you must agree that there is only a small fraction of all those people that you really care about, whose fate matters to you, and who you would miss if you lost contact with them. Make a list of those people for whom you truly care. Is your list really much longer than 150 names?

London, Bangkok, and Chicago are quite modern phenomena. Only during the most recent moment of human history have we been numerous enough to build cities with thousands and millions of inhabitants. Before the beginning of agriculture, humans lead a hand-to-mouth existence in small tribes or clans, and it was under these conditions that the human brain evolved its current structure. Therefore, only in this perspective does a comparison between the capacity of the cerebral cortex and group size become relevant. Suddenly, the figure of 150 people seems completely reasonable. This is the normal size for tribes or clans of people that live outside the influence of modern civilization today. Humans are adapted for living as hunter-gatherers, and it is a lifestyle that presupposes small groups and low population densities. Agriculture led to a ten to one hundred-fold increase in the number of people per square kilometre.

This limitation of our brain capacity, cognitive ability, and social competence, explains our tendency to organize or join appropriately sized groups: the local association of householders, motorcycle gangs, trade unions, sports associations, fraternal orders, or other collectives. It becomes very important for each of us to signal that we belong to some group via our clothes, by exhibiting some unmistakable equipment, using special jargon, or by participating in certain rites. We shouldn't forget dialects in this context. When travelling, I am often accosted by people who hear my dialect and who insist on associating and getting to know me because 'we come from the same region'. Certain theological scholars argue that religion is a superior way of strengthening a collective and setting up boundaries between those who are members and those who are outsiders.

Although creatures are impressively adapted for certain ways of life—the streamlined shark, the cheetah's speed, and the chimpaan nzee's intelligence—many organisms fail in their activities and die long before they have begun to feel the effects of age. Is there something wrong with baboons that leave their troop for a certain death? Or a zebra that ends up in the jaws of an attacking pack of wild dogs? Or an elephant that falls down a steep slope, breaks its leg and has a slow, painful death?

There was nothing wrong with these animals, other individuals were simply better adapted or luckier at that particular moment. Through the use of physical violence or social harassment, baboons can be chased away by individuals that are in some way superior to them. The zebra that is torn apart by wild dogs is for some reason slower or less attentive than the other zebras that survived: some inherited defect in construction, pregnancy, reduced immune defence resulting in poorer condition, or whatever. The elephant simply had an accident: no organism has managed to evolve a foolproof defence against accidents. The dinosaurs became extinct because a meteorite struck the earth. There is no defence against such an event. The evolutionary process lacks any trace of advance planning. Accidents and problems can lead to adaptations that tone down their effects—but not until these effects have become tangible.

Adaptations supply relative advantages. They do not make an individual over-whelming, infallible, invulnerable, or immortal. They exist because they have made, and continue to make, certain individuals better able to succeed in certain types of positive activities (reproduction) and to postpone death. With the exception of modern human populations, an early death and total failure to reproduce are the most common fates for animals. Considering this severe sorting-out process, it is not so strange that natural selection has generated so many remarkable adaptations.

The distribution of many animal populations can be explained because females like places where food and other resources are abundant, while males like places where females are abundant. For female mammals, in order to manage the great costs entailed in reproduction, they must have abundant and reliable access to food, since it is this above all else that determines their reproductive success. Male success on the other hand is determined by how many females he can fertilize. Chapter 6 considered the factors affecting the lifestyles of several of the savannah's herbivore species. In the case of primates however, the situation is more complicated, although the rule of thumb, that females are interested in food and males are interested in females, still applies.

Permanent camaraderie between a number of females is a framework in the social structure of primates that has very old origins. Although the struggle for better protection from predators was one of the original reasons for group living it lead to increased competition over food. Living among relatives might offer an advantage as they might be a little more generous with food in times of famine and be loyal bodyguards in conflict situations. Consequently, a nucleus of related females is established—which can compare with the 'ladies clubs' among elephants.

However, groups of primates are not ladies clubs, and include both females and males. Among mammals, males lack the prerequisites for contributing to the feeding of newly born offspring. Since male reproductive success is primarily limited by the number of females they manage to fertilize, they have no reason for remaining in the company of a female after they have made their quick but important contribution; however, they have an excellent reason for leaving, so that they can search out new, willing partners.

In many species of primates, females and males may live together to prevent infanticide. Immediately after taking over a pride of females, male lions begin killing the females' offspring (Chapter 9). The evolutionary reason for this behaviour is that the dead cubs' mothers will quickly come into heat again giving the killers the opportunity to father the next litter. The disposition towards infanticide is strikingly high in many species of primates. Both in langurs, an Indian relative to the African colobus monkeys, and gorillas from the misty mountains of Central Africa, impatient males who want to fertilize females kill at least a third of all of the females' offspring. The equivalent figure for South American red howler monkeys is an amazing 64 per cent. One reason why infanticide is so common among primates is that young stay helpless for such an unusually long time, and must remain continually with their mothers. Consequently, a male can easily see which baby must be killed to enable a certain female to become receptive for fertilization.

This significant risk for infanticide by unfamiliar males is a possible explanation to why, after mating, males remain with one or more females in a group and are able to defend their young against other potentially infanticidal males. Females gratefully accept the offer: their young have a reduced risk of dying, group size increases, and males can be good to have around, not only as defenders against homicidal males of their own species, but also against all kinds of predators. The males' enormous strength and canine teeth are extremely useful, even if they evolved as weapons to be used against each other in competition over access to females.

There is a risk of infanticide when two or more males join a group. Females deal with this risk in various ways, and one of these is to copulate with all the males. If all can be the father, no one wants to take the risk of killing his own offspring. This was also suggested as the explanation for the promiscuous sexual behaviour of female chimpanzees (Chapter 11). Several related females with an overlapping genetic interest may establish an aggressive sisterhood that repels males with suspicious intentions, or new mothers may establish a special relationship with one or more powerful males to protect her from other males. She can later pay back this protection by allowing her protector(s) first priority when she next comes into heat. This is similar to the behaviour of savannah baboons (Chapter 10).

Conflicts between neighbouring groups often lead to infanticide among savannah baboons, chimpanzees, vervets, as well as a few Indian species of primates. It is advantageous for one group to limit the growth of the neighbouring group. Females who have lost their young tend to move to the victorious group—if you can't beat them, join them. Prospects for individual success become undeniably better in a winning group. Consequently, males have extremely good reasons for defending their group territory to the utmost, using physical violence or by engaging in demonstrations of power along their territorial borders.

To be included in a group of just the right size and composition is the desire of every baboon, chimpanzee, and undoubtedly also *afarensis, habilis, erectus,* and *sapiens*. An individual who ends up in a favourable social situation has a significantly better prospect for long life and successful reproduction than the poor soul who lives alone or in a small gang excluded from society's collective. Effectively functioning groups don't originate by chance but as a result of the selfish efforts of a number of individuals to maintain their mutual social situations. Teams are dependent on their individual members, and few of these are without fault regardless of whether they are made up of humans or of clever members of other species.

## STATUS, PRESTIGE—AND LOSS OF FACE

The group, the troop, the team, or the gang enables individuals to attain the goal common to all organisms that have evolved via natural selection: to maximize reproductive success. Those genes that build carriers with lower success become fewer and fewer with each generation, whereas those that build effective carriers will make up an increasing fraction of each generation. Evolution is this simple. Although it is vital for an individual to live in a group and, therefore, worth a sacrifice or two to keep the group together, it is also important to hold one's own in the competition within the group. The most important resources for all organisms that practice sexual reproduction are partners. Generally, females make a greater and more long-term investment than males to achieve successful reproductive results. Thus, a female will give birth to far fewer offspring than the male can father. Women rarely give birth to more than a dozen children during their lifetime, and most give birth to many fewer. The current record for men however is more than 850 'official' children: the Moroccan sultan, Ismail the Bloodthirsty, ended up in the *Guinness Book of World Records* for this reproductive feat. At any given time in a population, there are more males ready to reproduce than there are females and so they must compete with one another. Biologists refer to this as a skewed 'operational sex ratio'.

However, there are many reproductive costs beyond the production of eggs and sperm. Not only women but also men must invest in the care of offspring during several years of adolescent growth and since the number of offspring produced during a lifetime is limited every reproductive effort becomes important. As a result it is essential that the correct genetic choice of partners is made. Ismail the Bloodthirsty and several other potentates, both past and present, had an unusual reproductive strategy for our species, one that can only occur under extremely dictatorial political and economic conditions. Equality and democracy are generally met with sympathy because they even out reproductive success among men. Despots arouse animosity, particularly when they behave like Ismail.

Women should therefore be very particular in their choice of mate, and men as well (though to a lesser degree), and competition would be expected between men for the best women, as well as between women for the best men. Since through pregnancy and nursing women experience a much greater physiological stress than men do, their condition is of particular importance in order for reproduction to succeed. Thus, males should consider the female condition carefully when choosing a mate. Men lack the ability to take on physiological costs such as pregnancy and nursing and therefore can only indirectly contribute to the success of the reproductive project by supplying additional sources of nutrition to both his partner and offspring. Accordingly, women are likely to place more importance on differences between material wealth in men when they choose a partner, whereas men place more importance on the observable physical condition of women. Thus, men should be expected to signal that they have a good economic situation while women signal that they are youthful, in good health, and fertile. On average, this is the case and the principle is similar regardless of which species one studies. Mate selection is one of the most important decisions an individual makes during his or her lifetime. No wonder that a careful testing of the different aspects of the tentative partner's qualifications occurs, or that some dishonest advertising goes on.

Within the theory of evolutionary biology, there are two different selection processes—natural selection and sexual selection. Natural selection generates adaptations that, for example, increase an individual's ability to swim or run fast and hide from predators, or catch prey and effectively convert food consumed into offspring. Sexual selection, however, leads to adaptations that either favour an individual's chances to assert itself in competition with others of the same sex for partners of the opposite sex, or that increase his or her attractiveness in mate choice situations. Sometimes a behavioural or physical attribute can function in both contexts as with the giraffe's long neck (Chapter 5).

Many of our sexual patterns were formed as early as *afarensis* or *erectus*. Some species of hominids exhibited far greater sexual dimorphism in body size than modern humans. This indicates that during that time, competition between men was very intensive; it was important that a male could defeat his rivals in physical battle. The victors experienced greater reproductive success while the losers had almost none. The level of sexual dimorphism acts as a predictor of the kind of mating system a certain species may exhibit. Gorillas have enormous sexual dimorphism and live in polygamous constellations with the old silverbacks as sultans of their respective harems, which their sons may inherit when the time comes. Gibbons, on the other hand, exhibit no sexual differences in body size and live in strictly monogamous relationships. The size differences between men and women indicate that the mating system that has dominated our evolutionary line for a long time is most commonly exhibited today is 'mild polygyny': monogamy with a tendency for one man to remain with one women or be chosen by one or a very few women simultaneously or in succession.

In addition to physical appearance and signs of material wealth and status, prestige and reputation play an important role in an individual's reproductive success. In our closest relatives, chimpanzees and bonobos, males, and to some extent females, spend time and energy advancing within the group's hierarchy. However, in many other species, males in particular are willing to make great sacrifices and take substantial risks for nothing more than a promotion in status. Having status means that there are individuals in your surroundings that are affected by the decisions you make. By definition, an individual who is known for having access to resources that he or she can use in order to help or harm his or her comrades has status.

The individual that reaches the top level in a group of primates is doing well for him- or herself. If there is competition for food, then he or she has priority. High-ranking males experience greater success with females. Social status is inherited to some extent, and a young primate that has a high-ranking mother often has better chances for a long life and many offspring than the one who does not.

An individual searching for a mate is after certain things on behalf of its future offspring. Good genes make an excellent gift. If the status of individuals is partly a function of their genes, the one who chooses a high-status individual as co-parent will increase the likelihood that their offspring will in turn become a high-ranking individual and become parent to several offspring. Consequently, those who hope to be chosen must demonstrate their high status to those who are choosing. One must look attractive. A primate boasts its excellent quality by being plucky or by generously giving away food, a peacock by exhibiting its splendidly decorative feathers, a toad by croaking in the lowest bass voice possible...

A favourable environment with enough good quality food is necessary for growing up. Since high status individuals generally control richer resources, it is wise to choose a mate who will be an effective co-worker in supplying food.

In order to be chosen, an individual—and it is usually males—must signal that he has good genes, many resources and therefore a high status. Since it is impossible to demonstrate the quality of genes and difficult to present many resources, status is used as an indicator of the individual's general excellence. Humans and individuals of other species have evolved an infinite variety of characteristics or ornaments to signal their excellent qualities to the other sex.

But how can cheating be prevented? False promises of generous contracts are not unknown. How can a female searching for a mate trust that the individual displaying in front of her and signalling that he is healthy and of good quality will live up to his promises?

The honesty of signals can only be guaranteed if they are so handicapping and costly that they can't be displayed by individuals other than those who are truly of the best quality. Perhaps one can signal physical strength with an inflated posture and padded clothing—however, even someone who is feeble can afford such signals. On the other hand, trekking off into the wilderness with a 35 kilogramme backpack on your back for a speedy climb up the nearest mountain deserves admiration. Anyone can talk about heroic deeds—but the individual who throws himself (or herself) into the roaring river to save someone in distress is the one that is awarded the medal, is pictured in the local newspaper, and receives admiring glances. The individual that repeatedly leads the group to fresh water, fig trees loaded with ripe figs, and predator-free resting places, gains prestige— but the one who boasts about his/her skills and then fails is diminished in everyone's eyes. Success is vital. The larger the handicap, the greater the odds and the more impressive my achievement—if I succeed. This is the simple principle for the honesty of signalling that has recently been comprehensively presented in an interesting book by the Israeli biologist couple, Amotz and Avishag Zahavi.

Imagine all the people, mostly young men, and so many hominids before them, who have fallen because they tried to bluff their way to a higher status and attractiveness than they could actually manage. The world is full of lost reputations. Of course, individuals don't want to be cheated and incoming information is assessed for its honesty. Thus, a conflict develops between the ability to cheat and the ability to discover cheaters. This takes up a significant portion of the working capacity of our brains. As an important aid, we have consciousness, which, by allowing us to see ourselves as if in a mirror, helps us to know what others look like inside and how they might react in various critical situations.

## MACHIAVELLI'S DARKER AND LIGHTER SIDES

Our brain doesn't have the capacity to handle all the necessary relationships if our immediate social world includes more than 150 people. Groups of primates in general, and the more recent hominids in particular, are not temporary bands of anonymous individuals, but are woven together in more or less stable networks where all individuals have long-term relationships with one another and a historically conditioned culture in the form of shared knowledge.

What is a relationship? Clearly the relationship between individuals in a group of primates is of a completely different nature to that between buffaloes on the savannah. Primate relationships are characterized by extreme flexibility and are strongly influenced by which individuals are interacting and their previous behaviour. Every relationship between two or more individuals has a unique history. In addition, many primate groups persist over long periods, often longer than the life span of an individual, and they are comprised of individuals of both sexes from several generations. Many members of a primate group, but not all, are related to each other. One basic characteristic is that the nucleus of the primate group comprises several closely related females, but the males are unrelated and immigrate from other groups. There is an interesting exception to this rule: in both chimpanzee species as well as in humans, the framework of the group is made up of several related males/men, and it is primarily the females/women that move from group to group or tribe to tribe.

The complex social game within hominid groups on the African savannah was probably the most important factor behind the evolutionary development of the brain (especially the cerebral cortex) during the past few million years. Within groups of primates an individual might profit significantly from being able to manipulate others for their own purposes. Increasingly the idea of Machiavellian intelligence has been raised, because deception, manipulation, corruption, the construction of alliances and coalitions, and complicated conspiracies with several participants would all demand a particularly large social intelligence or ability to think socially. This kind of thinking was named after the Italian political author, Niccolo Machiavelli (1469–1527), who wrote a guide for young noblemen about how they could more easily ascend the complicated Italian hierarchies of their time by using various tricks of deceit and deception.

Humans use many means to increase their status. Keeping on the right side of our superiors, repeating popular opinions that are quickly altered depending on who one is addressing, being seen with the right people, distributing gifts and thus retaining debts of gratitude, and building cliques and alliances to remove people standing in the way of one's own advancement, in short, to participate in conspiracies. All these kinds of behaviours are more or less recognizable in everyone, everyone except for oneself of course. This is the finesse—that each of us honestly believes that we are free from all those despicable cheating tendencies that are so obvious among our fellow-beings. The better we are at fooling ourselves, the more convincing we can be when trying to tempt or convince others to behave in a manner that is in our own interest but not in theirs. I am willing to believe that car salesmen, advertising executives, politicians and preachers, and others who try to foist off articles or opinions on us are, for the most part, honestly convinced that what they offer is superior. The human aptitude for manipulation, intrigue, and deception is not something that Machiavelli invented. On the contrary, it is an ancient inherited quality that we carry with us from our original home on the savannah, and judging by how things have developed, it has been very useful. There are no indications that our inclination for cheating is on the decline. A man of vision and a contemporary of Machiavelli, Sebastian Brant, coined the aphorism '*mundus decipi vult, ergo decipiatur*', which means, 'the world wants to be deceived, consequently, I will deceive it'.

There is a certain measure of Machiavellian intelligence in our closest relatives, chimpanzees and bonobos, as well as in other apes and perhaps a hint of it in certain monkeys. The phylogenetic timetable for the growth and development of the brain indicates that this intelligence evolved when the common ancestor to both chimpanzee species and to hominids lived on the edges of the rainforests. The expansion of the brain must have provided exceedingly important advantages to those individuals that deviated by having larger brain capacities. A positive feedback process or chain reaction provided every change with incentives for further changes until we reached today's thoroughbred practitioners of intrigue.

Many of the qualities that we most admire about ourselves and that we usually claim as being uniquely human are by-products of the evolution of Machiavellian intelligence. For example, it is difficult to manipulate others without having some idea of how these other individuals think and feel and how they might react. It is also useful to be able to imagine the consequences of one's own behaviour as well

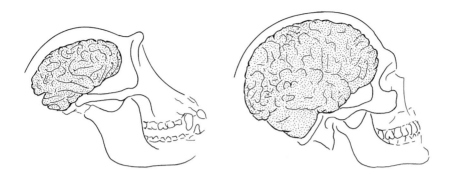

*Figure 26.*
*The cerebral cortex and the frontal lobes are particularly over-sized in humans, as can be*
*seen in this comparison with a modern chimpanzee.*

as the behaviour of others and compare this with other possible scenarios. If you fiddle with one component of a machine, something might go wrong in another part of it. Thus, Machiavellian intelligence doesn't simply mean skill at cheating and deception, but also the ability to sympathize, empathize, and fantasize. If the dark sides go far back in the phylogenetic history of primates, certainly these lighter sides do as well.

## With Eyes Sensitive to Green

What was a normal working day like for a group of *Homo erectus* out on the savannahs of eastern Africa? Speculation about how they might have lived is based on how modern savannah organisms exist. As they woke from a chilly night and rubbed the sleep from their eyes, the group of *erectus* people had simple demands and ordinary restrictions on their day. First and foremost, they had to secure sufficient food and water for the dawning day. Certainly, there were mornings when they woke beside a water-hole or river where they could easily quench their thirst as well as find the plant foods that constituted their staple diet—nuts, fruits, berries, and roots. If the water level was receding, perhaps they might find a dead or dying fish with which to supplement their diet. Life was good and our friends could take it easy and spend time engaging in social interactions. It is easy to imagine how their children played along the water's edge, overseen by their mothers and grandmothers. The only thing clouding their day was perhaps an uneasiness that a neighbouring group with bad intentions might appear, or that a hungry predator would be attracted to the water and abundance of prey, including *erectus* themselves. It was undoubtedly important for these people to choose locations with expansive views and climber-friendly trees.

However, no idyllic spot endures forever. Inevitably, resources have a tendency to run out. When drought comes upon the region, if not sooner, it will be necessary for this group to move on and look for a new temporary place to live. Peacefully resting alongside a spring was probably something the *erectus* group could only indulge in now and then. Most days were probably filled with foraging for different kinds of food, looking for water, and searching for shelter. Thirst, hunger, disease, accidents, and sudden death in the jaws of a crocodile or lion were reality for them.

Water, food, and shelter are necessities that are extremely unevenly spread across the savannah landscape, which is often a mosaic of different vegetation types, each with their opportunities and dangers. It was just as important for *erectus* hominids as well as their predecessors and followers to find those regions that provided the best conditions for survival, for maintaining good physical condition, and storing resources for costly reproductive efforts. Similar to other animals, the species of *Homo* were and are supplied with an inherited programme that directed them to prefer certain types of living environments or biotopes to others.

Since we aren't able to study the habitat choice of extinct hominids, we can instead look at the choices of humans living today. Gordon Orians, an American behavioural ecologist, has investigated the kinds of landscapes humans consider attractive or would like to live in. Regardless of which part of the world the people tested were from, their preferences indicated a surprising level of agreement, but with certain interesting differences in age classes. Most people preferred the open savannah landscape with groves of trees and bushes spread out over an expansive plain as opposed to rainforests, deciduous forests, coniferous forests, and deserts. The preferences for the savannah decreased with increasing age, with the older test people preferring the type of habitat found in their home regions. We are clearly born with a habitat-choosing mechanism that attracts us to the savannah, but our preferences are also influenced by our experiences—a pattern we have seen in several other situations.

Orians and others have continued with the study and have identified several factors involved in the kind of landscape to which we are attracted. Among these features are bodies of water, trees that branch at or just above ground-level (children's climbing trees), altitudinal variations, and especially, green vegetation. If the scene also includes large, tasty animals such as zebras or sheep, the positive classification of the landscape increases. Even quite discretely presented technological objects, like a distant power line, decrease the attractive value of the landscape considerably.

When living organisms choose a place to live, naturally they must not only consider immediate needs, but also think about the future. Both existing and future resources can be difficult or impossible to observe directly and instead must be estimated using different signs. For example, clouds in the sky herald rain showers, sprouting grass, abundant flowering, and the approaching rainy season. Other signs might indicate that a certain nutritional source is ready for exploitation. There is no doubt that life on the savannah demands a large amount of 'ecological intelligence', one of the most important building blocks in the evolution of the characteristic intelligence of modern humans.

The millions of years spent on the savannah have made a lasting impression on humans' psychological capacity; even today people from Texas, Argentina and Korea are attracted by savannah landscapes—a good example of the significance of previous adaptations in evolutionary history. As an effect of this inheritance, consider how modern people design areas meant for recreation rather than those for industry. What does the city park in your home town look like? Or in the cities you might have visited on different continents? Exactly, they look like savannahs, complete with grassy lawns and groves of trees, (artificial) cliffs and hills, and preferably a pond with quacking ducks and decorative goldfish. A playground is constructed for children; we furnish trees for climbing and build caves and crannies where they can crawl around. The vegetation includes as many different species as possible. A botanical garden with tens of thousands of plant species is considered by many as something especially attractive.

The attraction value of a landscape increases if it contains large, tasty animals. The strong interest many people have in animals has been interpreted as yet another expression for our ancient, programmed environmental preferences. Following this argument through, it isn't so very strange that we prefer landscapes with game animals. Large edible animals aren't particularly abundant and usually try to remain hidden in areas where they are exposed to hunting or persecution by humans. However, circumstances often reveal their presence even when they try to remain hidden. Circling vultures or ravens signal the location of a predator's kill and thus advertise that game species, carnivores and therefore meat are all nearby. In the same manner, the chattering of a troop of vervet monkeys or baboons, or a flock of birds in the distance can signal the availability of fruits and berries, or possibly a waterhole. Having the ability to identify the various opportunities and risks within a landscape via different kinds of indicators is an excellent adaptation.

Is this fascination with animals an additional manifestation of our long life on the savannah? What other explanation is there for the astounding fact that zoological gardens, aquariums, and other 'animal exhibits' in the USA are visited by more people each year than all the professional sporting events taken together?

It is good to treat animals as positive features in our images of a landscape. On the other hand, there are many animals that, from a human perspective, do not provide food or any other benefit, but instead pose threats. Humans, particularly in groups, have a fairly good ability to discover these animals in time, and are able to retreat to safety or defend themselves. Inevitably, certain other animals remain undetected until the last second, and then the only hope is to jump or sprint away as quick as lightening. Natural selection has developed an inherited programme that causes us to run first, and only after that to think about what the danger was and what its intentions were. Professor Arne Öhman, who early on understood the significance of the evolutionary background of human actions, wrote: 'Therefore, it is natural to accept that our genes have given us an ability to quickly associate fear and avoidance with animals that appear in threatening situations.'

Snakes and other reptiles are only some of the animals that cause fear and abhorrence in many people, even those who have never had any terrifying contact with them. Reptiles, from *Tyrannosaurus rex* to puff adders and spitting cobras, have been and still are serious threats to mammals since the time before primates entered the scene. Our innate fear of reptiles was perhaps established in mammals that lived tens of millions of years ago. At the same time, many people have a great fascination for these animals, as long as they are under some kind of control and can't make a surprise attack on us.

It is remarkable that most people throughout the world, even in areas with few or no snakes, carry in their genes an inherited fear of snakes—while children have to be taught to 'abhor' cars, live electric wires, scissors, and all the other dangerous objects in our modern environments.

Even if landscape architecture cannot be described as the world's oldest profession, it satisfies one of our oldest needs. Humans are calmest in open landscapes because they are adapted to them and have experienced their best reproductive success while living in them. In this respect, that which is optimal for us is what we are programmed to be attracted to, dream about, and praise.

## TOOLS OF STONE

As humans stood up and began walking on two legs, their forelimbs were gradually freed from their role in four-legged (quadrupedal) transportation and became specialized for new functions. The distribution of body weight that characterized the climbing, arboreal animals happened to prepare the hominid's ancestors for the conversion into animals that walked upright on two legs. The hind legs went through a thorough reconstruction; in particular the long, soled feet with short toes that we walk on today differ greatly from the 'back hands' of the other apes. The forelimbs however, thanks to the previous arboreal lifestyle, didn't need such a radical reconstruction, although they too required some changes in order to become adapted to their new tasks. Primates other than hominids are also equipped with hands that can accomplish many wonderful things. Baboons, vervet monkeys, and chimpanzees are quite 'handy' and are able to handle objects with impressive manual dexterity. Two or three adolescent baboons, for example, can easily dismantle all detachable parts on a car during a coffee break, the driver's coffee break that is. However, certain changes in the hands occurred during the time between *afarensis* and *sapiens*: our thumbs and the last segment of our fingers are proportionally longer than Lucy's, who had fingers that were more curved than ours, enabling her to grasp branches better. She was bipedal— but also a good climber. In addition, our thumbs are more opposable and our entire hand more mobile.

Certainly, the bones in the hand have become modified during the four million years of life on the savannah that lie between Lucy and today's humans, but in reality, even more radical changes have occurred in the musculature and nerves of the hand as well as in hand–eye co-ordination. Although such changes aren't apparent in the fossil record they are inferred from the development of artefacts—tools and other items—that hands have formed for various practical purposes.

The oldest artefacts found and dated thus far were made using the Olduwai technique, referring to the location in northern Tanzania that has supplied many of the fossils and artefacts related to hominid evolution. The creators of these objects were either late *Australopithecus* or early *Homo habilis*, and they lived between 2.5 and 1.5 million years ago. The tools are made of stones from which the craftsmen or craftswomen chipped off shards to obtain sharp edges. This kind of simple tool was all that was produced during several hundred thousand years. After that, people belonging to the species *Homo erectus* began producing double-

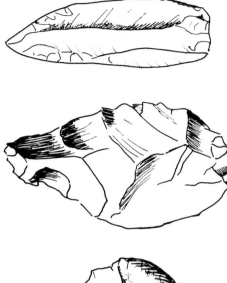

Figure 27.
From the bottom upwards, these
stone tools represent approximately
one million years of technical
advancement, encompassing
hominids from *Homo habilis* to
*Homo erectus*.

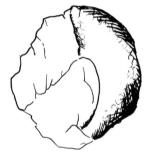

edged axes and other more refined tools using what is called the Acheul technique
(named after the Saint Acheul region in France).

The archaeological findings made in Africa and in many other places around
the world indicate two interesting facts. First, one is struck by the exceptional slowness with which stone technology changed, and second, how little progress the
Olduwai technique represented when compared with what some chimpanzees
are able to produce today. Even they can make several different kinds of extremely
simple tools, such as sticks to poke down holes in order to fish out termites. They
also use stones to crush nuts, although they don't modify the stones. The manufacture of simple objects from wood and the use of natural objects as tools or

perhaps weapons are accomplishments that the common ancestor to the chimpanzee and hominid lines may well have achieved and, consequently, should also have been present in early hominids, although no such objects have been preserved from that time or have yet been found. Many new fossils and artefacts are being found and interpretations may be modified accordingly.

According to one model, human intelligence can be described as a building with several rooms. Two of these rooms have already been visited: the room for social intelligence, with a portrait of Machiavelli on the wall, and the room for ecological or natural history intelligence with a portrait of Carl von Linné. We are now entering the room for technological intelligence. Almost all the furniture in this room is modern, because the furnishings arrived only recently. It is impossible to say whose picture decorates the walls: modern painters don't always put recognizability of the model high on their list of priorities.

The origination and spread of agriculture signified the definitive end to the lifestyle that characterized hominids from the time of the missing (or rather connecting) link, to the time 10–20 000 years ago when humans in Mesopotamia began growing crops, thus laying the foundation for a stationary way of life, a fast growing population, and opportunities for a greater division of labour and social stratification in the growing society. The hunter-gatherer lifestyle was gradually replaced by an agricultural lifestyle, which by 6000 years ago had reached all continents with the exception of Australia. Not all people converted to an agricultural way of life. In many regions, people continued to live as hunters-gatherers in parallel with the expanding farming societies, although they were often relegated to areas where climatic conditions were harsh or where the soil was less productive. Today, remnants of this ancient way of life remain in some places, even if modern techniques and culture affected them.

As far as human lifestyles are concerned, agriculture is the most revolutionizing technical innovation that has occurred during our history. Agriculture brought to a close the period when humans—like all other organisms—were completely dependent on existing natural resources. With agriculture, humans began a large-scale reconstruction of the earth's biological production system in order to benefit themselves. This innovation has been a fantastic success and has led to the increase of world population to a level that far surpasses the 'pre-technological' era. The time taken to reach this population explosion with its accompanying global rearrangement of the earth's ecosystems is only a tiny fraction of the time that has passed since the hominid line evolved in the African rainforest.

## DELICIOUS MEAT

Once upon a time, an ape that probably looked much like today's chimpanzees or bonobos was forced or tempted to leave the rainforest. These would have been difficult times for the first savannah pioneers. Savannah predators in particular would have posed a great threat to the small hominids. With fewer trees they would be more vulnerable to hyenas, sabre-toothed cats, lions, and other voracious hunters. One defence against these dangers was to live in larger groups, which required a larger and better-equipped brain. This in turn placed new demands on their diet.

The human brain is a remarkable organ—one of the most remarkable of all biological instruments or organs that natural selection has formed. To accomplish all the important tasks demanded of it, the brain requires a steady supply of high-quality nourishment. In practice, this means a protein-rich diet of meat. How could a small, rather poorly equipped hominid acquire the meat that its brain demanded? In the same way that they avoided becoming dinner for a predator: by living in larger and more co-ordinated bands and by using more sophisticated tactics. In some circumstances, cleverness can compensate for the lack of bulging muscles, sharp claws, long canine teeth, and fast legs.

Naturally, we don't know to what extent *Australopithecus afarensis* (Lucy and her friends) or early *Homo* hominids ate meat, and if they did, how they obtained it. However, we do know how chimpanzees obtain meat: they hunt. As hunters, they behave with a strange mixture of skill and clumsiness. Occasionally, there is apparent co-ordination within the hunting team, which is comprised of all or some of the males in the group. If the quarry suddenly turns on the chimpanzees and drives them away the hunt will fail. Hunting forays are often the result of improvisation instead of planning, and once the quarry is captured many chimpanzees are unskilled in the act of killing. The end of a chimpanzee hunt often leaves a gruesome impression on the human observers. For example, after they capture a young baboon they may carelessly pull at its limbs until suddenly an arm or leg comes off, then they tentatively bite on the bleeding body, and only after some time is the unfortunate victim dead, quartered, and eaten. Some chimpanzees however, are more effective in their killing; biting their prey in the neck or banging it on the ground, crushing its head.

Of the three chimpanzee populations that have been intensively studied, two in the forest savannahs on the eastern shore of Lake Tanganyika (Gombe and Mahale) and one in the Tai rainforest on the Ivory Coast, the Tai chimpanzees are the only ones that truly hunt in co-ordinated groups. Chimpanzees in Tanzania hunt alone or in small groups of two or three, often with poor or no tactical co-ordination.

For many years, the prominent Swiss primatologist Christophe Boesch has studied chimpanzees in the Tai forest. Both in Tai as well as in Gombe, the location of Jane Goodall's pioneering research, the chimpanzees' favourite prey animals are red colobus monkeys. In Tai, the chimpanzees hunt both adult and young colobus in the treetops in a co-ordinated and decisive manner, while the few successful hunts in Gombe are accomplished when one or two chimpanzees almost accidentally manage to grab a careless young colobus. In Gombe, some of the colobus have adopted the strategy that the best defensive tactic is to attack. The Gombe colobus often conduct preventive attacks against chimpanzees, whereas the Tai colobus do just the opposite—they become silent and sneak away when they hear chimpanzees approaching. Boesch believes that the differences between chimpanzee and colobus behaviour in Tai and Gombe are due to differences in the vegetation. In Gombe, the forest is open with miombo trees that are only 10 or 15 metres tall and are without leaves during a large part of the year. Consequently, it is difficult for the colobus to hide. They have a better chance of concealment in the towering and dense Tai rainforest where the chimpanzees must co-operate in order to have any chance in their hunts.

Chimpanzees seem to prefer hunting monkeys, but other quarry is occasionally found on their dinner menus. Among most species of antelope, females hide their calves in long grass or under bushes while they graze. If a gang of chimpanzees discovers an unattended calf or the piglets of bush pigs, they are quick to take advantage of the free food. Similar to savannah baboons, chimpanzees are mostly herbivorous; however, both baboons and chimpanzees clearly show their delight when they manage to kill an animal. Meat means a party.

Among chimpanzees, meat is not significant merely for its proteins and calories. The successful hunter is expected to share and has good reasons for doing so. He is often so harassed that an exceptionally aggressive chimp may steal a piece of the meat. The thief then runs away and is exposed to persistent begging by other members of the group. Generally, a successful chimpanzee shares willingly with other group members. His generosity is particularly aimed at females, with whom, if they are of a lower social rank, he does not need to ingratiate himself. However, they are the potential sexual partners for males and older females are instrumental in deciding the outcome of disagreements between different contenders for the throne. Generosity with meat can therefore be a wise investment. A male chimpanzee who has succeeded in killing his quarry gives out a special call, similar to his human counterparts, signalling his success and calling the other members of the group. The triumphant fanfare of the hunting-horn may well cause a knowing grin on the face of an experienced male chimpanzee.

If a successful hunter is too stingy towards his hunting partners, they may be unpleasant towards him on the next hunt, or simply refuse to allow him to join. The mutual exchange of goods and favours is one of the most important rules of conduct among chimpanzees as well as many other social animals. The individual who shares meat rises in status within the group: look, I contribute to the survival of the group and its general health, and I can manage fine even though I give away precious food. Special competence brings with it indispensability, and that results in a high status within the group. A dominant male chimpanzee confirms or raises his rank not only by appropriating the largest portion of available food, but also by apparently unselfishly giving away food to the 'masses'. Through such social 'investment' he promotes his own future reproductive success.

The chimpanzee appetite for meat shows that it is not a human invention, but an ancient primate characteristic: success in hunting brings with it status, and hunting is an activity that helps in establishing good relations between males in the group. Wild chimpanzees have never been observed sharing vegetable foods (with the exception of mothers sharing with their young), since such plain food is too easy for anyone to obtain. However, Frans de Waal reported that the chimpanzees in the Arnhem Zoo ritually shared the food that their caretakers brought once or twice a day. In zoos, chimpanzees can't eat when they want to; since food is served in infrequent but large portions the chimpanzees make a great deal of fuss over 'green' food as well.

There are hardly any confirmed reports of chimpanzees eating from dead animals that they happen to come across. They don't seem to be scavengers in that sense, whereas humans gladly take advantage of leftovers from kills by larger carnivores and will actively drive them away to obtain a delicious eland or oryx fillet. This habit is not forgotten in those regions where there are still large carnivores and large herbivores.

No human characteristic is foreign to chimpanzees. On the one hand their days are filled with actions that resemble friendliness, which to some extent they are—even if they are ultimately based on a *quid pro quo*. On the other hand, some behaviours, if seen amongst humans, would be considered terrible. Some primates commit infanticide, and if that isn't enough, they eat the victim after the murder. This kind of behaviour also occurs among other animals. Infanticide has been known among human cultures both among hunter-gatherers and in higher technological civilizations. Children with defects and those born too soon after their older siblings have had poor chances of survival in some societies. They have either been put to death directly after birth, or are not looked after properly with death soon following. In some cultures the sex of the child dictates whether it is welcomed and allowed to live.

The hunting behaviour of chimpanzees provides support for the hypothesis that hunting for meat is an ancient primate characteristic that probably contributed to increasing the size and unity of hominid groups on the savannah. There is a possible 'hitch' in this theory. Among chimpanzees and humans, males constitute the framework of the groups, whereas in most other modern primates females make up the nucleus. The increasing need for meat caused by the brain's increase in size may have forced this change, so that instead of mothers and daughters, fathers and sons became the group's special troops. The unbroken rule is that hunting is an exclusively male occupation—it unites males. However, hunting behaviour may not have been the primary cause for the increase in hominid group size. Benefits per individual tend to decrease even at quite small group sizes—a lion pride doesn't have several dozen lions. Instead, it was partly the need for protection from predators and partly—and perhaps primarily—competition and aggression between different groups or societies that forced hominid group sizes to increase uncontrollably.

## CHATTERING HUMANS

'I have never met a person who is not interested in language. I wrote this book to try to satisfy that curiosity. Language is beginning to submit to that uniquely satisfying kind of understanding that we call science, but the news has been kept a secret.' So begins a book by one of the most prominent of the evolutionarily informed language psychologists, Steven Pinker. The gift of speech is without doubt one of the characteristics that differentiates humans from all other animal species alive today. A normal person spends an amazing amount of his or her waking time talking to other people (in addition to sometimes talking to him- or herself). Talkativeness is such a distinct characteristic in our species that we should have been named *Homo garrulus* (the chattering human) instead of *Homo sapiens* (the wise, discerning, and knowledgeable human).

Although human language has attained a unique level of complexity, it nevertheless has prototypes or preliminary stages in other species. Perhaps a kind of linguistic communication began to develop as early as the transition between *Homo heidelbergensis* and *Homo sapiens*, who eventually became the ancestors of all modern humans, migrated out of Africa, and populated the earth. Unlike the ability to write or the beginning of agriculture, language did not originate within a certain ethnic group. Vocal language is a basic component of human nature.

Recent archaeological findings indicate that *Homo erectus* were the first people to colonize the island world between Asia and Australia, as well as some islands in Polynesia. They could not have arrived there without seaworthy boats. Could they really have developed the advanced technology necessary for building such boats without being able to communicate with one another via a language with nuances and a reasonably large vocabulary? There is no definite answer to this question; however, some researchers are willing to interpret the occurrence of a relatively advanced technology among *erectus* humans as an indication that these humans talked to each other. When humans or our ancestoral species actually began to talk is still unknown. One reason is that speech gradually developed over tens of thousands of years or even longer. Speech is one of our adaptations and has evolved via the usual selective mechanisms. It is not a miracle that can be dated to a specific time.

Human language is an adaptation, a genetically programmed ability, comparable with the navigational ability of a migrating bird or the sonar mechanism of a bat. Children speak fluently and construct sentences using advanced grammatical structure as early as three years old—without having received any formal training. Some speech impediments are inherited from generation to generation. The left half of the brain contains the speech centres in an area of the cerebral cortex known as Broca's centre. (Hence the joke that humans talk with the left half of their brain while the right half keeps silent and feels embarrassed.) Brain damage results in specific language impediments depending on where the damage occurs. The human upper respiratory system and auditory apparatus have species-characteristic components that are adaptations for improved vocal

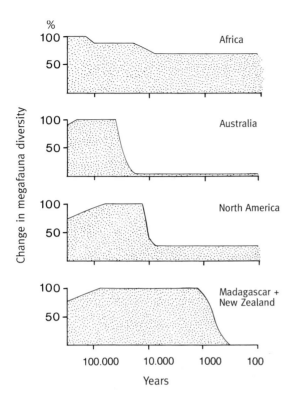

Figure 28.
When *Homo sapiens* arrives
on a continent or island,
the existing megafauna
populations decline fast.
Large edible animal
populations are rapidly
reduced or eliminated by
meat-hungry humans, as are
carnivores that compete with
humans or threaten human
lives. Few African species
have become extinct so far;
but almost all are drastically
reduced in number and
sidelined to small pockets of
land relative to when
Africa's natural history was
first explored a century and
a half ago.

communication. There is no connection between the level of technological complexity in different ethnic groups and their languages, and within a group of people factors such as intelligence, social class, or level of education play no measurable role in the individual variation in language ability. Language ability means the ability to apply certain basic rules of speech; it does not refer to the size of the vocabulary, which varies greatly with the different life situations of individuals. Of course, the ability to speak a specific language such as Chinese, Swedish, or Swahili is not an expression of an inherited programme; however, the ability to speak at all and thus obey certain common rules is part of our genetic baggage. The language, dialect, and jargon that an individual adopts during his or her first few years depends on the language environment in which he or she grows up.

If the ability for language is programmed in our genes, it has presumably evolved via natural selection. It is unlikely that such a complicated phenomenon as human language could have originated by chance or as an evolutionary by-product of some other characteristic. The complexity of language suggests it is an adapted character: individuals who were slightly better at speaking clearly were at a slight advantage. Those parts of our brains that are responsible for our ability to speak have accordingly evolved via the same mechanism—variation, heritability, varied reproductive success—as our hearts, our kidneys, our intestines, and our eyes.

Human language undoubtedly originated on the African savannahs. There are differing opinions as to how and when the spoken language originated (as opposed to sign language or body language), whether it was in Lucy or *Homo erectus*, or as late as early *Homo sapiens*. Human speech may have begun with a system of special calls, similar to those of vervet monkeys for 'warning for martial eagle' or 'warning for unfamiliar person'. The American researchers Dorothy Cheney and Robert Seyfarth have studied this elegant little monkey in Amboseli in southern Kenya. They concluded that primates have a significantly larger vocal repertoire than suspected, and that many of their calls have clearly defined meanings. Vervet monkeys have specific words for a number of different kinds of threatening situations. They have alarm calls and contact calls that refer to objects (different kinds of predators, for example) and events in their surroundings. These calls are varied and are often understood or interpreted by the receivers in a very nuanced manner.

The vocal calls of primates, however, can also function in situations other than reporting observations. A small primate baby who is ill-treated by a larger adolescent primate or a female monkey who is harassed by another individual will scream out their distress and call for help using special calls. Both vervet monkeys and other primates make use of calls or 'words' that signal different problematic social situations and emotions—in short, rudimentary speech. Thus, it is reasonable to assume that primate grunting, screeching, and yelling could have been the starting point for hominid, and eventually, human language.

Genetic variation in addition to selective pressures must have existed, to favour some and disfavour other genetic variants. Allocating valuable brain capabilities to a certain purpose, in this case speech, is not without cost, but it is an ability that must be paid for. What advantage did language bestow on those who were better 'speakers'?

The tough competition for resources on the savannah resulted in a perpetual game, a kind of soap opera with intrigue, intricacy, deception, rivalry, and the building of alliances, as well as many other kinds of interactions. Those who succeeded rose in social rank and attained relatively better reproductive success. Having the good ability to send signals to other members of the group, either honest or dishonest, must have been an advantage within the group's social game—a game that was concerned with more important things than simply life and death.

Almost all primate species use grooming as their primary form of social communication. Anyone who has seen a gang of primates will have noticed the considerable amount of time they spend grooming one another. The hygienic significance of this behaviour is unknown. It is possible to understand group structure and dynamics by watching who grooms whom, and for how long. The alpha male safeguards the individual who grooms him from bullying and harassment from other individuals. A group of related females groom one another's fur intensively. When, in spite of everything, a conflict does erupt, an individual must try to obtain support, and establish alliances with influential individuals—they do this by grooming. Within groups of primates, long-term friendship relationships often exist between certain individuals—coalitions—and those who are included in a coalition continually reaffirm their trustworthiness by assiduously grooming their companions. After a fight, both winner and loser must work out their relationship so that life can return to normal. This may require a 'peace treaty' in the form of a grooming orgy. Several different kinds of reconciliatory behaviour have been described in chimpanzees as well as other primates. They might not be able to say, 'I'm sorry'—but they can show it.

The more individuals there are in a group, the more numerous the social inter-

actions. It is complicated keeping track of everyone's relationships and manoeuvring so as not to end up in a fight or fall down the rungs of the hierarchy. Accordingly, a large part of the day is dedicated to grooming. Since primates are generally
visually oriented animals and not keen on being active at night, they don't use the
night-time hours (12 hours in equatorial regions) for grooming. In addition, you
can only groom one friend at a time.

The savannah environment favours those who live in groups and larger groups
have better chances for survival particularly against attacks by predators. What
then do they do in such a situation? They make the transition to using vocal
communication. One can both talk to and scold more than one individual at the
same time, and one can even talk in the darkest hours of the night.

The British primatologist Robin Dunbar suggested that speech evolved as a
solution to the demands of living and functioning in large groups, in particular to
handle all the social contacts. According to Dunbar, the most important function
of speech is not to be able to report 'I saw a leopard at the waterhole', but to provide
a better means for detailed gossiping. 'Even though I gave Carl a handful of nuts
yesterday, I didn't get one bite of the colobus he killed today.'

There are several research reports that have investigated what people generally
talk about, whether they are students sitting at a university café or a group of San
('Bushmen') around their campfire in the Kalahari. People talk about interper-
sonal relations or—put more plainly—they gossip. American students talk
neither about Hegel's philosophy nor particle physics—but spend most of their
time gossiping about people they knew or had heard about. In the Kalahari, San
men and women often sit up all night talking about themselves and others and
about the relationships between different people in the clan's past or present.
Children sit with attentive ears and remember the things they hear. Many moonlit
nights underneath the Southern Cross have been spent talking about real or
imagined injustices and favours that failed to appear, trying to reach compro-
mises to different conflicts, so that life can go on. 'Say what you will about Peter,
but he is an excellent topic for discussion', was a very human comment I heard
once during a conversation.

Different levels of skill and elegance in the difficult art of oral expression would have brought status, influence, and popularity. Natural and sexual selection are sufficient to explain the success of sophisticated language among hominids. Increasingly critical receivers demanded increasingly more sophisticated messages (true or false), and this escalation eventually led to the unique, many-facetted modern human language and the enormous expansion of the cultural domains. Our symbol-filled language and culture are so different from that of other species that these phenomena are still held by many as unexplainable using ordinary processes of evolutionary biology. Some people are just not willing to accept the creative power of evolution.

Opinions differ considerably regarding the role language has played in the level of human consciousness, in the understanding of other people's intentions, and in our ability to think, remember, and construct scenarios of future events. As humans developed the ability to consider the future, they were also able, to some extent, to influence it. For example, they could formulate rules and laws meant to uphold the interest of the group against the individual. Perhaps fantasy—the art of imagining different scenarios—and the ability for long-term planning are what have given subsequent hominids and especially *Homo sapiens* their unique successes.

When our predecessors on the savannah evolved spoken language to deal with their social problems, they took the definitive step towards the evolution not only of a new species among the millions of other species, but a species with power over all other species.

## FAMILY PROBLEMS

Our most important clues as to how hominids lived during the long time span between leaving the rainforest and emigration from Africa come from comparisons with our closest relatives, particularly chimpanzees that inhabit savannah regions, and groups of humans who, in the past and a few still today, pursued a hunter-gatherer lifestyle on the African savannah. All modern groups of humans have exceptionally similar genetic constitutions. The obvious difference between the lifestyles of Swedes and the San people in Africa, for example, is a result of their different environments and not of their genetic make-ups. Whereas the San people live in a savannah environment greatly resembling the one in which almost the entire history of hominids has occurred, Swedes live as recent immigrants in a cold, damp climate zone, habitable only after a thorough reconstruction of the ecosystem and enormous energy consumption. Consequently, it is more helpful to observe the San way of life to form a picture of how hominids survived the ecological conditions of the African savannah where many of our adaptations developed.

Savannah hominids, especially *Homo* species, lived in fairly small groups, bands, or tribes that were nomadic within a fairly well-defined area. Different groups within the same region would have had some contact (possibly hostile) with one another; but when young individuals reached sexual maturity, they may have left the groups where they were born and joined one of the neighbouring groups. In most species, only adolescents of one sex disperse from their natal groups to reduce the risk of inbreeding. It doesn't matter which of the sexes leaves and which remains, and this can vary from species to species. Within most primates, females remain in their natal groups whereas males emigrate. However, among chimpanzees, bonobos, and humans the opposite occurs: males remain and females immigrate. The result is a nuclear group of closely related males—fathers and sons. The group's females are related to individuals in neighbouring groups and have the opportunity to maintain contacts with them. We don't know how much this occurs among bonobos and chimpanzees, but amongst humans this is a characteristic behaviour (which benefits telephone companies).

Within groups of chimpanzees and humans, kinship ties constitute an invisible but stable network. A close relative wishes the best for a chimpanzee or human—or at least some good, depending on how closely related they are. In addition, primates generally live according to the principle of 'give a favour—receive a favour' (the tit-for-tat principle). Give me some food today—remember that I gave you food the other day when you were hungry! Come rescue me from my attacking enemies—I promise to help you if you get into trouble tomorrow! Help me to attain the alpha position in the group—I will share all the benefits I receive, especially since we are half-brothers! These are only imaginary fantasies, but they are plausible examples of primate politics...

Primate groups become more tightly knit as a result of this tit-for-tat principle. The individual who is most skilled at using the political game to climb upwards in the status hierarchy is most successful. Success requires a sharper ability than one's comrades in remembering favours and disservices, in recognizing individuals, and in balancing immediate egoistic tactics against long-term group preservation strategies. The tit-for-tat system requires that the group remains together over a long period and that the individuals who receive favours and gifts without paying back can be identified and chastized. In fact, new detailed field studies of diverse extremely social animals have demonstrated that deceivers and freeloaders are identified and punished in some way or another, or are thrown out of the group.

Naturally, there is great temptation to win selfish advantages by using pirate tactics: wandering between groups, grabbing favours, and then quickly disappearing, moving on to the next group... However, since primates have a well-functioning intellect, newcomers are identified and either held outside the collective or controlled during a trial period. There are interesting accounts and filmed evidence of how young male baboons or young female chimpanzees have been forced to spend a certain amount of time in a 'waiting room' before finally being accepted as new group members—starting out at the bottom of the hierarchy. Gossip probably has its roots in its function of keeping cheats and pirates outside the tit-for-tat network.

Severe competition may exist between different primate clans, as well as a latent state of war that can explode into terrible acts of violence including bloodshed and heavy casualties. Researchers have noted a high frequency of threats and acts of war among practically all peoples that have been studied before they converted to the kind of lifestyle usually termed western civilisation. Even among peoples that have been described as relatively peaceful, violent deaths among men have had similar or higher frequencies in the worst criminalized big-city slum areas. Among chimpanzees and pre-technological peoples, only males/ men go to war and almost only males/men resort to violence in their conflicts. Amazons are figments of the imagination. Peaceful 'primitive people' living in balance with nature are also fantasies. Human societies that practice sustainable exploitation of their natural resources are more common in political manifestos than in reality.

Leftovers from a larger predator's kill probably made up a large part of the hominid meat supply: the habit of leopards to hang the leftovers from their kills in a tree would hardly deter the agile hominids. Whether it was stealing leftovers or hunting that was the most common means of obtaining meat, hominids clearly gained an advantage when working together as a team. The ability to travel great distances was necessary in both cases. Many researchers support the hypothesis that the need for meat and the methods used by humans to obtain it contributed to the increased division of labour between the sexes. Because of pregnancy, nursing of young, and smaller size, females did not travel as far as males and tended to remain near the camp-sites.

Unlike chimpanzees and bonobos, humans have a strong tendency to 'keep track of paternity'. Within most peoples, some kind of 'marriage' or long-term permanent pair bonds exist, which are initiated with special ceremonies often involving economic transactions between the two families. These marriages may be monogamous (one man, one woman), polygynous (one man, two or more women), or polyandrous (one woman, two or more men). The latter occurs very rarely and when it does, usually takes the form of two or more brothers having to join together because of economic difficulties in order to be able to afford a woman—an almost over-explicit illustration of the significance of kinship. The formal marriage system may, but does not necessarily coincide with the pattern of sexual relations. A proportion of children are the fruits of 'extra-marital' affairs. Consequently, the child's genetic and social fathers are different people.

One fundamental biological inequality between the sexes is that a female/

woman always knows which children are hers. A male risks sacrificing resources for an individual who will not pass on his genes—a terrible blunder from the evolutionary biology perspective and a reason for jealousy that can lead to serious crimes—or great literature.

Naturally, this is only a problem in those species where males make a significant investment in the care of the young. Among most mammalian species, there is no such investment, the father absconds as soon as he has completed his task of fertilization. Not so the males among social primates however. Although they cannot nurse the young, they contribute by defending the territory and the group, particularly from males of the same species. Recent research indicates that infanticide is very common among many animal species, including several species of primate. In the past, the killing of one's own species was interpreted as abnormal or sick since it did not benefit the 'survival of the species'. However, the killing of a certain individual is an understandable behaviour in certain situations. If a male kills the offspring of another male, in many cases the mother becomes receptive to a new fertilization attempt and can become the mother of the murderer's offspring. Even within our own species men have a greater tendency to abuse and kill stepchildren than their own children.

The one who really loses out when an unknown male turns up and commits infanticide is the father of the dead offspring. Maybe this factor was important in influencing the evolution of the nuclear family. Male hominids on the savannah could increase their relative reproductive success by defending their offspring from other males who were after the mothers as sexual partners. Females with partners that could effectively fend off infanticidal attacks became winners. Consequently, it became important to these females to be, or at least appear to be sexually monogamous. If a male begins to suspect that he is not the genetic father of the young, he may become less interested in defending the female and her offspring—in fact, he might himself become an infanticidal male. Sexual monogamy occurs where both the male and the female benefit from remaining together for a while after the birth of their young.

However, a female may also benefit from not being completely monogamous.

Females of many species flirt and mate with males other than their social partners because good genes and rich resources can't always be found with only one male. To obtain good genes and sufficient resources, a female may require at least two partners. A female may increase the reproductive investment made by her primary partner by 'hinting' that she finds other males interesting and that they are interested in her. To prevent being deceived about genetic paternity, the primary partner can maximize his time with her, providing her with a valuable bodyguard as well as providing her with a generous supply of resources, thus reducing the need to do business with other courting males. Life is full of complications, both for humans and for all other extremely social animals.

Within hominid groups we begin to see a possible motive for the origination of a system of nuclear families; large-brained offspring require increasingly greater care to survive. Those males who participate in the care of their young inevitably pay more attention to paternity and differentiate between their own offspring and the offspring of others.

It is perhaps from this perspective one should consider concealed ovulation in humans and certain other primates. As this technical term implies, females of these species do not signal when ovulation occurs and thus when they are receptive for fertilization. Female chimpanzees and baboons indicate their receptive status via a grotesquely swollen and brightly coloured rump, in addition to alluring behaviour and (probable) odours. Female gorillas provide more discrete signals. Among gibbons and humans, females don't appear to provide any information as to their receptive status.

The two possible explanations proposed are that concealed ovulation in combination with a liberal sex life prevents the males of a group from knowing the paternity of the offspring, although they might all believe that they are the father or else that it is a trick to keep her partner at home. Since he invests time and resources in the offspring, he must ensure that they are actually his genetic offspring. He does this by remaining at home and copulating with his partner as often as possible. If he were to go prowling after other females, another male might fertilize his partner. One or two flirtatious glances by a female towards an interested neighbouring male should be enough to remind her partner of the advantages of staying at home. Both explanations consider that concealed ovulation is a female tactic to convince one or more males to provide assistance in raising her offspring, or at least to refrain from killing them.

So our ancestors on the savannah lived, congregated into bands or groups via kinship and tit-for-tat connections under the continual threat of conflict with other clans over important resources. Within every clan there was a game where males in particular would do anything to manipulate their way up the hierarchy, and to ensure the survival of the group. Power was won by brutal violence, but also via calculated altruism. Competition might even have taken place for the most altruistic individuals as partners. Under some circumstances, altruism may have become an ornament—a sexual attraction and signal of genetic excellence, laying a foundation for altruism to become a runaway characteristic; just as costly, but also as profitable for its practitioner as a peacock's tail is for the peacock.

An editorial about compulsory military service for the Swedish Daily News (*Dagens Nyheter*) read 'Society is an organization of people who have joined together because togetherness provides them with advantages; those belonging to the organization must participate in its maintenance and defence; this is included in the primary obligations of membership. Also included in this obligation is the defence of one's country without any special compensation.' The people sitting around camp-fires on the savannah—*habilis*, *erectus*, or *sapiens*—would all nod in agreement. That is exactly how it is, they would say to each other. What about the oldest and wisest of chimpanzees in Gombe or Mahale—wouldn't a gleam of understanding flash through their thoughtful eyes if they could somehow read this editorial?

## HUMAN NATURE

Natural selection favours those individuals in the population who survive and reproduce better than others in the same temporary conditions—*unequal*

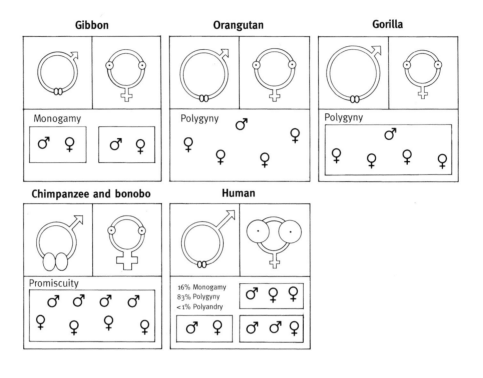

*Figure 29.*

*An overview of some aspects of the sexual biology of modern anthropoid apes. For each species or group of species, the symbol in the left-hand square represents males and the symbol in the right-hand square represents females. The difference in size between the two circles illustrates the difference in body size between the sexes. The arrow on the male symbol indicates the relative size of the penis and the ellipses at the bottom of the circle indicate the size of the testicles. The circles on the sides of the female symbol indicate the relative size of female breasts, and the cross at the bottom of the circle indicates the extent to which their external genitalia increase in visibility when they are in heat. The bottom rectangles show a schematic representation of the reproductive group's composition. In species where females copulate with several males in quick succession, the males must deliver a large quantity of sperm, which is why the chimpanzee's testicles are relatively enormous.*

*reproductive success.* The proportion of different genes in the population changes gradually allowing adaptations to the fluctuating conditions of the environment. However, a characteristic of life on earth is that everything changes, and that conditions today may be radically different tomorrow. When changes in the environment are slow, plants and animals have time to adapt, but when changes in the environment are fast in relation to the speed of evolutionary change, it becomes difficult for plants and animals to keep up with the times. In some cases organisms may run or move away from the problems, for example, organisms might counteract the effects of global warming by following the optimal temperature zone as it moves northwards, or counteract the effects of a global chilling by following the warmer climate southwards. An organism may have flexibility in its behaviour or patterns of living and thus be able to withstand the changed conditions. Not all living organisms are locked into a specific unwavering way of life in a specific narrowly defined environment. Such rigidity would be catastrophic in a world that is continually changing. Many species have considerable ability to modify individual behaviour, to survive new challenges and take advantage of new opportunities. The idea that an individual's genes decide the course of his or her life to the smallest detail—*genetic determinism*—lacks any support within modern evolutionary biology research. The individual variation that occurs in the various traits in a population of humans or any other species depends on the interaction between the genetic variation and the environmental conditions under which the individual has lived and continues to live. Genes establish certain limits; however, within these there is space for many alternative behavioural patterns. What life will look like for a specific individual is decided by the interaction between the initial genetic capital and the continuous influence of the surrounding environment regardless of the species.

Living organisms can react quickly to changes in their environments, especially through changes in their behaviour, and if a species or a certain local population manages to survive a critical period of radical change, then natural selection may evolve genetic adaptations. Some individuals would have a few more offspring than others, and the genes providing this advantage would increase in frequency within the population. However, if the species was too slow in adapting to the changing world, then sooner or later they would become extinct. It is estimated that 99 per cent of all species that have ever lived on the Earth are extinct, mainly because they were unable to compete successfully in life's race.

Throughout their history, the more recent hominids have exhibited an excellent ability to adjust their behaviour and thus survive both large and small changes in their environment. Had *Homo erectus* been unable to do this, they would hardly have become the cosmopolitan species that they were. Neanderthals, who according to the most recent findings were a geographically isolated and highly specialized race of *Homo erectus*, survived under such trying external conditions that they must have had an impressive ability to improvise and find new solutions to the multitude of problems surrounding survival. We probably do our relatives—not ancestors—a great injustice when we think of them as dense muscle-bound oafs who became stuck in the ice age's snowdrifts, even if their technological inventiveness was modest.

However flexible and recently environmentally formed we human *sapiens* are, our most important anatomical and behavioural adaptations evolved on the African savannah where our species and our ancestors spent most of their existence. Five to seven million years have passed since the ancestors of hominids left the rainforest, and about four million years since the evolution of bipedalism. It may be three million years since true humans in the form of *Homo habilis* first appeared and our own species turned up between 150 000 and 400 000 years ago. It was perhaps only 100 000 years ago that our own species began moving out of the African savannah. Even though these colonizers adapted rapidly to their different living environments and now look different in different parts of the world, humans as a species have many characteristics in common which were in our genetic baggage when we wandered out of Africa. The sum of these universal characteristics is human nature. Almost all these qualities have evolved via processes of natural selection. No other process or mechanism with the capacity to form or adapt organisms able to solve complex problems in their environment has so far been discovered—despite a determined search.

That our physical construction and behaviour are the results of a process that has been going on for millions of years doesn't mean that living organisms—humans, gorillas, buffaloes, or hyenas—are inflexibly fixed in a particular way of life. On the contrary, an individual is formed based on the continuous interaction of their genes (genotype) with their environment. Genes provide their bearers with certain limitations or reaction norms, but the existing environment is then responsible for the individual design. Genes and the environment play an eternal game with individual lives as the stakes.

Although humans are adapted to the environment where our predecessors spent most of their phylogenetic history and universal human qualities exist, this doesn't mean that we are all identical in behaviour or construction. With the exception of identical twins we are genetically unique, which means that we have inborn differences and live in unique life situations. These universal characteristics vary in their design, but within certain limits or within a certain 'superstructure'. Unique genotypes in combination with unique individual surroundings produce infinite variations for humans and all other animals. Those individuals who end up in, or find the ideal environment for their genes, have the best chances for survival. Populations with great genetic variation are best at managing future trials. Although natural selection can accomplish much, it cannot plan or establish goals. Deliberate (artificial) selection has been developed by humans to improve milk production in cows or the ear colour of Airedale terriers. Successful and goal-oriented breeding programmes for domestic animals constitute a worthwhile pedagogical parallel to the fundamentally and completely different process of natural selection.

It is impossible to make a complete list of all the qualities that are universally human. The American anthropologist Donald Brown has attempted to deal with the question of human nature. One of the most important universal human qualities is the advanced ability of the transference of knowledge, skills, ideas, and regulations from generation to generation—what we call *culture*. The most important means of conveying culture is the spoken language, which is used both to bring culture to other individuals and to direct and manipulate their behaviour. Speech sounds different among ethnic groups, local populations, and individuals, but all languages have certain fundamental similarities in structure. In all languages, the meaning of words can be modulated through intonation and facial expressions. All people have a clear self-awareness and an awareness of their relationships with other people and can imagine how various actions or words might affect those relationships. Simply speaking, humans have imagination. They are self-aware and assume that others are as well. Humans make tools that are used to construct other tools, they use fire, have some kind of home, and make weapons, even if they are simple. Humans live in social groups, they carefully differentiate between relatives and non-relatives, they impose taboos on various things such as the number of children within a family, make rules about marriage and sexual habits, as well as fight (go to war) with neighbouring groups over their home regions and other resources. It is almost exclusively men that participate in acts of war, and who have the greatest political influence in the group. While men tend to remain in their home groups, women move or are moved to other groups, which leads to regional networks that function via female kinship ties. Men and women have clearly differentiated work specializations. Women supply a larger part of the vegetarian component of the basic diet, whereas men obtain the meat, which is considered particularly desirable and is often divided and distributed according to special rituals. Humans construct detailed concepts about inexplicable powers that affect their lives, and about the unavoidable approach of death. Within the group, many people tend to develop individual specializations, and accordingly will perform different functions within the society. Sometimes these roles become socially inheritable. The quest to acquire a specialization or to become indispensable is one of the most important components of an individual's, and particularly a man's industrious, sometimes frenetic struggle to rise in status and attain the alpha position; women tend to be attracted to men who succeed at this. People tend to divide into groups that mark their unity, but that also mark their demarcation via special, culturally distinctive features.

The list would be longer if it included all universal human qualities, but shorter if it contained only unique human qualities. Some—though not all—of the features of human nature are found in more or less simplified versions even in species other than *Homo sapiens*. Several different animal species have a culture in the form of non-genetic transference of knowledge and local traditions and many are also toolmakers.

Typically, a hominid group comprises approximately equal numbers of both sexes and nuclear families including individuals from three or four generations can usually be identified within the group. Judging from the conditions under which pre-technological groups of people lived, mortality among small children as well as among young men who were fond of fighting and indulging in dare-devil acts was much higher than in most modern western societies. Since many young men became victims of their own aggressive and daring inclinations, more women than men reached adulthood. Although the average life span was shorter than in modern welfare states, some individuals did reach old age.

The menopause (when women lose the ability to reproduce prior to outward signs of age-related deterioration) may be a unique human characteristic. This is puzzling since selective mechanisms put a premium on the greatest ability to produce children. Maybe these older women gain more (with regards to transmission of genes to the next generation) by helping their children and their children's children. Among humans and certain other primates, individuals whose mothers are still alive have, on average, somewhat higher social status and reproductive success than those who can't depend on this special support. It is difficult to prove but far from unlikely that a group of primates would enjoy a better than average reproductive sucess by including a few old experienced and knowledgeable 'cultural bearers'.

Jared Diamond (American physiologist, evolutionary biologist, ornithologist and one of the most interesting writers about human evolution) emphasizes that the sexual biology of our species is in many respects unique among animals. He points out six elements that in combination cause *Homo sapiens* to look like a sexual biological curiosity among mammals. Most men and women enter long-term and publicly recognized pair bonds within which all or most of their sexual activity occurs. This system is common during the reproductive period but does not necessarily continue throughout an individual's life. Both men and women invest in the care of their offspring, although not to the same degree or in the same way. The pair lives as part of a larger group of individuals with whom they co-operate or compete, and with whom they defend a common group territory. Sex in humans is a very private matter that is shielded from public view. Sexual activity is not limited to or even intensified during the periods during which fertilization is possible, but instead is disengaged from reproductive purposes. Since ovulation occurs without any outer signals (concealed ovulation), this is somewhat inevitable. Lastly, women relinquish their own reproductive ability well before death. Diamond argues that the unique human sexual biology, which is an adaptation to the conditions on the African savannah during our origins, have had an exceedingly strong effect on the origin and design of such important human characteristics as our tendency to form societies, our morals, and our culture.

The group has become vitally important for an individual's prospects of survival and reproduction. The social lifestyle of hominids has evolved via the same general mechanisms that are thought to explain the origination of sophisticated social behaviour, namely kin selection and the tit-for-tat principle. However, these factors cannot totally explain the unselfishness (altruism) and the co-operative spirit that characterizes human societies. The American anthropologist Christopher Boehm has proposed that the 'leadership' must listen to the attitudes and interests of the 'rank and file' if the success of a group is dependent on a certain size and some individuals are willing to make short-term sacrifices in favour of a longer-term interest in the survival of the group. The primate inclination and ability to form alliances and thus carry out revolutionary changes in group hierarchy means that the powerful alpha male of today may tomorrow lie bleeding and dying after having been attacked by an alliance of dissatisfied subordinates. Boehm's argument is that those genes that programmed their bearers to behave so that the group ran smoothly became crucial for the average reproductive success of individuals and their kin, and therefore also benefited. If their groups were more successful in wars with neighbouring clans their genes were more likely to be directly or indirectly passed on. A prerequisite for the acceptance of this model is that individuals with extremely egotistical and disloyal behaviours can be identified, punished, and suffer reduced relative reproductive success.

Struggles over rank and prestige in chimpanzees and hominid groups on the savannah are generally between males. Similarly, males go to war with neighbouring clans. However, male reproductive success is dependent on who the females choose as mating partners. It is possible to quarrel and fight, hunt and kill—but the male who is seldom or never accepted as a sexual partner is and remains an evolutionary fiasco. The power of sexual selection is great. Thus, male behaviour is chiefly guided by female preferences. In some animals, behavioural ecologists have shown that extremely dominant 'macho' males are not necessarily preferred by mate-hunting females; those who convincingly signal their ability and willingness to invest in the care of coming offspring are selected.

Why then do some males invest in costly and risky macho behaviour? Different individuals have different qualifications and therefore play their own individually formed games. Perhaps the macho roll is played by males who lack the qualities that would make them suitable for the softer role that would lead to even greater success with the opposite sex. One thing you want, but the other you shall have, as Queen Christina said to her son Gustaf Adolf II in a situation where love and politics pulled him in different directions.

Sexual selection has played a significant role in the evolution of the behaviour dominant males exhibit towards one another in many species. If a male only behaves such that the female's offspring survives, she doesn't care about the details. Masculine qualities, which aid in the female's own reproductive success, are attractive. Beauty certainly lies in the adapted brain of the beholder.

A male that is attractive to a female is one who is powerful enough to protect her from harassing and pushy young males, who is capable of protecting their mutual offspring from the infanticidal tendencies of other males, who is skilled at obtaining nutritional resources for the nuclear family, who via special talents and skills can cement his leadership position, and who is accordingly capable of passing on his social status to his offspring. Since all of this constitutes a substantial cost for him, he must limit himself. This causes competition between females over the best males. Females compete primarily by signalling—truly or falsely— optimal age, sexual monogamy, good genes (through the lack of defects such as asymmetrical physical characteristics for example), and good physiological condition (health).

Such mate choice criteria as these occur in all species where both sexes make significant investments in the care of offspring. The similarity in the size of the investment does not mean that both sexes make the same kinds of investments. For example, a male can increase his reproductive success by—perhaps together with his brothers and sons—fighting to retain or increase the size of their territory. A female wins more perhaps by storing up for the nutritional demands of the intended demanding pregnancy.

Social and sexual patterns don't have to coincide. In species after species, behavioural ecologists have discovered how social monogamy (one male and one female that share duties of caring for the young) occurs parallel with sexual polygamy. Males always profit from fertilizing females, and particularly so when they manage to shift the resulting costs of care for the young onto another male. A female can profit from a furtive copulation with a male other than her social partner if that male has genes that seem to be better than those of her own 'fellow', even if she can't claim him as her social partner. However, this must take place discretely, because if her mate discovers that he is not the father of her offspring, he will drastically reduce his interest in providing resources.

Anthropologists have reported an unusual level of equality and altruism between men, and between men and women, in the San or Bush people of the Kalahari. The atmosphere is often described as peaceful and friendly, and violent crime is said to be unusual. However, more recent investigations have indicated that these accounts were much too idyllic, possibly wishful thinking. The San are indeed quite helpful towards one another—but not if the welfare of themselves or their kin is in jeopardy. It is bad to brag about success during a hunt—but 'if a hunter has a particularly successful period, he remains at home in the camp and rests allowing someone else the opportunity to bring home the meat and be praised by the women', according to the Swedish anthropologist Wilhelm Östberg. Territory is clearly divided between the different groups and there are strict rules as to how hunts should proceed near these borders. One may help a group of neighbours in need—but only if there is a long-term, unwritten 'contract' of service in return. Men represent the group in all contacts with other groups. Women never participate in hunting and are not allowed to touch the men's weapons. Östberg writes: 'Being co-operative and generous are good qualities, but it is considered unbecoming to be aggressive. Lions are not the heroes in the tales of the Bush people, rather the crafty jackals that get up to tricks and flourish—and survive.' Exactly. Machiavelli smiles as he watches from above.

The biological criterion for equality is equal reproductive success. This varies much more among males than it does among females in most species of animals. Ismail the Bloodthirsty who ended up in the *Guinness Book of World Records* for being the most successful begetter of children throughout human history has already been mentioned. If the Bush people live in equality, then paternity of the children in a group should be divided equally among the men.

This is not the case. The Canadian sociologist, Nancy Howell, has reported that of the men in the Dobe!Kung group of Bush people (the exclamation point indicates a click sound) 10 per cent are responsible for fathering 45 per cent of the children. Thus, a large number of men live out their lives without leaving any genetic traces. Even among women reproductive success was surprisingly unequal: 10 per cent of the women produced 30 per cent of the children.

Such data show that a relatively unselfish and co-operative society allows individual differences in ability to use that society for egotistical purposes. Why do people with low or no reproductive success remain in the group? Why not simply leave? In many cases they do embark on a risky venture out into the world. The degree of adaptation among individuals to existing conditions will always vary. These different qualities lead different individuals to follow different strategies.

Regarding the San—as well as other human groups—presumably the young people who have the best genetic and social qualities manage to remain in the group and profit from remaining, whereas individuals who don't function well in the existing conditions or who are born into poorer social conditions are forced to emigrate. Their chances for reproduction in their home group are zero, even though there is the chance that they will survive longer in the security of their home group. The risk of death is extremely high when individuals emigrate—at least they were in pre-technological societies—but those emigrants who find unoccupied and habitable territories or find a group that is willing to accept them, will perhaps have a chance of reproduction. Natural selection has supplied all living beings with a series of reaction norms that generally increase individual reproductive opportunities: remain at home and lay low; or fight and engage in intrigues; or leave, there may be a nice new world just over the mountain.

Within most animals species there is great variation in behaviour between males and females. In many, the sexes are almost 'two different species' with extremely different living habits. Among most primates and, in particular, more recent hominids, groups are composed of both females and males; groups composed of only one sex are almost an unknown phenomenon. It would be wrong, however, to conclude that individuals in these groups have sexually neutral behaviour. Millions of years of adaptations have provided females with different psychological equipment from the males.

# 14

## Small steps, long journey

MODERN EVOLUTIONARY BIOLOGY has shown that humans are characterized by a history much older than our own species—the result of millions of years of accumulated adaptations to a precarious, savage, and dangerous world. Unlike the universe, we didn't come into being via a dramatic Big Bang, but rather—to quote the British evolutionary anthropologist Robert Foley—via a long series of hiccups. Our physical and psychological qualities show repeated cycles of variation and rejection. The remarkable adaptations in all living creatures, including the human brain, have arisen and evolved through differences in individual reproductive success. Biology originated from the bowels of physics and chemistry via this simple mechanism. From each generation, some survive and go on to influence future generations, while most disappear without a trace. Each being alive today can proudly state: all my ancestral mothers and fathers lived long enough to pass on their genes to the next generation.

Take any living creature and investigate its origins, searching farther and farther back in time; the result will always be the same—physics and chemistry. The origin of life was most certainly complicated; however, in that environment and at that time it was also a completely natural chemical reaction. The origin of molecules with the characteristics of life (reproduction, heritability, and variation) in what is sometimes called the 'primordial soup' is no stranger than the fact that certain chemical changes occur in your breakfast egg during the five minutes it spends in boiling water. Life still obeys the laws of physics and chemistry. Because of this, organisms have evolved many adaptations as a result of variations in temperature, humidity, the magnitude of seasonal variations, and many other environmental factors.

Savannahs are biological phenomena, biomes, which arise anywhere on earth where the appropriate combination of environmental factors exists. They dictate what kinds of adaptations the plants and animals that live there must evolve in order to increase their survival under those particular conditions. However, it is not sufficient to be able to survive the physical and chemical stresses such as heat and drought, wind and fire. Living organisms are programmed by their genes to reproduce, and with implacable automation, their reproduction leads to competition over different kinds of resources. Plants compete with other plants for access to sunlight, water, pollinators, and other necessities. Animals compete over grass and meat, partners and other commodities. Generally, demand is greater than supply. The result is a runaway competition that leads to the extinction of most organisms. When individuals don't reproduce quickly enough to compensate for losses, populations decrease and die out. Extinction has been the destiny of most of the species that have ever evolved on this earth.

Imagine any living creature—a stag beetle, a common gull, a house mouse... or even a human. Richard Dawkins presented the following thought experiment in one of his books.

Ask a girl to stand on the beach of the Indian Ocean, just south of Mombasa in Kenya, with her right foot in the water and her left on the beach and then ask her to stretch out her left arm. Place her mother beside her and ask them to hold hands and beside them, the girl's grandmother. Form a chain of women holding hands. The farther from the coast we come and the deeper inland, the more different the women will look from the girl on the beach. We are running the evolutionary film backwards.

Now we take a young female chimpanzee and ask her to stand opposite the human girl, with her left foot in the water and her right foot on the beach. Then her mother stands to her right and holds her hand, and then the grandmother, and so on. Thus, a chain of chimpanzees grows parallel with the line of women stretching across the savannah towards Kilimanjaro. The farther inland we go, the more different the chimpanzees become compared with the young female chimpanzee on the beach, and here again, we run the evolutionary film backwards.

When these two chains reach the foot of the mountain, they are about 600 kilometres long and are composed of 400 000 links, that is, generations. If all these women, on average, gave birth when they were 12 years old, the distance between Mombasa and Kilimanjaro would represent a time span of about 5 million years.

By the time we reach the famous National Park of Tsavo—a third of the distance between ocean and mountain—it would start becoming difficult to identify which chain began with a human girl and which began with the young female chimpanzee. As we approach the white-capped mountain, those in the chain facing north and those in the chain facing south are identical. The chimpanzee lineage and the hominid lineage were still united at that time, even if separation was imminent.

Let us now continue our journey westwards towards the heart of Africa. Eventually, the ancestors of gorillas join up with the joint chimpanzee–human lineage and farther down the line, lineages from other primates also join the chain, until one day there are no recognizable primates, only a kind of peculiar mammal that doesn't resemble anything living today. Now we are approximately 60 million years into the past and on its westbound journey our chain has long left the African continent behind. If each generation is 3 years long (we are talking about quite small animals), then this chain, which began with the two young females— a human and a chimpanzee—at 40° east longitude on the beach south of Mombasa, has grown to 20 000 kilometres long. The animals that now make up the other end are located at 90° west longitude where they are climbing onto land on one of the Galapagos islands (which didn't actually exist at the time) and are being welcomed by a young British gentleman with a burning interest in geology and biology—Charles Darwin. To his great relief he has just stepped onto land from the eternally rolling brig (where he has spent years being seasick) that is now anchored off the uninviting beach covered with lava rocks.

I am sure that he would have enjoyed following this living chain eastwards and forwards in time so that he could, with his own eyes, witness how primitive mammals became primitive primates. He would see how they gradually became more advanced in their intelligence and their way of life via continuous adaptations, sometimes in one direction, sometimes in another, in answer to the various problems and opportunities that met them along the way. After a long trek, Darwin would have found himself on the savannah of East Africa and would have been able to understand how this special environment formed each link and, step by step, made the beings in the one line more like the young chimpanzee female on the beach, and the beings in the other line more like the human girl.

Small steps and a long journey lead to powerful and mighty humanity. It was that simple.

# Cameos of the key species

ORDER: PRIMATES

Superfamily: Hominoidea (apes and humans)

**Chimpanzee** *Pan troglodytes*

*Pan* = Greek Arcadian God, who lived in meadows and groves; *troglodytes* = cave dwellers, based on an eighteenth century notion that chimpanzees were degenerate 'cave people'. The word 'chimpanzee' comes from a language spoken in the Congo.

DISTRIBUTION: West and Central Africa, from Senegal to Uganda and Tanzania. Divided into three geographical races with considerable genetic differences but few differences in appearance.

HABITAT: Rainforest, as well as mosaic landscapes that include rainforest, woodland savannah, and more open terrain with a special preference for gallery forests and secondary growth forests.

DESCRIPTION: Males are up to 170 cm tall and weigh up to 45–50 kg; females are 10–20 per cent smaller and lighter. Live in trees (arboreal) or on the ground (terrestrial); extremely social and live in clans of related males plus unrelated females; hold group territories and are aggressive towards neighbouring clans; diverse vegetarian diet that is complemented with hunted prey in the form of monkeys and other smaller mammals; promiscuous sexual behaviour and no pair-bonding; matings conducted in the open; males do not participate in the raising of young.

In most places, all three races show negative population trends and are threatened by deforestation and hunting pressures; the total population is uncertain but estimated at 100 000 to 200 000 individuals.

**Bonobo** *Pan paniscus*

*Pan*, see previous species; *paniscus* = diminutive of genus name. The word bonobo comes from a language that is spoken in the area where the species is found. It was previously called pygmy chimpanzee.

DISTRIBUTION: Found only in the Congo, south of the Congo River; do not co-exist anywhere within their range with either chimpanzees or gorillas; no clear race divisions.

HABITAT: Rainforest.

DESCRIPTION: Marginally smaller than chimpanzees but more slender in build; males and females are about equal in size (150 cm tall and weigh 30–40 kg); arboreal or terrestrial; extremely social, live in large communities and in a constant state of solidarity; contrary to the previous species, males are not clearly dominant over females; little violent aggression within the group as well as between neighbouring groups; vegetarian; extremely promiscuous with frequent sexual contacts between not only adults of the opposite sex, but also in all imaginable constellations; no pair-bonding; matings conducted in the open; males do not participate in the raising of young.

In a large part of their range, their numbers are diminishing due to deforestation and hunting pressures; the situation is considered to be grave since the total population is estimated at only 10 000 to 20 000 individuals.

**Human** *Homo sapiens*

*Homo* = human being; *sapiens* = wise.

DISTRIBUTION: After recently emigrating from Africa, the species is now cosmopolitan; the relatively young age of this species is probably the reason for the genetic differences between populations in different geographic regions being small despite there being considerable variation in appearance.

HABITAT: Their original habitat was forest savannah interspersed with gallery forests and more open areas, preferably near water; the unique ability to manipulate the environment and exploit its resources enables humans to live in all kinds of biotopes, from the arctic to equatorial regions.

DESCRIPTION: Males are up to 2 m tall with a maximum body weight of over 100 kg; females are generally 10 per cent shorter and 20 per cent lighter, although the degree of sexual dimorphism varies between different populations; large geographic variation regarding physical appearance; terrestrial and walk upright on two legs; extremely social with tribes or clans that co-exist in large aggregations; females are more apt to leave their birth clans than males; omnivores; great variability of mating systems, but usually both parents care for the young and at least periodic social and sexual monogamy; extremely developed vocal communication abilities; skilled in the production and utilization of tools and can modify the surroundings for own advantage.

Rapid population growth with a global population that exceeds 6 000 000 000 individuals; no risk from a species preservation point of view.

## Superfamily: Cercopithecoidea (Old World monkeys)

### Red colobus *Colobus pennanti,* also called *Colobus badius*

*Colobus* = maimed, which alludes to the fact that species in this genus have greatly reduced thumbs; *pennanti* after a British zoologist; *badius* = chestnut brown.

DISTRIBUTION: Widely distributed over much of Africa's forest and woodlands; systematic complications prevent accurate determination of range of this and related species.

DESCRIPTION: Variable but usually with a rich chestnut on the the back; body length up to 80 cm and an equally long tail; maximum weight 10 kg.

HABITAT: Rainforest or other permanently green forest; in fact, this species is included in this book only because of its importance as the main prey species of meat-greedy chimpanzees.

It is reported to be greatly decreasing in many areas due to the usual reasons: deforestation and hunting pressures.

### Western black-and-white colobus *Colobus polykomos*

*Colobus*, see previous species; *polykomos* = with abundant fur, which alludes to the long and soft fur that forms an enormous tail tuft and mantle of long white hair.

DISTRIBUTION: Central Africa and (locally) eastward to Ethiopia, Kenya, and Tanzania.

HABITAT: Rainforest and other permanently green forests.

DESCRIPTION: Body length up to 120 cm, plus a 75 cm tail; maximum weight of up to 12 kg.

Black-and-white colobus belong to a sub-family called leaf-eating monkeys, as they can feed on a diet of nutritionally poor leaves. In order to manage this, they have developed a digestive mechanism that is similar to that of ruminants in certain respects. All colobus species are characteristically arboreal. They live in groups composed of a dominant, territorial male and a number of mutually related females and their offspring. Some populations seem to be managing quite well while others are being decimated for the usual reasons, particularly hunters who covet their fur.

### Savannah baboon *Papio cynocephalus*

*Papio* from a late Latin word for baboon, which in turn is of unclear origin; *cynocephalus* = dog head.

DISTRIBUTION: All of sub-Saharan Africa excluding rainforests and some mountainous and desert regions; divided into four geographic races that have such distinct appearances that they are often perceived as separate species, which is contradicted, however, by the fact that they can interbreed in areas of contact. There are two additional baboon species in Africa, the hamadryas (*Papio hamadryas*) and the gelada (*Theropithecus gelada*), both limited to Ethiopia and Eritrea.

HABITAT: All types of savannahs; sometimes even in smaller clusters of trees or gallery forests in desert-like regions; frequent visitors to agricultural fields.

DESCRIPTION: Males are up to 90 cm tall in addition to a 60 cm long tail; males weigh up to 30 kg; females weigh about half that of males; there are also many other sexually dimorphic traits; live more on the ground than in trees, but sleep either in trees or on steep slopes; extremely social with troops that can include several scores of individuals and may include several dominant males with every group of females (who are all related); females remain in their birth troop whereas males emigrate; no distinct territorial defence; primarily a vegetarian diet but also eat insects and hunt and kill small mammals and young birds.

The savannah baboon also manages well in densely populated areas where they have an advantage because of the decimation of the leopard population.

### Vervet or green monkey *Cercopithecus aethiops*

*Cercopithecus* = tailed ape; *aethiops* = Ethiopian, which in the olden days was synonymous with African.

DISTRIBUTION: All of sub-Saharan Africa excluding rainforests; for some curious reason they are also absent from a large area in the south-west despite the occurrence of an apparently suitable environment; divided into a number of geographical races of dubious validity based on details in fur colour.

HABITAT: Savannah with abundant trees; favours zones of acacias along sporadic water-courses; also found in densely populated regions.

DESCRIPTION: Males can attain body lengths of 65 cm plus an equally long tail, and a maximum weight of 7 kg; females are about one-third smaller; apart from the difference in size, sexual differences are small; arboreal and terrestrial; strict vegetarians; extremely social with group size varying between 5 and 75 individuals; females remain in their birth groups, males emigrate; both sexes help in defending a group territory; males dominant to females; females establish alliances to counteract male aggression.

Common in most places.

## ORDER: CARNIVORA

### Family: Canidae

#### Black-backed jackal or silver-backed jackal *Canis mesomelas*

*Canis* = Latin for dog; *mesomelas* = half black.

DISTRIBUTION: Eastern and southern Africa with a curious gap in the region approximately encompassing Angola, Zambia, and Mozambique; one race north of this gap and one race to the south; three additional *Canis* species in Africa.

HABITAT: Savannah with groves or galleries of acacias.

DESCRIPTION: Slender, long legs, with a fox-like head; body length up to 100 cm excluding the tail, which is 40 cm long; live in nuclear family groups with a male, female, and offspring from several generations, of which the oldest help in the care of the younger ones; defend territories; omnivorous: insects, small rodents, young mammals and birds, berries, and fruits; steal from the kills of larger carnivores.

Common in appropriate habitats.

#### Wild dog (African wild dog) *Lycaon pictus*

*Lycaon* = wolf-like; *pictus* = painted on, which alludes to the colourful fur patterns; hyena dog is a name previously used, which is completely misleading.

DISTRIBUTION: Now reduced to small pockets in central, eastern, and southern Africa; four geographic races.

HABITAT: All types of savannah.

DESCRIPTION: Body length can reach 110 cm, plus a 30–40 cm tail; average body weight of 25 kg; insignificant or no differences between the sexes in size or colour; extremely social with packs including up to 50 or so members of which only a few actually produce young; collective care of the pups; males remain in their home pack and make up most of the pack, while females emigrate; hunting consists of co-operatively chasing down smaller or medium-sized antelopes and zebras; hunts are preceded by long and intensive 'friendly behaviour'; are forced to relinquish many kills to lions and spotted hyenas.

The total population is estimated at between 2000 and 5000 individuals; ruthless persecution by livestock farmers and others in combination with diseases transmitted by domestic dogs has pushed this species to the brink of extinction; superior competition from dense populations of lions and hyenas can be, at least in some places, additional causes of the acute crisis situation; substantial and vigorous populations occur perhaps in only two or three preserves in Tanzania, Botswana, and South Africa.

## Family: Hyaenidae

**Spotted hyena** *Crocuta crocuta*

*Crocuta* = yellow, as in the *Crocus* flowers; the word hyena comes from Greek and means pig-like, which alludes to the bristly mane.

DISTRIBUTION: All of sub-Saharan Africa excluding rainforests; however, hyena are eradicated from large parts of southern Africa; no recognized geographical races; the family Hyaenidae has an additional three species in Africa; hyenas are closely related to the mongoose family and have occasionally been included within the family Viverridae.

HABITAT: Most types of savannah; also in densely populated areas.

DESCRIPTION: Body length can reach 140 cm plus a 30 cm tail; weigh up to 90 kg; females are somewhat larger and heavier than males; more active during the night than during the day; they are carnivores that hunt for themselves as well as steal meat from the kills of other carnivores; can succumb to eating garbage; live in clans of related females; males from other groups join the female groups; females socially dominant to males; a clan can include over a hundred individuals, although they never appear all together; individuals act on their own or in small groups; care of offspring only by mothers.

Hyena populations are declining in many places because of active extermination campaigns; they are one of the many species that hardly have any future except within reserves and National Parks.

## Family: Felidae

**Leopard** *Panthera pardus*

Both the genus and species names mean panther, which is the same as leopard. Leopard is a curious combination of lion + panther.

DISTRIBUTION: Originally found throughout the entire continent, but now exterminated or greatly decimated across large regions; the only distinctive race is found on Zanzibar, where leopards have large black plate-size 'rosette' spots on the fur.

HABITAT: Rainforest, savannah, and desert (excluding only the most extreme deserts); found up to the tree-line in mountainous regions; also in densely populated areas and even in city suburbs where they prey on feral dogs.

DESCRIPTION: Males reach a maximum body length of 190 cm plus a 60–100 cm tail; males can attain body weights of up to 80 kg, females 55 kg; aside from the size differences, there are no other sexually dimorphic differences; hunt on the ground but are excellent climbers and drag their kills up into the trees; they are carnivores with a wide register, from small rodents to medium-sized antelopes, monkeys, and swine; solitary; defend territories; primarily nocturnal, even in areas where they are not persecuted.

Despite intensive extermination efforts in addition to hunting them for sport and for their furs, they are widely distributed and in some places quite common; however, some populations are severely decimated or threatened including, among others, the distinct Zanzibar race.

### Lion *Panthera leo*

The meaning of the name is self-evident.

DISTRIBUTION: Previously found all across Africa excluding rainforests and the driest deserts, however, now exterminated from a large part of its natural range; of the two races, the North African one is now extinct.

HABITAT: Savannah of all kinds that are rich in game.

DESCRIPTION: Males can reach a maximum body length of 250 cm and females a maximum length of 190 cm, plus a tail of 100 cm; maximum body weight of 250 kg and 180 kg respectively; males are equipped with a mane of variable colour; primarily active at night and live entirely on the ground; hunt medium-sized to large game including giraffe and buffalo; extremely social with a pride structure composed of related females and a group of immigrant males, often related to one another; when new males take over a pride of females, they kill the existing young; defend group territories; communal care of the young; females in heat accompanied by a male for several days during which they may copulate hundreds of times; males socially dominant to females, who do most of the hunting.

Exterminated in southern and northern Africa several hundred years ago; the population is on the decline except in reserves; dense populations in some National Parks, which will be the only safe haven for this species in the near future.

### Cheetah *Acinonyx jubatus*

*Acinonyx* = with un-retractable claws; *jubatus* = fitted with a mane (referring to the young); cheetah goes back to an ancient word that can be derived from Sanskrit and alludes to the spotted fur.

DISTRIBUTION: Have been present in all savannah and semi-desert regions across the entire continent, but are now greatly reduced in most places; no geographic race differentiation but rather the contrary, an unusually high degree of genetic uniformity across the entire population.

HABITAT: Open savannah with good visibility and abundant game.

DESCRIPTION: Body length reaches 140 cm plus 100 cm tail; weigh up to 65 kg; males about 10 per cent larger than females, but no other sexually dimorphic traits; females are solitary or together with their offspring; males are either solitary or form coalitions comprised of two or three brothers; great geographic variation with regard to their social habits; hunt by running down their prey, which includes smaller antelopes, hares, and gallinaceous birds; lose many of their kills to other carnivores; males do not contribute to the care of the young.

Like all predators, the cheetah is intensively hunted by livestock farmers; the population has dramatically decreased during the last few decades; it is controversial as to whether the species' low genetic variation has contributed to this population crash; unlike lions and leopards, it has been difficult to breed cheetahs in captivity.

## ORDER: ARTIODACTYLA (Even-toed ugulates)

## Family: Hippopotamidae

### Hippopotamus *Hippopotamus amphibius*

The genus name is a compound of two Greek words that mean horse and river, while the Greek species name means 'lives in both ways', that is, both on land and in water.

DISTRIBUTION: Originally found in wetlands across the entire continent including the Nile up to the Mediterranean Sea.

HABITAT: Rivers and lakes surrounded by wetlands (which hippos help to create and enlarge).

DESCRIPTION: Body length can reach up to 4 m, including a 50 cm tail; males weigh a maximum of 3200 kg, females are 20 per cent smaller; males have larger incisors and canine teeth that are used in bloody battles over territories and females in heat; matings take place in the water; a male either alone or together with several other males defends a territory containing several females, in which case there is a clear dominance hierarchy; on land they are exclusively grazers, but they also eat a significant portion of aquatic vegetation; rest during the day either in or near water and return to land at night in order to forage; 'the mouth of a hippo is big enough, and its teeth sharp enough to be able to bite a three metre long crocodile in two'.

Declining sharply in agricultural regions but has the potential for re-introduction as well as semi-domestication for meat production or to prevent overgrowth of vegetation in dams in places such as power stations.

## Family: Suidae

### Warthog *Phacochoerus aethiopicus*

The genus name is a compound of two Greek words meaning wart and pig; *aethiops* = Ethiopian, which in the olden days was synonymous with African.

DISTRIBUTION: Previously found throughout Africa except in rainforests and deserts; several geographic races; Africa is home to an additional two species of swine, bushpig (*Potamochoerus larvatus*) and giant forest hog (*Hylochoerus meinertzhageni*).

HABITAT: Savannah and vegetation mosaics of different kinds.

DESCRIPTION: Male body lengths are up to 150 cm plus 50 cm tails, and weigh up to 125 kg; females are only half the size of males; the 'warts' and tusks of males are much larger than those of females; active during the day (diurnal); one or more females and their offspring gather in small, loose groups, while the males live a more solitary existence; males do not participate in the care of young; a large portion of their diet is composed of underground roots and other vegetation which they dig up.

Decimated or exterminated from large areas where agriculture and livestock occur, but numerous in reserves and sparsely populated regions; can become quite unafraid in places where it is not persecuted and should therefore have a potential for domestication.

## Family: Giraffidae

### Giraffe *Giraffa camelopardalis*

The genus name is based on the Arabic name for this animal; the species name means roughly 'leopard-spotted camel'—perhaps an instance of Linnean humour?

DISTRIBUTION: Previously, all of Africa except the rainforests and the driest deserts, but now pushed back greatly; several races whose validity are dubious; great regional and even individual variation in the pattern of spots.

HABITAT: Bush and woodland savannah.

DESCRIPTION: Males can reach heights of over 5 m and females over 4.5 m; weighs up to 1900 kg and 1200 kg respectively; loosely social without territorial behaviour; males use their long necks and heavy heads to fight over rank and females in heat; active during the day with an intensification in activity at dawn and dusk; diet consists of bushes and trees, particularly fond of the different *Acacia* species; needs to drink daily and therefore cannot stray far from water.

They are now mainly restricted to reserves and certain sparsely populated regions; they are considered to be a potential species for semi-domestication for the production of meat, hides, etc., particularly since they would not compete with cattle nutritionally speaking.

## Family: Bovidae

### Buffalo *Syncerus caffer*

*Syncerus* = with horns grown together; *caffer* after an old name for Africa's inhabitants.

DISTRIBUTION: West, Central, and East Africa; two very distinct races: *Syncerus caffer caffer* in savannah habitats, and *Syncerus caffer nanus* in rainforests; have sometimes been considered separate species.

HABITAT: Lush savannah and rainforests, including mountain rainforests up to 4000 m; require access to an abundance of water.

DESCRIPTION: Males attain body lengths of up to 350 cm, plus a tail of 75 cm, and weigh up to 900 kg; females are significantly smaller with proportionally smaller horns; the rainforest buffaloes are much smaller (maximum body weight of 350 kg), are redder in colour and have smaller horns; the savannah buffalo often live in large, dense herds, although bulls may sometimes occur alone or in small groups; related cows with their offspring make up the 'structural unit' of the herd; no territorial behaviour; exclusive grazers; both diurnal and nocturnal.

Versatile species that occurs in very diverse environments; the rinderpest epidemic during the 1890s affected buffaloes worse than any other wild species; decreasing locally due to hunting pressures and intensified livestock farming, but managing well in reserves.

### Bushbuck *Tragelaphus scriptus*

The genus name is a compound of two Greek words meaning goat and deer; the species name alludes to the fact that its white spots look like written characters; an older name of hieroglyphic antelope also alludes to this fact.

DISTRIBUTION: All of sub-Saharan Africa excluding deserts.

HABITAT: Forest savannah and dense bush savannah, gallery forests; preferably near rivers and lakes.

DESCRIPTION: Body length up to 145 cm in males and 125 cm in females; weigh up to 75 kg and 45 kg respectively; males have spiral horns with only one twist; solitary males defend territories and harems with a few females; prefer dense vegetation; can reach large population densities and become quite unafraid when they are left alone.

They are fairly common even in densely populated and disturbed areas.

### Greater kudu *Tragelaphus strepsiceros*

*Tragelaphus*, see previous species; *strepsiceros* = with twisted horns.

DISTRIBUTION: From South Africa to Ethiopia and southern Sudan, rare or absent near the equator; three races; the lesser kudu (*Tragelaphus imberbis*) is a closely related species found only in East Africa's drier regions.

HABITAT: Forest savannah and sometimes bush savannah, preferably in hilly terrain.

DESCRIPTION: Body length in both sexes can reach up to 275 cm plus a 50 cm tail; males have twisted (cork-screw) horns that can reach lengths of up to 180 cm (measured along the curvature); males also have a long beard along the underside of the neck (absent in the lesser kudu); males weigh up to 300 kg, females seldom over 200 kg; females gather in small herds of about a dozen individuals and are periodically visited by one or more males; males also gather in small groups; no territorial behaviour, but males accompanying females attempt to drive away competitors; chiefly browsers.

Like most other large savannah species, the greater kudu has a fragmented distribution; the population is healthiest in southern Africa where kudus are tolerated on livestock ranches as game for hunting and as meat-producers; during the rinderpest epidemic in the 1890s, kudu populations in Kenya were severely decimated and have hardly recovered even today.

## Common eland *Taurotragus oryx*

*Taurotragus* = bull + goat; *oryx* = a general Greek name for gazelle or antelope.

DISTRIBUTION: From Kenya, south to Botswana and north-eastern South Africa; farther to the north it is replaced by the Derby eland (*Taurotragus derbyana*).

HABITAT: Savannahs, including quite open areas.

DESCRIPTION: The largest of the antelope species and the most similar to domestic livestock; males attain lengths of 350 cm, females 280 cm, in both cases exclusive of the 75 cm tail; maximum weight is 950 kg for males and 600 kg for females; spiral-shaped horns in both sexes, the females' horns are as long as the males' although thinner; variable vegetarian diet; live in wandering herds without territories; usually 20–50 animals in a herd, although favourable grazing conditions can attract hundreds of individuals to the same location; age and size determine dominance relationships; females co-operate in defending their offspring from predators and are often successful, even against lions; this behaviour is more similar to 'cattle-like' animals than it is to antelope.

Manage to survive even in relatively densely populated regions, although local hunting pressures can lead to declines; the possibility of domestication has often been discussed, but has not yet been put into practice despite the fact that the species has many characteristics that make it suitable for such purposes.

## Kirk's dik-dik *Madoqua kirkii*

*Madoqua* is an Amharian (a language spoken in Ethiopia) word for small antelope; *kirkii* = after a British military officer who had an interest in zoology and was stationed in what was then British East Africa.

DISTRIBUTION: Two separate areas of distribution with two separate races: one in Kenya and Tanzania, the other in Angola and Namibia; two or three other species of the same genus inhabit north-eastern Africa; the systematics of the group is uncertain.

HABITAT: Dry bush savannah.

DESCRIPTION: Body length 50–75 cm; weight 4–7 kg; the only sexually dimorphic traits are the pointed horns up to 10 cm long which the males bear; live in pairs in territories; browsers that consume leaves, bark, and fruits; diurnal and nocturnal, the latter particularly when it is very hot; surprisingly good survival rate despite the fact that the species is vulnerable to many different predators.

Locally decimated due to degradation of the environment, hunting, and harassment by semi-feral dogs, but generally unthreatened.

### Kob *Kobus kob*

*Kobus* is a Latinized Bantu word that connotes this antelope and other related antelope species.

DISTRIBUTION: From Senegal to southern Sudan and western Uganda; three geographical races.

HABITAT: Grass savannah near permanent water sources.

DESCRIPTION: Males reach a maximum of 180 cm, plus a 15 cm tail; maximum weight is 120 kg; females are considerably smaller, reaching a maximum weight of 80 kg; males have lyre-shaped, coiled horns; variation in mating behaviour: sometimes males form leks (a number of males occupy small territories alongside one another and are then visited by females who choose among them) and sometimes males defend larger territories and are visited by groups of females; both individual status and population density play a part in determining which behaviour a male chooses; can reach very high population densities in favourable biotopes, Queen Elizabeth Park in Uganda for example; some populations undertake seasonal migrations.

In many areas they are pushed aside and decimated by the expansion of agriculture and livestock farming, however, they have amazing recovery and colonization abilities; the species is in no general danger; they seem to have characteristics that are favourable for semi-domestication and use as meat-producing animals.

### Puku *Kobus vardoni*

*Kobus*, see previous species; *vardoni* after an English hunter and naturalist who was a friend of David Livingstone.

This species is the counterpart of the Ugandan kob, somewhat smaller and paler; distribution is concentrated around Zambia and Zimbabwe; locally abundant and in no acute danger.

### Lechwe *Kobus leche*

*Kobus*, see Kob; *leche* after a Bantu word meaning antelope.

DISTRIBUTION: Approximately the same distribution as for puku; several distinct races.

HABITAT: Wetlands near marshes and in river valleys.

DESCRIPTION: Similar to both of the previous species regarding size, appearance, and habits, but also have large and splayed hooves as an adaptation to the marshes that are its usual habitat.

Several local populations have recently been exterminated and others are threatened by the expansion of agriculture and livestock farming in the relatively lush biotopes that make up lechwe habitat; will probably not survive outside reserves.

### Waterbuck *Kobus ellipsiprymnus*

*Kobus*, see Kob; the species name alludes to two white half-moon shaped rump patches that together form an elliptical pattern.

DISTRIBUTION: From Senegal to Ethiopia and south to north-eastern South Africa and southern Angola; waterbuck with the rump patches described above occur in the south-east; another race, *Kobus ellipsiprymnus defassa*, occurs in the north and west. This race does not have the two half-moon shaped rump patches, but instead has a white full-moon rump patch; some researchers believe that these two races should be considered separate species.

HABITAT: Savannah near permanent water sources.

DESCRIPTION: Body lengths up to 240 cm, plus a 40 cm tail; males weigh up to 275 kg, females are considerably smaller; males have coiled horns up to 1 m long; characteristic long and shaggy fur; grazers who sometimes resort to browsing in times when grass is scarce; indistinct and loose social system; no territorial behaviour; herds are generally small with individuals leaving and rejoining; often occur as solitary or with two or three adult males together; meat from waterbuck has a strong and pungent smell which has falsely led to the assumption that the species is shunned by lions and other predators.

Local population decreases, but generally a species that manages quite well.

### Thomson's gazelle *Gazella thomsoni*

*Gazella* originates from Arabic and means wild goat; the species name honours a British explorer, Joseph Thomson, who is thought to have been the first European to cross Masailand.

DISTRIBUTION: High plains in East Africa; there are several unsolved systematics problems within the genus *Gazella*, which makes classification difficult.

HABITAT: Short grass savannah.

DESCRIPTION: Body length up to 110 cm plus a 25 cm tail; males weigh up to 35 kg, females 25 kg; males have S-shaped, rather thick horns up to 40 cm long, female horns are somewhat shorter, thinner, straighter, and often have defects, or are sometimes completely absent; occur in large, indeterminate herds of hundreds or even thousands of individuals that leave and rejoin the herd; males establish territories and try to attract receptive females; some populations undertake partial seasonal migrations; fast, but no endurance, because they are unable to maintain a low body temperature when they run; vulnerable to many different predators.

Many populations have been reduced due to hunting and expanding agriculture and livestock farming, however, other populations are completely unthreatened as in the Serengeti.

### Grant's gazelle *Gazella granti*

*Gazella*, see previous species; *granti* after a British explorer who, in 1858, was one of the two men who discovered that Lake Victoria was the source of the Nile.

DISTRIBUTION: East Africa; three races.

HABITAT: Dry savannah with short grass; often occur together with the previous species.

DESCRIPTION: Body length up to 165 cm; males reach a maximum weight of 80 kg, female barely 70 kg; males have horns up to 80 cm long, thick, coiled, and S-shaped; females have thinner and straighter horns; diet and reproduction very similar to Thomson's gazelle.

### Springbok *Antidorcas marsupialis*

*Antidorcas* means equivalent to *Dorcas*, which is Greek for gazelle; *marsupialis* = equipped with pouch or pocket, which alludes to a fold of skin on their backs that is supplied with several glands and can be turned inside-out.

DISTRIBUTION: Parts of South Africa, Botswana, and Namibia.

HABITAT: Sparsely vegetated, dry savannah to semi-desert.

The springbok's lifestyle is similar to the previous two gazelle species; particularly in the past when the springbok was still quite common, long migrations or eruptions were common when food became scarce and conditions became too difficult even for this animal that is extremely adapted to arid environments.

The population trend in some areas is still negative due to the expansion of livestock farming, but in other areas the springbok has been semi-domesticated as a meat and hide producer and is thought to have a large potential as such in the drier regions of southern Africa.

## Impala *Aepyceros melampus*

*Aepyceros* = with giant horns; *melampus* = black-footed.

DISTRIBUTION: Their range of distribution is divided: one section includes eastern Africa from Kenya to Transvaal in South Africa (*Aepyceros melampus melampus*), the other section is much smaller and includes south-western Angola and northern Namibia (*Aepyceros melampus petersi*); occasionally these two races are accepted as separate species.

HABITAT: Sparse forest and bush savannah, preferably along the edges bordering open areas.

DESCRIPTION: Males reach body lengths up to 150 cm and females 125 cm; maximum weight is 60 kg and 45 kg respectively; only males have horns; horns are lyre-shaped, coiled, and up to 90 cm long; browsers; must drink everyday, at least during the dry periods; males defend territories; wandering herds of females and bachelor males; herds usually include from 10 to 100 individuals that move about within a limited area; no long-term relationships between individuals; seasonal reproduction in some areas, year-round reproduction in others; males smell strongly during the rut.

They are surviving quite well in many regions and in some areas are quite abundant; however, the race found in south-west Africa is small in number and threatened.

## Topi *Damaliscus lunatus*

*Damaliscus* is Greek for young cattle; *lunatus* derives from the Latin *luna* (moon), alluding to the fact that from a certain angle the topi's horn can be shaped like a crescent moon.

DISTRIBUTION: Divided into several sometimes fairly distinct races with their own popular names, for example, tsessebe (*Damaliscus lunatus lunatus*) in southern Africa, korrigum (*Damaliscus lunatus korrigum*) in the inner regions of West Africa, and topi (*Damaliscus lunatus topi*) in East Africa.

HABITAT: Grass and mixed savannah; prefer tall grasses in wide river valleys.

DESCRIPTION: Males can reach body lengths of 220 cm and weigh 140 kg; females are 20 per cent smaller and lighter; both sexes have coiled, curved horns; variation in mating system, dependent at least in part on population density: either males are solitary in widely dispersed territories, or many males close together in leks; mostly stationary, but in some places make seasonal migrations that can stretch over hundreds of kilometres; characteristic grazers.

Abundant in many reserves, but exterminated from large areas; however, in general the species is not in danger.

### Kongoni *Alcelaphus buselaphus*

The genus name is a compound of the Greek words for elk (moose) and deer, and the species name is a compound of cow and deer (so full of fantasy!); a common name for this species is hartebeest, a name used by the Dutch immigrants in South Africa, meaning 'deer'.

DISTRIBUTION: Divided into about ten more or less distinct geographic races and range over a large part of Africa's savannah regions.

HABITAT: Mosaic biotopes with grass and forest savannah.

DESCRIPTION: Somewhat larger and heavier than topi; both sexes have horns that attach to the head so close together at the base that they look like they have grown together; offspring remain an unusually long period with their mothers (sometimes over 2 years); as with other antelopes of this size class, sexual maturity is reached at around 3–4 years old; males intensively defend territories, which they are forced to leave after only a short time due to exhaustion or because they are driven away by other males; battles over attractive territories can last for over an hour and end with the winner chasing the loser, sometimes over several kilometres; exclusive grazers.

Many populations are exterminated or greatly decimated, but in general the species is not in any acute danger; kongoni are preferred game for both legal and illegal hunters, as the meat is considered extremely tasty.

### Wildebeest (gnu) *Connochaetes taurinus*

The genus name is based on the Greek words for beard and fluttering, flowing hair; the species name means 'bull-like'; the species is often called striped gnu in order to differentiate it from the white-tailed gnu (*Connochaetes gnou*) that now only exists in a semi-domesticated form in South Africa.

DISTRIBUTION: Eastern and southern Africa.

HABITAT: Grass savannah and mosaic landscapes; not far from water.

DESCRIPTION: Males reach body lengths of 250 cm and weigh up to 300 kg; females are only slightly smaller; both sexes bear outward curving, 'buffalo-like' horns; prefer short grass; often nomadic or migratory, like in the Kalahari and Serengeti regions; males occupy temporary, individual territories where they perform peculiar antics trying to attract receptive females; during fights, males often kneel as they angrily butt horns; while most newborn calves of other antelope species lie hidden and are occasionally visited by their mothers for bouts of nursing, gnu calves are up and running with the herd only hours after birth; both rutting and parturition times are often short and synchronized.

Even though the species as a whole is not threatened, the situation in the long run is disquieting since gnus are dependent on land that is also attractive to the livestock industry;

in addition, it only seems to be able to survive successfully at relatively large population densities; in the future it will probably be relegated solely to reserves and game ranches.

### Roan antelope *Hippotragus equinus*

*Hippotragus* = Greek for horse + wild goat; *equinus* = Latin for horse-like, which alludes to the supposed horse-like posture.

DISTRIBUTION: Mostly limited to two transverse strips across Africa: one stretching from Senegal to Ethiopia, the other from Angola to Mozambique; four or five rather diffuse races.

HABITAT: Woodland savannah with miombo or other deciduous trees.

DESCRIPTION: Powerfully built with a body length in males up to 250 cm and a weight of 300 kg; females slightly smaller; both sexes have backwards pointing, coiled horns, which in males can reach lengths of one metre but half that in females; sensitive to both predation and competition and seem to occur primarily where predators and other large herbivores are few in number; have never been very abundant in any part of their range; grazers that complement their diets with some browsing; occur in herds of a maximum of 30 females, with one male that furiously repels all other males in the vicinity; other males form bachelor herds; home ranges are marked with dung piles and glandular secretions placed on twigs and branches.

Expansion of livestock farming has decimated or eliminated this species from large areas; however, overall they are not acutely threatened.

### Sable antelope *Hippotragus niger*

For the genus name, see the previous species; the species name means black, which is particularly fitting for adult males.

DISTRIBUTION: South-eastern Africa, north to the equator; two geographical races.

HABITAT: Woodland savannahs.

DESCRIPTION: Body size is similar to that of the roan antelope, however, horns of the sable antelope males can reach lengths of up to 150 cm (they are longest in a race found in central Angola, which is somewhat larger and sometimes considered to be a separate species); herds can reach sizes of up to 100 individuals; behaviour similar to the previous species.

The Angola race (species?) is severely threatened although their situation is uncertain after the many years of war that this country has experienced; the eastern race is hard pressed and decimated due to the expansion of livestock farming, but is not acutely threatened.

**Oryx** *Oryx gazella*

*Oryx* is Greek for gazelle or antelope, while *gazella* has its roots in Arabic and means wild goat; especially in southern Africa, the oryx is often called gemsbok, which alludes to chamois (*Rupicapra rupicapra*) in the mountains of southern Europe.

DISTRIBUTION: Kalahari region; the beisa oryx (*Oryx beisa*), a closely related species, occurs in East Africa, from northern Tanzania to Eritrea; sometimes these two species are considered to be a single species.

HABITAT: Dry grass savannahs and desert-like regions.

DESCRIPTION: Males are up to 2 m long and weigh up to 250 kg; no significant size differences between the sexes; both males and females have very long, pointed and almost straight horns; wandering herds of females or mixed flocks with both males and females, seldom with more that 25 individuals; grazers, that in difficult times complement their diet with browsing and by digging up roots; do not need much water; some males are stationary and defend territories; despite their impressive horns and characteristic aggressiveness between males, serious injuries are seldom observed.

   Their range has greatly diminished, but the oryx is abundant in many reserves and is often tolerated on land belonging to livestock ranches since they are popular game and meat-producing animals; no serious danger of extinction.

## ORDER: PERISSODACTYLA (Odd-toed ungulates)

### Family: Equidae

**Plains Zebra** *Equus burchelli*

*Equus* = Latin for horse; W. J. Burchell was an English zoologist who completed a successful collecting expedition to Africa in 1811; the word zebra is of unknown origin.

DISTRIBUTION: The plains zebra ranges from Ethiopia to northern South Africa and Namibia; like many of Africa's large mammals, zebra systematics is somewhat uncertain; some believe that the plains zebra belongs to the same species as the extinct quagga (*Equus quagga*); if this is accepted then the plains zebra's scientific name must be changed to *Equus quagga burchelli*; in addition to this complex of species, there are two other distinct zebra species, the mountain zebra (*Equus zebra*) in southern Africa, and Grevy's zebra (*Equus grevyi*) in north-eastern Africa.

DESCRIPTION: Maximum body length is up to 275 cm and stallions can weigh up to 325 kg, mares up to 250 kg; the striped markings exhibit great regional and individual variation; live in nuclear herds (harems) of, at the most, six mares dominated by one stallion who furiously turns away all approaching stallions; several such groups can merge into larger herds, however, they maintain their internal integrity; the stallion also defends his harem from predators; zebras draw tightly together at the approach of danger and the stallions utter a characteristic yelping neigh; zebras are extremely social and spend great amounts of time nibbling or biting on each other's hide and hair, which does not exclude the fact that there is a tense atmosphere between stallions, particularly in bachelor herds; other females in the herd often disrupt copulations, particularly if the female in heat is a low-ranking mare; characteristic grazers that prefer short grasses; some populations are migratory; make daily trips to water.

Apart from reserves and other protected areas, the plains zebra has been exterminated or decimated in many places; however, the species as a whole is not in danger.

## Family: Rhinocerotidae

### Black rhinoceros *Diceros bicornis*

Both names mean 'two-horned' in Greek and Latin respectively.

DISTRIBUTION: Their original distribution covered the entire African continent excluding the rainforests and the driest desert areas; several diffuse races exist (or have existed); they are now limited to smaller pockets of their original range.

HABITAT: Extremely broad range of biotopes and successful in all types of savannah, although they prefer areas with dense bushes and thickets; daily access to water is a necessity.

DESCRIPTION: Body length can reach almost 4 m and they can weigh up to 1400 kg; females are slightly smaller than males; both sexes have two horns that vary greatly in shape and size (record length of nearly 1.5 m); live alone or in small groups; calves accompany their mothers for two years or more; 3–5 year interval between births; males do not have a chance of coming near a female in heat until they have reached at least 10–12 years old; rely primarily on their senses of smell and hearing; diurnal and nocturnal; characteristic browsers, although they do like certain herbs (not grass); they require daily access to water and in some places are dependent on the wells dug by elephants in dried-up river-beds.

Catastrophic population decline during the twentieth century; this decrease has accelerated during the past three or four decades mostly due to illegal hunting of rhinos for their horns, which fetch an enormous price in certain Arab countries and in East Asia; as recently as the 1960s, the black rhinoceros was common in many areas, but now the population across the entire continent has been reduced to between 2000 and 5000 individuals, with the largest populations in South Africa and Namibia.

**White rhinoceros** *Ceratotherium simum*

*Ceratotherium* = mammal with a horn; *simum* = wide, blunt, which refers to the wide nose.

DISTRIBUTION: In the past, their extensive distribution included Central Africa between Lake Victoria and Lake Tsad, and southern Africa from Mozambique to Namibia; the race *Ceratotherium simum cottoni* in the northern region is probably extinct; *Ceratotherium simum simum* in the southern population was down to only a few hundred individuals, but was saved at the last minute and has increased to about 7000 individuals.

HABITAT: Grass savannah with groves of trees; near water.

DESCRIPTION: Body length up to 420 cm and males weigh up to 2200 kg, females 1600 kg; both sexes have two horns, which are thick but relatively short; males occupy territories that are marked with dung, urine, and scrape marks; young rhinos follow their mothers for up to 3 years; females have their first offspring at 6–7 years old; females with young gather in small cohesive herds; characteristic grazers, prefer short grasses in broad river valleys; as opposed to the black rhinoceros, the white rhino is a docile animal that is relatively easy to work with.

It is uncertain whether the northern race is still in existence; however, the southern race is out of danger in South African reserves where they are effectively protected from poachers; both species of rhinoceros, and particularly the white rhino have been successfully reintroduced in some areas where they previously existed.


## ORDER: PROBOSCIDEA

## Family: Elephantidae

**African elephant** *Loxodonta africana*

*Loxodonta* means 'with sloping teeth'; the species name is self-explanatory.

DISTRIBUTION: Historically, elephants have ranged across the whole of Africa with the exception of the driest desert regions; now its distribution is greatly fragmented and it is restricted to savannah and rainforests from Niger and Ethiopia to north-eastern South Africa and northern Namibia; there are two distinct races: *Loxodonta africana africana* in savannah regions and *Loxodonta africana cyclotis* in rainforests (the race name means 'with round ears'). Recently the two races have been elevated to species rank.

HABITAT: Elephants are at home in all biotopes, from the deepest rainforests to the Namib Desert, and even high up in mountainous regions; one condition is that they must have access to water—if there is an abundance of lakes, watercourses, and marshes, then there is a good chance there will also be a healthy (and dense) population of elephants; they dig their own waterholes in dried-out riverbeds and in this manner provide necessary water to many other species in the areas which might not otherwise survive; dense populations have tremendous effects on vegetation.

DESCRIPTION: Males can weigh over 6000 kg, whereas females seldom weigh more than 3500 kg; both sexes have tusks, but they are much larger in males; large regional and individual differences in tusk size and shape; some elephants lack tusks; elephants live in separate male and female herds; female groups are composed of related individuals led by a matriarch; female herds have contact with one another and meet regularly at waterholes or along rivers; nuclear herds typically have twenty or so members, but much larger aggregations can be observed during long wanderings; male herds are more loosely organized; extremely intricate social patterns and behaviour; females give birth at 3–9 year intervals and gestate for about 650 days; prefer to browse on trees and bushes as well as on lush aquatic vegetation; can also forage on grasses and roots; they are extremely fond of fruits of different kinds; much of the evidence indicates that elephants were originally exclusively rainforest animals, and have only relatively recently colonized drier biotopes.

Elephants disappeared from North Africa during the fifth century, probably due to climate changes in addition to hunting pressures; the extreme population decline began during the nineteenth century, slowed down during the first half of the twentieth century, but then accelerated again during the latter half of that century when the total number of elephants declined by 80 per cent; the total population today is estimated at about 500 000 individuals, the savannah race constituting half and the rainforest race half; however, the rainforest elephants in particular are difficult to count; their decline has been due to the intensified use of land for agricultural purposes; elephants and farmers do not easily coexist; poaching for the valuable ivory has also contributed to the death of hundreds of thousands of elephants; the prognosis is that elephants will only survive in the future within reserves and under continual population management.

# Suggested further reading

Below are two lists including a few of the publications from which I have benefited during the writing of *Savannah Lives*. The first list of books are both highly interesting and offer numerous further references. The second list provides a selection of scientific articles containing important factual information or giving an interesting picture of the present situation within evolutionary biology and ecological research.

## A-LIST

Alcock, J. (1998). *Animal Behavior. An Evolutionary Approach*. Sinauer, Sunderland, Mass.

Andersson, C. J. (1861). *The Okavango River: A Narrative of Travel, Exploration, and Adventure*. Hurst and Blackett, London.

Andersson, M. (1994). *Sexual Selection*. Princeton University Press, Princeton, New Jersey.

Barkow, J. H. *et al.* (ed.). (1992). *The Adapted Mind. Evolutionary Psychology and the Generation of Culture*. Oxford University Press, New York and Oxford.

Betzig, L. (ed.). (1997). *Human Nature. A Critical Reader*. Oxford University Press, New York and Oxford.

Bickerton, D. (1995). *Language and Human Behavior*. UCL Press, London.

Brown, D. E. (1991). *Human Universals*. McGraw-Hill, New York.

Brown, L. (1965). *Africa. A Natural History*. Hamish Hamilton, London.

Byrne, R. (1995). *The Thinking Ape. Evolutionary Origins of Intelligence*. Oxford University Press, Oxford.

Cheney, D. L. and Seyfarth, R. M. (1990). *How Monkeys See the World*. University of Chicago Press, Chicago and London.

Cloudsley-Thompson, J. L. (1969). *The Zoology of Tropical Africa*. Weidenfeld and Nicolson, London.

Darwin, C. (1859). *On the Origin of Species by means of Natural Selection, or the Preservation of Favoured Races in the Struggle for Life*. John Murray, London.

Darwin, C. (1871). *The Descent of Man, and Selection in Relation to Sex*. John Murray, London.

Dawkins, R. (1986). *The Blind Watchmaker*. Longman, London.

Dawkins, R. (1989). *The Selfish Gene*. 2nd edition. Oxford University Press, Oxford.

de Waal, F. (1996). *Good Natured*. Harvard University Press, Cambridge and London.

de Waal, F. and Lanting, F. (1997). *Bonobo. The Forgotten Ape*. University of California Press, Berkeley.

Desmond, A. and Moore, J. (1991). *Darwin*. Michael Joseph, London.

Diamond, J. (1991). *The Third Chimpanzee*. Radius, London.

Diamond, J. (1997). *Why is Sex Fun?* Weidenfeld and Nicolson, London.

Dunbar, R. (1996). *Grooming, Gossip and the Evolution of Language*. Faber and Faber, London.

Estes, R. D. (1991). *The Behaviour Guide to African Mammals*. University of California Press, Berkeley.

Foley, R. (1995). *Humans before Humanity*. Blackwell, Oxford.

Fortey, R. (1997). *Life. An Unauthorized Biography*. HarperCollins, London.

Gaston, K. J. and Spicer, J. I. (1998). *Biodiversity. An Introduction*. Blackwell Science, Oxford.

Goodall, J. (1986). *The Chimpanzees of Gombe*. Harvard University Press, Cambridge, Mass.

Gould, J. L. and C. G. (1994). *The Animal Mind*. Scientific American Library, New York.

Grzimek, B. and M. (1965). *Serengeti shall not die*. Collins, London.

Howell, N. (1979). *Demography of the Dobe!Kung*. Academic Press, New York.

Huntley, B. J. and Walker, B. H. (ed.) (1982). *Ecology of Tropical Savannas*. Ecological Studies 42. Springer-Verlag, Berlin and Heidelberg.

Höglund, J. and Alatalo, R. V. (1995). *Leks*. Princeton University Press, Princeton, New Jersey.

Jones, S. *et al.* (ed.) (1992). *The Cambridge Encyclopaedia of Human Evolution*. Cambridge University Press, Cambridge.

Keeley, L. H. (1996). *War before Civilization*. Oxford University Press, New York.

Kingdon, J. (1993). *Self-made Man and his Undoing*. Simon & Schuster, London.

Kingdon, J. (1997). *The Kingdon Field Guide to African Mammals*. Academic Press, San Diego.

Klein, R. G. (1989). *The Human Career. Human Biological and Cultural Origins.* University of Chicago Press, Chicago.

Kruuk, H. (1972). *The Spotted Hyena. A Study of Predation and Social Behavior.* University of Chicago Press, Chicago.

Leakey, R. (1994). *The Origin of Humankind.* Weidenfeld and Nicolson, London.

Lee, R. B. (1979). *The !Kung San.* Cambridge University Press, Cambridge.

Lewin, R. (1997). *Patterns in Evolution. The New Molecular View.* Scientific American Library, New York.

Maynard Smith, J. and Szathmáry, E. (1995). *The Major Transitions in Evolution.* Freeman/Spektrum, London.

McClanahan, T. R. and Young, T. P. (ed.) (1996). *East African Ecosystems and their Conservation.* Oxford University Press, New York.

Mellars, P. and Stringer, C. (ed.) (1989). *The Human Revolution.* Edinburgh University Press, Edinburgh.

Mithen, S. (1996). *The Prehistory of the Mind.* Thames and Hudson, London.

Moss, C. (1988). *Elephant Memories.* Elm Tree Books, London.

Nishida, T. (ed.) (1990). *The Chimpanzees of the Mahale Mountains.* University of Tokyo Press, Tokyo.

Owen-Smith, R. N. (1988). *Megaherbivores.* Cambridge University Press, Cambridge.

Pinker, S. (1994). *The Language Instinct.* Penguin, London.

Plotkin, H. (1997). *Evolution in Mind.* Penguin, London.

Poole, J. (1996). *Coming of Age with Elephants.* Hodder and Stoughton, London.

Prins, H. H. T. (1996). *Ecology and Behaviour of the African Buffalo.* Chapman and Hall, London.

Ridley, M. (1993). *The Red Queen. Sex and the Evolution of Human Nature.* Viking, London.

Roosevelt, T. (1910). *African Game Trails.* Charles Scribner, New York.

Ross, K. (1987). *Okavango.* BBC Books, London.

Schaller, G. B. (1972). *The Serengeti Lion. A Study of Predator–Prey Relations.* University of Chicago Press, Chicago.

Sinclair, A. R. E. and Arcese, P. (ed.) (1995). *Serengeti II. Dynamics, Management and Conservation of an Ecosystem.* University of Chicago Press, Chicago.

Skinner, J. D. and Louw, G. N. (1996). *The Springbok.* Transvaal Museum Monograph 10. Pretoria, South Africa.

Smuts, B. B. (1985). *Sex and Friendship in Baboons.* Aldine, New York.

Sommer, V. (1989). *Die Affen. Unsere wilde Verwandtschaft.* Geo Verlag, Hamburg.

Stanley, S. M. (1986). *Earth and Life through Time.* Freeman, New York.

Stevenson-Hamilton, J. (1947). *Wild Life in South Africa.* Cassell and Co., London.

Tattersall, I. (1995). *The Fossil Trail. How We Know What We Think We Know about Human Evolution*. Oxford University Press, New York.

Trivers, R. (1985). *Social Evolution*. Benjamin/Cummings, Menlo Park, California.

van Lawick Goodall, J. (1971). *In the Shadow of Man*. Fontana/Collins, London.

Whiten, A. and Byrne, R. W. (ed.) (1997). *Machiavellian Intelligence II*. Cambridge University Press, Cambridge.

Williams, G. C. (1966). *Adaptation and Natural Selection. A Critique of some Current Evolutionary Thought*. Princeton University Press, Princeton.

Wilson, E. O. (1971).*The Insect Societies*. Harvard University Press, Cambridge, Mass.

Wilson, E. O. (1975). *Sociobiology*. Harvard University Press, Cambridge, Mass.

Wilson, E. O. (1978). *On Human Nature*. Harvard University Press, Cambridge, Mass.

Wrangham, R. and Peterson, D. (1996). *Demonic Males*. Bloomsbury, London.

Wrangham, R. W. *et al.* (ed.) (1994). *Chimpanzee Cultures*. Harvard University Press, Cambridge, Mass.

Zahavi, A. and A. (1997). *The Handicap Principle*. Oxford University Press, Oxford.

## B-LIST

Abbate, E. *et al.* (1998). A one-million-year-old *Homo* cranium from the Danakil depression (Afar) of Eritrea. *Nature*, **393**, 458–460.

Aiello, L. C. and Dunbar, R. I. M. (1993). Neocortex size, group size, and the evolution of language. *Current Anthropology*, **34**, 184–193.

Alberts, S. C. and Altmann, J. (1995). Balancing costs and opportunities: dispersal in male baboons. *American Naturalist*, **145**, 279–306.

Alexander, R. D. (1989). Evolution of the human psyche. In *The Human Revolution* (ed. P. Mellars and C. Stringer), pp. 455–513. Edinburgh University Press, Edinburgh.

Arnason, U. *et al.* (1996). Pattern and timing of evolutionary divergences among hominoids based on complete mtDNAs. *Journal of Molecular Evolution*, **43**, 650–661.

Bergström, R. (1992). Browse characteristics and impact of browsing on trees and shrubs in African savannas. *Journal of Vegetation Science*, **3**, 315–324.

Bergström, T. F. *et al.* (1998). Recent origin of *HLA-DRB1* alleles and implications for human evolution. *Nature Genetics*, **18**, 237–242.

Boehm, C. (1992). Segmentary 'warfare' and the management of conflict: comparison of East African chimpanzees and patrilineal-patrilocal humans. In *Coalitions and Alliances in Humans and Other Animals* (ed. A. H. Harcourt and F. B. M. de Waal), pp. 137–173. Oxford University Press, Oxford.

Boehm, C. (1997). Impact of the human egalitarian syndrome on Darwinian selection mechanisms. *American Naturalist*, **150**, S100-S121.

Boesch, C. (1996). Hunting strategies of Gombe and Tai chimpanzees. In *Chimpanzee Cultures* (ed. R. W. Wrangham *et al.*), pp. 77–91. Harvard University Press, Cambridge, Mass.

Borgerhoff Mulder, M. (1991). Human behavioural ecology. In *Behavioural Ecology*, 3rd edition (ed. J. R. Krebs and N. B. Davies), pp. 69–98. Blackwell, Oxford.

Buss, D. M. (1989). Sex differences in human mate preferences: evolutionary hypotheses tested in 37 cultures. *Behavioral and Brain Sciences*, **12**, 1–49.

Cerling, T.E. *et al.* (1993). Expansion of C4 ecosystems as an indicator of global ecological change in the late Miocene. *Nature*, **361**, 344–345.

Coley, P. D. *et al.* (1985). Resource availability and plant antiherbivore defense. *Science*, **230**, 895–899.

Coppens, Y. (1994). East Side Story: the origin of humankind. *Scientific American*, **5**, pp. 62–69.

Cronin, H. (1997). How do we select mates? Why do we like hamburgers? Darwin's evolutionary theory may have the answers. *Time Special Issue*, Winter 1997/98, 'The New Age of Discovery', pp. 92–99.

Daly, M. and Wilson, M. (1994). Some differential attributes of lethal assaults on small children by stepfathers versus genetic fathers. *Ethology and Sociobiology*, **15**, 207–217.

Dawkins, R. (1993). Gaps in the mind. In *The Great Ape Project: Equality beyond Humanity* (ed. P. Singer and P. Cavalieri), pp. 80–87. Fourth Estate, London.

de Waal, F. B. M. (1997). The chimpanzee's service economy: food for grooming. *Evolution and Human Behavior*, **18**, 375–386.

Dublin, H. T. *et al.* (1990). Elephants and fire as causes of multiple stable states in the Serengeti–Mara woodlands. *Journal of Animal Ecology*, **59**, 1147–1164.

Dunbar, R. I. M. (1996). Determinants of group size in primates: a general model. *Proceedings of the British Academy*, **88**, 33–58.

Enquist, M. *et al.* (1998). The logic of Ménage à Trois. *Proceedings of the Royal Society of London B*, **265**, 609–613.

Frank, L. G. *et al.* (1995). Masculinization costs in hyaenas. *Nature*, **377**, 584–585.

Fritz, H. and Garrine-Wichatitsky, M. (1996). Foraging in a social antelope: effects of group size on foraging choices and resource perception in impala. *Journal of Animal Ecology*, **65**, 736–742.

Gorman, M. L. *et al.* (1998). High hunting costs make African wild dogs vulnerable to kleptoparasitism by hyaenas. *Nature*, **391**, 479–481.

Gosling, L. M. (1986). The evolution of mating strategies in male antelopes. In *Ecological Aspects of Social Evolution* (ed. D. I. Rubenstein and R. W. Wrangham), pp. 244–281.

Princeton University Press, Princeton, New Jersey.

Gowda, J. H. (1996). Spines of *Acacia tortilis:* what do they defend and how? *Oikos,* **77,** 279–284.

Grafen, A. (1990). Biological signals as handicaps. *Journal of Theoretical Biology,* **144,** 517–546.

Grinnell, J. and McComb, K. (1996). Maternal grouping as a defence against infanticide by males: evidence from field playback experiments on African lions. *Behavioral Ecology,* **7,** 55–59.

Hamilton, W. D. (1964). The genetical evolution of social behaviour. I, II. *Journal of Theoretical Biology,* **7,** 1–16, 17–52.

Hamilton, W. D. (1971). Geometry for the selfish herd. *Journal of Theoretical Biology,* **31,** 295–311.

Heinsohn, R. and Packer, C. (1995). Complex cooperative strategies in group-territorial African lions. *Science,* **269,** 1260–1262.

Hill, K and Hurtado, A. M. (1997). The evolution of premature reproductive senescence and menopause in human females: an evaluation of the 'Grandmother Hypothesis'. In *Human Nature, A Critical Reader* (ed. L. Betzig), pp. 118–137. Oxford University Press, Oxford.

Hofer, H. and East, M. L. (1993). The commuting system of Serengeti spotted hyaenas: how a predator copes with migratory prey. I, II, III. *Animal Behaviour,* **46,** 547–589.

Holekamp, K. E. and Smale, L. (1995). Rapid change in offspring sex ratios after clan fission in the spotted hyaena. *American Naturalist,* **145,** 261–278.

Jarman, P. J. (1974). The social organisation of antelope in relation to their ecology. *Behaviour,* **48,** 215–267.

Johnstone, R. A. and Grafen, A. (1992). Dishonesty and the handicap principle. *Animal Behaviour,* **46,** 759–764.

Komers, P. E. (1996). Obligate monogamy without paternal care in Kirk's dik dik. *Animal Behaviour,* **51,** 131–140.

Krackow, S. (1995). Potential mechanisms for sex ration adjustment in mammals and birds. *Biological Reviews,* **70,** 225–241.

Lamprey, H. F. *et al.* (1967). Invasion of the Serengeti National Park by elephants. *East African Wildlife Journal,* **5,** 151–166.

Leakey, M. G. *et al.* (1998). New specimens and confirmation of an early age for *Australopithecus anamensis. Nature,* **393,** 62–66.

Legge, S. (1996). Cooperative lions escape the Prisoner's Dilemma. *TREE,* **11,** 2–3.

Lummaa, V. *et al.* (1998). Adaptive sex ratio variation in pre-industrial human (*Homo sapiens*) populations? *Proceedings of the Royal Society of London* B, **265**, 563–568.

Madden, D. and Young, T. P. (1992). Symbiotic ants as an alternative defense against giraffe herbivory in spinescent *Acacia drepanolobium*. *Oecologia*, **91**, 235–238.

McKinney, M. L. (1998). The juvenilized ape myth–our 'overdeveloped' brain. *Bioscience*, **48**, 109–116.

McNaughton, S. J. (1992). The propagation of disturbance in savannas through food webs. *Journal of Vegetation Science*, **3**, 301–304.

Orians, G. H. (1998). Human behavioral ecology: 140 years without Darwin is too long. *Bulletin of the Ecological Society of America*, **79**, 15–28.

Packer, C. *et al.* (1990). Why lions form groups: food is not enough. *American Naturalist*, **136**, 1–19.

Packer, C. and Pusey, A. E. (1997). Divided we fall: cooperation among lions. *Scientific American*, **5**, pp. 32–39.

Pimm, S. L. *et al.* (1995). The future of biodiversity. *Science*, **269**, 347–350.

Plomin, R. *et al.* (1994). The genetic basis of complex human behaviors. *Science*, **264**, 1733–1739.

Pusey, A. E. and Wolf, M. (1996). Inbreeding avoidance in animals. *TREE*, **11**, 201–206.

Roberts, G. (1998). Competitive altruism: from reciprocity to the handicap principle. *Proceedings of the Royal Society of London* B, **265**, 427–431.

Rodseth, L. *et al.* (1991). The human community as a primate society. *Current Anthropology*, **32**, 221–254.

Sillén-Tullberg, B. and Möller, A. P. (1993). The relationship between concealed ovulation and mating systems in anthropoid primates. *American Naturalist*, **141**, 1–25.

Simmons, R. E. and Scheepers, L. (1996). Winning by a neck: sexual selection in the evolution of giraffe. *American Naturalist*, **148**, 771–786.

Sinclair, A. R. E. (1985). Does interspecific competition or predation shape the African ungulate community? *Journal of Animal Ecology*, **54**, 899–918.

Skarpe, C. (1992). Dynamics of savanna ecosystems. *Journal of Vegetation Sciences*, **3**, 293–300.

Stander, P. E. (1992). Cooperative hunting in lions: the role of the individual. *Behavioral Ecology and Sociobiology*, **29**, 445–454.

Tooby, J. and Cosmides, L. (1990). On the universality of human nature and the uniqueness of the individual: the role of genetics and adaptation. *Journal of Personality*, **58**, 17–67.

Trivers, R. (1971). The evolution of reciprocal altruism. *Quarterly Review of Biology*, **46**, 35–57.

van Schaik, C. P. (1996). Social evolution in primates: the role of ecological factors and male behaviour. *Proceedings of the British Academy*, **88**, 9–31.

Vesey-FitzGerald, D. F. (1960). Grazing succession among East African game animals. *Journal of Mammalogy*, **41**, 161–172.

Ward, R. and Stringer, C. (1997). A molecular handle on the Neanderthals. *Nature*, **388**, 225–226.

Wheeler, P. E. (1991). The thermoregulatory advantages of hominid bipedalism in open equatorial environments: the contribution of increased convective heat loss and cutaneous evaporative cooling. *Journal of Human Evolution*, **21**, 107–115.

White, T. D. *et al.* (1994). *Australopithecus ramidus*, a new species of early hominid from Aramis, Ethiopia. *Nature*, **392**, 558–559.

Wood, B. (1997). The oldest whodunnit in the world. *Nature*, **385**, 292–293.

Zedler, P. H. (1995). Are some plants born to burn? *TREE*, **10**, 393–395.

# Index

*Numbers in italics refer to pages with more detailed information*